BIG GAME

BIG
GAME

THE NFL IN DANGEROUS TIMES

Mark Leibovich

RANDOM HOUSE
LARGE PRINT

Published in the United States of America by Random House Large Print in association with Penguin Press, an imprint of Penguin Random House LLC, New York.

Cover design and photograph by Darren Haggar

The Library of Congress has established a Cataloging-in-Publication record for this title.

ISBN: 978-1-9848-2768-5

www.penguinrandomhouse.com/large-print-format-books

FIRST LARGE PRINT EDITION

Printed in the United States of America

10 9 8 7 6 5 4 3 2 1

This Large Print edition published in accord with the standards of the N.A.V.H.

In loving memory of great friends:
my father, Miguel Leibovich,
and brother, Phil Leibovich

Contents

Introduction

FOOTBALL, IN SPITE OF ITSELF

February 4, 2018

It fell to the Brazilian First Lady to settle the punch-drunk scene. She strutted in with the self-assurance of someone who knew her aura preceded her, even in defeat. "Great game," she said, not aware of the player's name (he was out of his jersey, a lineman by the size of him). He knew hers. Gisele Bündchen was working the big game after chaos in a back hallway of U.S. Bank Stadium in Minneapolis, seeking out Philadelphia Eagles to stun with her classy attaboys. I watched them flinch—**"Uh, thanks, thanks very much."** Super Bowl 52 had just ended in a hail of confetti and an unanswered Hail Mary from her husband, New England quarterback Tom Brady.

He was already being criticized across the Hot

Take Village for not sticking around the field long enough to congratulate his Philly counterpart, Nick Foles. So his supermodel wife, in Brady's stead, was taking on his celebrity grace duties. She moved from Eagle to sweaty Eagle, representing Brady both as a sportsmanship ambassador and—in a sly way—as a killer consolation trophy to brandish over the new champs. She was the last power play in his playbook. And the Eagles had no answer for Gisele. She caught another one leaving the locker room. "Good game," she said, startling him. "Uh, your guy's amazing," the Eagle muttered back.

Brady himself was behind a curtain dealing with the media. "Losing sucks," he confirmed. "But you show up and you try to win, and sometimes you lose and that's the way it goes." The game had finished only fifteen minutes earlier, he reminded everyone.

Brady is an empire, like the league he plays in. Empires fall eventually, but one of their best moves is to sell the illusion of timelessness. Normal limits don't apply. How many more big games did Brady have left? He kept getting asked this question, in so many words. "I expect to be back but we'll see," he said.

Four years earlier, in the Almighty's den, Brady and I had discussed the "How much longer" question too: issues of age, mortality, and the actuarial tables that he knew were running against him in the NFL, or "Not for Long" as players call a league where the average career lasts 3.3 years. Barely anyone still plays in these big games—much less excels—past forty, Brady's present age.

I wondered why he kept doing this, and whether he worried about confronting a void after he finished. "When I don't have the purpose of football, I know that's going to be a really hard thing for me," Brady told me then. There was melancholy to him when he said this, one I've sensed in Brady sometimes, even in his pinnacle moments—of which this batshit shootout in Minnesota was not one. He headed off his temporary stage and met up with his football goddess in a hallway. They shared a group hug with the kids, Instagrammed for proof.

Brady's Patriot teammate Rob Gronkowski walked by en route to another makeshift podium. Gronk appeared dazed, more so than his usual stupor. He also had processing to do. Only twenty-eight, the tight end had filled up an impressive share of stat sheets and medical charts over his eight seasons. How much more? He got that question, too. "I am definitely going to look at my future, for sure," Gronkowski said, maybe more candidly than he expected. "I am going to sit down the next couple of weeks and see where I'm at."

No one could blame him if he quit. His working life had been a pained procession of broken bones, concussions, surgeries, and rehabs. Even when health allowed, he performed under a doleful tyrant of a coach for a below-market contract in what sure looked to be a cheerless work environment. He had plenty of money, two Super Bowl rings, and Hall of Fame credentials. He could move into any number of Gronk-suitable existences—WWE, action movies, or some reality show.

But Gronkowski was also born to play this game, as much as any mortal body can be. He was Peak Football, both in size (six foot six inches, 260) and temperament (beast). He could still dominate if he wanted to or—more to the point— he **should** still dominate **because I really wanted him to still dominate**. Yes, I want Gronk to keep playing because he helps my team win. That's my selfish disclaimer: the Patriots are a disease I contracted early, growing up in Massachusetts. I still root for them, and am still trying to grow up (no longer in Massachusetts). The team has been great and interesting and despised for a long time. They make me feel like a winner, superior to my friends who root for other teams, and that's important, God knows.

Allegiance to the Pats can be tricky. We lead the league in crosses to bear. Our owner can be a whiny star-fucker and sniveling in victory. Everyone who follows pro football outside of New England is sick of us (excluding Donald Trump,

Jon Bon Jovi, and maybe a few others). Big portions of the Patriots' fan base have become entitled assholes. And yes, I might be one of them. Yet I am loyal to the Pats pretty much unconditionally, give or take the odd cheating rap or occasional Aaron Hernandez.

If anything, my infatuation with pro football has only deepened, even as I've supposedly become instilled with more mature priorities and a fuller knowledge of how the game operates and the kinds of people who operate it. It started in second grade, when my best friend, Josh, and I wrote a letter to our favorite player, Jim Plunkett, and invited the young Patriots quarterback to Josh's house for dinner (he never responded). This attachment has endured through the years and withstood a steady helmet-slapping of cognitive dissonance over whether I should know better than to keep following this sport as closely as I do. Scary research on posthumous football brains has been as impossible to miss as the testimonials from still-living retirees about the sad state of their bodies. (To wit: "My life sucks," Jim Plunkett, then sixty-nine, told the San Jose **Mercury News** in 2017. "Everything hurts.")

If you love football, you get good at blind spots and blind sides. NFL Network and NFL Films captivate with round-the-clock fairy tales: **"It starts with a whistle and ends with a gun!"** A football life can be irresistibly Hollywood and parable-ready—like the up-from-dirt saga of line-man Michael Oher, the protagonist in Michael Lewis's **The Blind Side**. But it's easier to ignore how his story ends, if anyone even noticed: Oher missed most of the 2016 season with the Carolina Panthers after a series of concussions. He posted a photo of ten pill bottles on Instagram and captioned it "All for the brain smh." Oher eventually deleted the post from Instagram, and the Panthers eventually deleted Oher from their roster.

The Lords of the League can appear overmatched by the moral and cultural moment that confronts them. Roger Goodell, the game's embattled commissioner, who in late 2017 received a contract extension that could pay him up to $200 million, always seems to be presiding over some self-inflicted mess. Under his watch, the NFL has gone from being one of the most unifying institutions in America to the country's most polarizing sports brand. Goodell himself seems not inclined to accept much blame for this trajectory. "I think it's a little more reflective of how somewhat divided our society is at this stage," he told me in his New York office a few weeks before the Super Bowl.

Still, my four-year incursion into the NFL has also led me to another impression: that for whatever reckoning might be in store for the sport—and whether that reckoning comes now or later—the game's appeal is powerful and durable, and its redemptions are never far away. The sport has a way of grabbing you back. It happened here in Minnesota three weeks earlier, when the Vikings quarterback Case Keenum threw a 61-yard touchdown pass as time expired to shock the Saints in the NFC Divisional Playoffs. The play sent Twin Cities fans into merry conniptions, lasting right up until the moment their team got spanked a week later by the Eagles. It would be re-lived and rehashed around the country for several days, no doubt by people who a few months earlier were declaring themselves "done" with football over some kneeling player, lousy ref's call, or other such outrage.

What to make of this beautiful shit-show of a league? I get asked existential versions of the "How much longer?" question myself. Which camp was I in? The true believer camp ("If we lose football," said David Baker, the president of the Pro Football Hall of Fame, "I don't know if America can survive") or the cataclysm camp ("In twenty-five years, no one in America will play football," said Malcolm Gladwell)?

Are we witnessing the NFL's last gasp as the great spectacle of American life? I'd probably put the game's long-term survival as a slight favorite over the doom scenarios. Pro football has prevailed too many times to bet against, in spite of itself.

Beyond that, I'm punting, or turning the question back on ourselves—the hundreds of millions of us who have made the National Football League the superpower it is. Why does this game still mean so much, and why are we still here?

THE WORST THING ABOUT PRO FOOTBALL IS that a lot of it has nothing to do with football. It has so much business and hair spray crusted over it: so many sideshows and expert panels "breaking things down for us" and a whole lot of people you don't want to deal with or watch on TV—and then you supersize all of it, stretch it over a week, and here we have the Super Bowl.

Our hosts did not disappoint. Neither did the weather. It was a frigid week in the "Bold North," as Minnesota is apparently now calling itself, courtesy of its Super Bowl 52 host committee. I hadn't heard "Bold North" before, just like I had no idea why Philly fans had taken to wearing German shepherd masks as their trademark identifiers instead of something, say, more majestic and bird-like (apparently the canine masks were meant to evoke the Eagles' underdog status—got it). This 2018 gridiron carnival played out in a dream sequence that featured the various parading werewolves of the NFL: **"I saw Bud Grant walking with the queen. I saw Odell Beckham Jr. walking with the queen. I saw (Boomer) Esiason**

drinking a Starbucks at the Loews Hotel. And his hair was perfect."

Both the Eagles and Patriots, and most of the international media, were based out at the Mall of America in Bloomington, next to the airport. By Friday, the warring Taliban factions from Mass-holia and Phillystan had descended on this retail colossus—big enough, by the way, to fit 7 Yankee Stadiums, 32 Boeing 747s, or 258 Statues of Liberty. The MOA also has its own in-house counter-terrorism unit for our safety. Fans pestered players at the food court, a Chinese TV crew broadcast from the Splat-O-Sphere (at the Mall amusement park), and armed SWAT teams prowled among the Buffalo Wild Wings, Kiehl's, and Benihana. Philadelphians were warned, as a security precaution, not to don their German shepherd masks inside the complex or to break into their menacing renditions of "Fly, Eagles, Fly." They appeared undeterred by the counterterrorism unit.

As happens whenever large bunches of media people assemble in one place, there was no shortage of bitching about something or another. This week's über-complaint, obviously, involved why on God's frozen earth we were here. As in, why would the league plunk down its marquee event in this NFC North Siberia? The consensus is that pro football has been overtaken by a "biblical plague of dickheads," to paraphrase the late writer Richard Ben Cramer (granted, he was talking about journalism).

Like many things with the NFL, the real answer included dollar signs. This was all bribery fodder, essentially, or a Bold North variant on the civic blackmail and corporate welfare model that's gotten many grand NFL edifices built and paid for. Football had awarded its grandest pageant to the Twin Cities in order to sweeten an already sweetheart deal in which state officials had agreed to subsidize a new billion-dollar stadium for the billionaire owners of the Vikings. And taxpayers would foot about half the bill for a football Versailles whose primary beneficiaries— a pair of New Jersey real estate barons—cared little about the cash-strapped predicament of Minnesota schools, roads, and "essential" services that were less essential than football.

And then came the extra point: local fans/ taxpayers were also forced to play host to the marauding followers of the team that two weeks earlier had defeated the Vikings in the NFC Championship Game in Philadelphia—and, for good measure, had pelted their kindly midwestern visitors with a Philly Special of profanity, hurled objects, and beer showers as they attempted to flee their beating.

All that said: the "Minnesota Nice" thing is legit. People are unfailingly friendly, even to outsiders who don't deserve it. "I will always live in

Minneapolis," Prince once told Oprah. "It's so cold it keeps the bad people out." Prince, however, did not live to see this invasion of Eagles and Pats fans at the Mall of America.

Yet just when you're ready to pronounce the NFL dead beneath an avalanche of its own greed and bullshit—hell, even declare the Super Bowl to be a trope for the decline of America—you hit the payoff. The game starts, and with it the best part of pro football: football.

THERE IS AN HONESTY ABOUT FOOTBALL THAT my day job—politics—could never match. No one tries to dress up or excuse a loss, which was refreshing after being lobotomized by so much political spin. No one tries to argue against numbers on a scoreboard, or convince a coach they deserve to start because they went to Harvard (or Alabama). "Football was an island of directness in a world of circumspection," Frederick Exley wrote in **A Fan's Notes**. "It smacked of something old, something traditional, something unclouded by legerdemain and subterfuge."

Super Bowl 52 was a glorious jailbreak. Both offenses ran circles around the opposing defenses. There was just one punt, few penalties, lots of big plays, and a few sandlot calls back and forth. The Pats tried a double-reverse pass intended for Brady, who had run wide open down the right sideline—only to drop the damn pass. This felt fateful, if not ominous.

Eagles coaches might have sensed the same because they called a similar play later in the half that Foles caught in the end zone. Philly fans were now beside themselves. They had dominated the stadium all night, outnumbering and outcheering smug Pats rooters by a ratio of about three to two. (We got **totally owned**, as the bros say.) Foles threw three touchdown passes, each requiring replays to confirm the balls were "possessed," the passes were "controlled," and the receiver "survived the ground." But it was Foles's touchdown catch that kicked the hysteria in the giant room up to decibels rarely heard from a Super Bowl audience in a neutral city.

At the start of halftime, I saw an older Eagles fan in a throwback Wilbert Montgomery jersey wheezing outside a men's room. He was resisting an oxygen mask from a paramedic and wanted no part of an ambulance. He had suffered too many years with the Eagles to miss this reward. Air is overrated.

I came to respect Eagles fans, grudgingly—very, very grudgingly—as their desperation added a visceral edge. Could they handle ultimate victory? What would the city look like in the aftermath? Philadelphia police slathered Crisco on city poles to discourage celebratory climbing after the Eagles' win in the NFC Championship Game.

The precaution—which based on news photos appeared not to work—joined an instant pantheon of nationally recognized "Philly things." Before the game, I spoke to many Philadelphia fans who fully expected calamity to intervene to ruin the ride. This is what being a Red Sox fan used to be like before we won in 2004, back in our lovable loser days (we are now neither).

In December, I was at the Eagles-Rams game in the Los Angeles Coliseum in which the Eagles' brilliant young quarterback Carson Wentz hurt his knee on a third-quarter scramble. The injury did not appear serious at first, but Wentz was replaced as a precaution by his backup, Foles, who managed to hold a late lead. Philly fans— a vocal majority in that stadium, too—were joyous as they filed out of the Coliseum after a 43–35 victory over the NFC West–leading Rams, only to get the news upon checking their phones that Wentz's injury was in fact a season-ending ACL tear. Elation to deflation, just like that. People were actually in tears. It was hard not to feel for the poor hooligans.

Nick Foles? Maybe a serviceable backup; but when posited as a viable Super Bowl quarterback, his name became a punch line. Foles had performed well as the Eagles' starter in 2013 and part of 2014, but had worn out his welcome by season's end—to the extent anyone ever gets "welcomed" in Philly to begin with. Not a single Eagles fan

I spoke to believed that the team had any hope without Wentz and with Foles. But somehow Philadelphia kept on winning with the journeyman backup. They were underdogs at home in the playoffs against Atlanta and Minnesota, but won both games. New England was solidly favored in the Super Bowl, despite the Eagles' being better at nearly every position—except for the most important one on the field, quarterback, where the Patriots and Brady held what looked to be a historic advantage.

This is why it can be hard to turn away from football. The most unlikely of performers can electrify on the biggest of stages, and when you least expect it. This game was just deranged. Thrills came nonstop—except when it all stopped.

A terrifying episode nearly ruined the whole party. In the second quarter, Patriots receiver Brandin Cooks caught a 23-yard pass over the middle, danced around for extra yardage, and never saw Eagles safety Malcolm Jenkins charging at him and **BOOM!** The helmet-to-helmet hit—deemed legal—elicited another category of football gasp, the sickened kind. Everything went quiet and Cooks was not moving and holy shit. Things got solemn fast.

Football is the "secret vice" of the civilized, wrote William Phillips in the journal **Commentary** in 1969. "Much of its popularity is due to the fact that it makes respectable the most primitive feelings about violence, patriotism, manhood." This is true enough, but the notion is predicated on damage staying within bounds. The year had been filled with serious injuries to star players (Aaron Rodgers, J. J. Watt, Wentz, and a host of others). But none of them threatened vital organs or functions, with the catastrophic exception of the Steelers' young linebacker Ryan Shazier, who suffered a spinal injury in a Monday night game against Cincinnati that jeopardized his playing career and (as of early 2018) his ability to walk normally again. Otherwise, even in the season-ending cases, the injuries remained in bounds. As long as the gladiator is still breathing—maybe favors us with a thumbs-up while being carted off—we know we've remained safely on the right side of what our football stomachs can digest. Pass the bean dip.

But Cooks was motionless for two, maybe three minutes. The silence in the stadium was becoming gruesome. Not respectable. To state the unspeakable, and at the risk of sounding glib: the Super Bowl would be a most inopportune stage to have a player die on—the NFL's worst nightmare. My colleague Joe Drape, who covers horse racing for the **New York Times** and sat next to me in the press box, mentioned at this moment a tragedy from 2008 in which a filly had died on the track after finishing second in the Kentucky Derby. Since then, the sport's leadership has lived in fear of a replay, believing horse racing might not survive another televised extravaganza that turned into a thoroughbred snuff event. It was obvious why Joe mentioned this now. Would they keep playing this game if Cooks died? Again, maybe this was needlessly glib and morbid (press boxes bring out the glib and morbid). But the NFL had almost certainly game-planned for this scenario, figured out some contingency in the event of sudden death.

Thank goodness, Cooks survived the ground and the blow that planted him there. He finally picked himself up and walked off and we could all get on with our fun. Cooks was ruled out the rest of the night with a head injury, but everyone else was free to resume pounding. It took just a few seconds to feel the game rumbling back to life, like a restarted locomotive. Drape headed off on a beer run.

Spoiler alert: The Eagles won, 41–33. Brady, who had been named the league's MVP for the third time the night before, was his usual New Age Ninja self, finishing with 505 yards and three touchdowns. His last-ditch 51-yard heave, intended for Gronk, was batted away in the end zone. As soon as the leather hit the turf, everyone's first instinct—mine, yours, Brady's—was to glance up at the clock to see if ticks remained. The zeros confirmed that time and Philly had beaten Tom, at least for this season.

"We never had control of the game," Brady was saying afterward to punctuate a season in which the NFL had itself felt at the mercy of uncontrollable events and actors—protesting players, rogue owners, and, not least, a U.S. president using our most popular sport as ammunition in the country's culture wars. Football no longer felt safely bubbled off from the messiness and politics of the larger American reality show.

This would all take time to process. The sport felt exhausted and unsettled, even as the Big Game euphoria spilled onto the arctic streets. Eagles fans were delirious and also dumbfounded. They were the underdogs who caught the car, and now what? Reckoning and redemption stories are always getting tangled up in football, boom versus doom in a grudge match. It felt strange to experience Peak Football and have it also feel like the end of something.

BIG GAME

Prologue

RESPITE

April 28, 2017

Goodell is a Douchebag!

—SIGN AT THE NFL DRAFT,
PHILADELPHIA

Again, Philly.

The season ended here with a parade and started with one, too—a parade of soon-to-be rookies ambling across a stage. The first NFL Draft ever to be held outdoors took place on a warm spring night, ten months and a very different identity ago for this proud and prickly town. Philadelphia had yet to achieve its unlikely Peak Football status. This was before Crisco poles and doggie masks and Nick Foles had also become celebrated Philly "things" (Foles had previously been a Philly "thing," for sure, but mainly just a thing to heckle).

I joined a sweaty throng outside the Philadelphia Museum of Art, near the Rocky statue. The City of Brotherly Love had been conferred by the NFL with the 2017 edition of its annual cattle call, kicking off a new tradition of the draft's being held in alternating cities (it was in New York for decades, then Chicago for the previous few years). Philadelphia, of course, makes a curious welcome center for a nervous young man. The town owns an ignominious reputation for drunken and derelict fan behavior—home to a population that allegedly booed Santa Claus and pelted him with snowballs during an Eagles game at Franklin Field in 1968. Local fans have disputed L'Affaire Santa/Snowball for years (thus "allegedly"), or at least the intensity of the invective aimed at the bearded saint. They can get pretty worked up about this alleged libel, too (as they do), but the city's reputation for fan loutishness has very much endured and been affirmed over the years. In 1997, the Eagles even established a court and jail in the bowels of Veterans Stadium to more efficiently deal with their unruly darlings.

Nearly two decades later, the prospect of an NFL Draft in Philadelphia shaped up as a potential dream matchup between the country's most abusive fans and the sports world's most abused commissioner.

My view was blocked by a guy in a Carson Wentz #11 jersey hoisting the aforementioned GOODELL IS A DOUCHEBAG! placard. Revelers chanted, screamed, and booed Commissioner Douchebag with impressive bloodlust. They included many drunken Eagles fans (redundant?) chanting "E-A-G-L-E-S EAGLES!" in responsive intervals. Face-painted toddlers chased around little green footballs. It was quite a scene, especially for a tableau whose primary action involved a stiff man in a suit reading young men's names off index cards and then hugging them.

NFL drafts have become like solstice festivals to mark the unofficial peak of the football off-season. "Off-season" has in fact become a misnomer and even a dirty word inside the modern NFL. "Off"-anything is an affront to the manifest destiny of a sport whose mission is predicated year-round upon the conquering of American downtime. No hour of the year should be safe from the league's revenue grabs. Previously low-key events like the NFL Draft, NFL Scouting Combine (March), and Hall of Fame inductions (August) have now become jacked-up merchandise and media extravaganzas unfolding over several days. The NFL is no longer just training camps, coaching carousels, and football games, but a series of highly produced set pieces, jubilees, and roving "fan experience" exposition parks in revolving venues.

The 2017 draft would be watched by 4.6 million people on two networks over three days, universes removed from the last time the draft was held in Philly, in 1960, when a few chain-smoking sportswriters showed up at a hotel ballroom. "C'mon, Philly, come on!" Goodell implored about twenty seconds after he took the stage, inciting louder boos. At an aide's suggestion, Goodell had considered a Santa-themed joke, something to the effect that "now I know how Santa felt," but opted against it—in keeping with the commissioner's general approach to humor (essentially nonexistent). He waved his hands toward his chest in the universal "bring it on" taunt. And it was on.

Sustained howls of derision. Greg Aiello, the NFL's longtime flack, scolded the ingrate masses via Twitter for their unpleasant reception. "If those 70,000+ fans in Philly like the Draft being there, they should cheer Roger Goodell," Aiello tweeted. Apparently we were all doing this wrong. "He's the reason the Draft is on the road," Aiello continued in defense of his battered boss. This did nothing to stop the booing.

Next to me on the grass stood a Cleveland Browns fan named Mike Carr, who had driven fifteen hours from his home in Lansing, Michigan. Carr was intent upon learning in person the identity of the player his team would select first overall. He could have watched from home, as he did over hours and days of coverage devoted to the previews, player capsules, and mock drafts in the run-up. He could have learned, in real time, what scouts were saying about the drafted players; that Ohio State cornerback Marshon Lattimore, for instance, was "genetically gifted," according to an NFL Network chyron.

But Carr preferred to be here, both to represent his native Cleveland and to shout down Goodell—the latter being as basic to this experience as candy on Halloween.

Carr does not care for the commissioner for many reasons. He mentions his bungling of the Ray Rice fiancée-battering episode from a few years ago. But mostly he spoke of jeering Goodell as a civic duty, a kind of proxy for the love-hate addiction our adrenaline-addled country has for this sport (that so many love) and this league (that so many love to hate). This was a Maximum American moment, courtesy of your favorite pro sports league and oligarchy.

"Freedom of association is a powerful thing," Michael MacCambridge wrote in **America's Game: The Epic Story of How Pro Football Captured a Nation.** "Every organization in America is someone's version of utopia." Even the Cleveland Browns. Carr will love them through thick, thin, and Johnny Manziel. He wore a

JOHNNY REHAB T-shirt to memorialize his team's
train wreck of a first-round pick from a few years
ago—a one-man reality show in his own right. "I
hope the Browns take Myles Garrett," Carr told
me, referring to the defensive end from Manziel's
alma mater, Texas A&M. "But I'm mostly really
looking forward to booing Goodell." It would
prove a satisfying night all around.

Goodell bear-hugged draftees as they walked
onstage. Every few picks, the commissioner
would bring human shields with him up to
the podium, maybe in an effort to discourage
booing: these were the Make-A-Wish Foundation kids, elderly Hall of Famers, and beloved
former Eagles whom no one would possibly
hate, even in Philly. Who could badger even
Roger when he was accompanied by a cancer-
stricken fourteen-year-old Ravens fan who read
the name of Baltimore's first-round selection? In
an upset, the mob behaved itself and gave the
kid a nice moment. The outdoor draft in general played to upbeat reviews, even evoked the Big
Game ambience of a fall Sunday at certain points.

"Especially when they played the national an-
them, I caught chills," John Ross, a University of
Washington wide receiver who was chosen in the
ninth spot by the Cincinnati Bengals, said later.
"I thought we were going to strap it up and play."
On nights like this, the NFL's iconic logo, or
"Shield," might as well be the American flag.

This being the twenty-first-century NFL, even these shiny scenes are destined to get shaded with something. The well-played draft followed an incomparable Super Bowl—with the Pats' overcoming a 28–3 deficit to stun the Falcons—but it was all being interspersed with one buzzkill or another. If it's Monday, we were learning that Dwight Clark, the great 49ers receiver, had been diagnosed with ALS, probably related to his career choice; Tuesday brings news that the Bears' Hall of Fame running back Gale Sayers is suffering from dementia. I caught brief word about the Clark and Sayers diagnoses on the NFL Network, which then moved seamlessly into another mock draft. Former Patriots tight end Aaron Hernandez, who was serving a life sentence for a murder conviction, was found hanging from a bed sheet in his Massachusetts prison cell on April 19. He died, at twenty-seven, with what researchers would later describe as the most severe case of CTE they had ever seen in a person his age. Hernandez also died, at the very least, with a dark sense of timing: that was also the day the Patriots were scheduled to make their post–Super Bowl visit to the White House.

Politics always seemed to be intruding somehow. This was very much a product of Donald J. Trump, and his ability to swallow up as much attention as possible from this bizarre American moment he was leading the nation through. Why should football be safe? Indeed, minutes after Super Bowl 51 ended members of the Patriots—a team Trump had very publicly adopted as his own—were being asked whether they would visit the White House, given the polarizing ways of the new president. Patriots tight end Martellus Bennett was the first to say no thanks, and a running tally would ensue over who else would demur. Six Patriot players said they would skip the traditional visit, and there were several additional blow-offs on game day. Brady himself came under heavy pressure to pass from his wife, his liberal Bay Area family, and assorted other anti-Trump friends (Brady had known Trump for years, judged a beauty pageant, and golfed with him a bunch of times). On the appointed day, Brady was a no-show, citing "personal family matters"—as in, his family, especially his wife, would have killed him if he had gone. Brady's absence put the starstruck Trump in a foul mood. He did not mention Brady in his Rose Garden remarks and did not take a phone call from the quarterback that night. Sad!

I HAVE WRITTEN ABOUT AMERICAN POLITICS and campaigns for sixteen years. Politics in that time has become a rolling entertainment spectacle, and perhaps the only real-stakes reality show that Americans were following as closely as they were the NFL. Politics grew hotter, as football did, under the raw nihilism of today's culture. And that was even before Donald Trump was running for anything.

Trump's presidential campaign featured many of the conditions that the NFL had enjoyed for years. He generated news every day, not all flattering, but enough to make him inescapable. He was covered by a pack of political reporters who often treated campaigns like Big Games themselves (with "pre- and postgame" coverage of debates), as opposed to complicated issue slogs with real-life consequences. Trump was his own Big Game, seemingly the only one people and media were paying attention to. He elicited passion pro and con. He appealed to a white male confirmation bias and sense of siege present in many who love football.

Every fan at some point becomes convinced the league office, other teams, referees, and announcers have it in for their utopia. The system is rigged against us. Like most Patriots devotees, I started hating Goodell for his punishment of Brady over Deflategate, the football air pressure debacle that (as Stephen Colbert correctly noted) was the rare sports scandal about shrinking balls that does not involve steroids. Did being mad at the league stop me from shelling out hundreds of dollars a year for tickets, DirecTV, NFL Sunday Ticket, RedZone, and the tools of dependence the cartel keeps pushing my way? That's funny.

As with any decent reality show, the NFL is juiced by controversy, in many cases of its own making. Deflategate provided a trivial diversion after the previous season's nightmare of a reality show, the one featuring the star running back cold-cocking his fiancée in an Atlantic City elevator and then dragging her limp body into the casino. Goodell suspended Ray Rice for two games only to have—plot twist—the security video of Rice's knockout turn up on TMZ. This led Goodell to make Rice's suspension "indefinite" and to months of recriminations over how the league could not have known about the video as it had claimed. It also raised **fundamental questions** about whether the NFL cared about domestic violence and—even more—about whether Goodell should keep his job. Reality TV does love a deathwatch.

Still, notwithstanding the NFL's year-round ability to be compelling, something was happening to this sport. Football felt less confident and more precarious, at least from the outside. I wanted to immerse myself to a point that exceeded my usual fan's engagement, beyond the preapproved all-access "experience" shows that bring us inside locker rooms and huddles and sideline confabs. For as ubiquitous as the NFL has made itself, there still remained a great mystery about the league. I had become especially curious about the closed cabal of "insiders" who owned, operated, and performed in the circus. The Rice case laid bare how little I knew about this world in a way I had not appreciated. It exposed a level of vulnerability in something that appeared so invincible. One day, a new season was set to begin, fresh with the promise of new ratings records and revenue horizons; next, this supposedly "existential crisis" hits the sport with the suddenness of a left jab on an elevator.

"Everything can change so fast in our society, for me or anyone else," Goodell told me in one of the sporadic conversations we had over the last few years. "Only the paranoid survive" is a favorite mantra of his, and a phrase you hear a lot around NFL headquarters. It's tempting to dismiss this as just another of the corporate clichés preferred by Goodell, someone who preambles many of his sentences with "As I say around the office . . ."

But "only the paranoid survive," a motto associated with Intel's Andy Grove, struck me as a telling conceit for the modern NFL. While Grove's assertion is meant as a call to vigilance and aggressiveness, the NFL's application of the phrase seemed more in tune with defensiveness and raw nerves. This also became clear to me as soon as I began peeking behind the Shield.

"It's like this thing I say around the office, 'Believe in better,'" Goodell was telling me in January

2016. We were standing on the sidelines at Bank of America Stadium in Charlotte, before that season's NFC Championship Game between the Arizona Cardinals and Carolina Panthers. Up on a Jumbotron, the Patriots and Broncos were playing in the AFC game with sound turned up to a level that accentuated the crunch of every tackle. Each blow echoed through the stadium, and a startled gasp went up in Charlotte after Patriots receiver Danny Amendola was knocked into next week by a Denver safety. Amendola appeared staggered.

Goodell kept talking. He is fond of words like "monetize." He also talks a lot about finding new revenue streams and "growing the pie." The league is always sharing—or leaking—its gaudy dollar-signed pie. Goodell said he wants the NFL to achieve $25 billion in gross revenue by 2027 (it stood at $14 billion as of 2017). Pete Rozelle, the NFL's commissioner from 1960 to 1989, who steered it on the trajectory of its exploding popularity and riches, preached that it was a bad look for the league to have financial figures in the news. Goodell's NFL has no such reticence. Today's owners have proven again and again how much they crave big numbers; so that's what their commissioner—their employee—serves up. Since Goodell became the league commissioner in 2006, most of the owners have seen the value of their franchises double (twenty-nine are now among the fifty most valuable sports franchises on the planet, according to **Forbes**).

Pie is delicious.

Yet it also felt like a moment when the beast might be getting fat, when the business and the pageant of the NFL could be overtaking the perfection of the game. Was football teetering on the edge of a darker future? Or was I just being breathless ("teetering," always a tell), trying to overhype this as a moment of truth and sell it as a showdown between World Domination and Sudden Death? Football is just football, after all; angst is for writers.

My expedition would kick off with an email from the great Brady himself ("Tom Brady here," the subject line said—a "yeah and I'm Santa Claus" moment if I've ever had one). This was a new and different caravan for me. I do not normally cover sports and have no history with any of these people. I embedded with the top executives of the sport, got drunk and passed out on Jerry Jones's bus, attended the league's committee meetings, parties, and tribal events, interviewed journeyman and superstar players and about half of the owners (sneak conclusion: billionaires are different from you and me). I would get doused by vomit at the draft, sprinkled by confetti at the Super Bowl, cried on by a spurned Raiders booster from Oakland, and hugged by a stricken Steelers fan I met at Heinz Field during a public viewing for the team's longtime owner, Dan Rooney, who died in April 2017. The woman wore a Troy Polamalu jersey, said a silent prayer, and rubbed a Steelers-issued "Terrible Towel" on Mr. Rooney's casket.

NFL evangelists are always couching their product as a gift of escape. Football provides its disciples "a chance to really celebrate and come together and get away from our everyday troubles," Goodell said in an interview with CBS's Bob Schieffer before the Super Bowl a few years ago. In Goodell's telling, life is hard, but Sundays liberate and give solace. Games are confined to about three hours and offer us a thrilling parenthetical escape from our "troubles."

"We offer a respite," the Dallas Cowboys' owner, Jerry Jones, told me. "We are a respite that moves you away from your trials and missteps, or my trials and missteps." Jones is in many ways the embodiment of today's NFL: rich, audacious, distracted, shameless, and a veteran of more than a few trials and missteps of his own.

For me football was a respite from my day job, and from Donald J. Trump, insofar as Trump could be avoided at all.

In 2013, I wrote a book about another cozy and embattled dominion, Washington, D.C. **This Town**, it was called. I wanted to capture that world at a moment when it seemed Washington had reached a saturation point of self-congratulation as the rest of the country looked on with venomous fascination. I wanted to portray life inside the debauched seat of the capital at a formative moment. The orgy felt overdue for a reckoning. Populist tension was getting too hot outside the Beltway, and conditions seemed primed for an invading agent. I was as shocked as anyone by Trump's election, but not that the puffed-up world of D.C. would ignite a counterforce that could blow up politics as we knew it.

I wanted to do something similar with the NFL: to take a fuller anthropological measure of an empire that seems impossible to imagine America without, and yet whose status quo feels unsustainable.

To much of the American heartland, in football hotbeds like Pennsylvania, Alabama, and Texas, the game represents a way of life under attack. Fans, coaches, and many players resent the boutique coastal sensibilities that they believe exaggerate the risks of brain injuries. Football's biggest critics, they say, never played the game or felt the passion of a **Friday Night Lights** town. I became conscious of this disconnect as someone residing in a Northeast media bubble that so badly missed where the country was headed during the 2016 election.

We are products of the tribes we inhabit and our groupthink assumptions. As sports fans, we self-select parochial enclaves. Every Pats fan

I know is certain that Goodell royally screwed our Greatest Quarterback Evah in Deflategate. Then there's the 90 percent of the rest of the country that roots for other teams and whose worldviews skew accordingly. Ravens fans held rallies in support of Ray Rice postelevator and still could be seen wearing Rice's #27 jersey all over Maryland. This is your brain on football.

Jerry Jones described the beauty of the NFL to me as a weekly Coliseum clash in which representatives from my town and your town met up. "And we'll just have a big old time, being relevant to one another," Jones told me. "Relevant" is a term you hear a lot around the league. It is a curiously timid concept given the financial and cultural dynasty the NFL has maintained for five decades (were the Beatles "relevant" to rock 'n' roll?). Why mention relevance? It goes to the insecurity, maybe, or paranoia at the thought that some disruption could come along as easily as Trump did, descending from an escalator and dragging norms down with him.

The NFL is a norm. It is also a swamp. You learn that soon enough, a roiled and interconnected habitat. Everyone up and down can be a part of the same Big Game.

Another thing I have learned writing about Washington: if you're well positioned, the swamp is a warm bath. I keep thinking, for some reason, of a story told by Leigh Steinberg, the once-high-flying agent who represented the league's elite players for about twenty-five years before plummeting into an abyss of lawsuits, bankruptcy, addiction, etc. Back when he was still a "Super Agent" in the 1990s, Steinberg negotiated a contract extension for Patriots quarterback Drew Bledsoe. To celebrate, he and Robert Kraft repaired to the owner's home on Cape Cod for a special champagne toast—together in Mr. Kraft's hot tub. "I can't think of another owner in the NFL I would have rather shared a hot tub with," Steinberg wrote warmly in his memoir. This, too, is football.

1.

THE SUPER BOWL
WITHOUT JOCK STRAPS

March 20, 2016

The Membership is not at all pleased with these accommodations. Who found this place? Heads need to roll. Kids on spring break keep running through the lobby in bathing suits, like this is Six Flags over Boca or something. They are carrying milk shakes and ice cream cones with rainbow sprinkles.

"What is this, summer camp?" said Steve Tisch, the film producer and chairman of the New York Giants. If you own a football team, yes, in a sense it is—summer camp for superrich postmenopausal dudes. The National Football League offers them round-the-calendar recreation, delicious food, and a dedicated counselor/commissioner to hold their hands and buckle their big-boy pants. Tisch is known among certain campers as "the Tush." He is a model bunkmate: well liked, good company, and always helpful about hooking his NFL partners up with party invitations and tickets to the big Hollywood award shows when they come through L.A. He introduced Bob Kraft to his kid girlfriend, the model-actress Ricki Noel Lander, at a party at Chez Tush. Tisch owns the distinction of having won both a Super Bowl and an Oscar (as a producer of **Forrest Gump**). He displays both trophies in the den of his home in Beverly Hills.

"Look at these," Tisch told me as he admired the twin booty when I visited him at his hillside mansion. "They were great to show off when I was dating." That was before Tisch met his newest trophy, the gorgeous Katia Francesconi, whom he celebrates with a photo display in his front entryway. She speaks five languages, Katia does, and for their first "serious" date, Tisch flew her to the Toronto film festival, then to Pittsburgh for a Giants-Steelers game, then to Spain. He proposed in Portuguese.

Tisch has a certain dumbfounded charm about him. You could even call it Gump-like in how he projects both a lurking detachment and an utter sense of belonging to the privileged jungles he occupies. He is easily amused. When I first met him, at a Super Bowl party, Tisch told me to call him on his cell phone. He would be more than happy to share with me his impressions of America's most successful sports league and the sanctified club he belonged to as an NFL owner ("Junior high school for billionaires," as he described this confederacy). I asked Tisch for his phone number. "Sure," he replied. "Just dial 310 Take-A-Hike." And the happy camper laughed a little harder than I might have expected him to. It's good to be the Tush. He told me to call anytime. Once, I asked Tisch if he was in fact the only person on the planet with both an Oscar and a Super Bowl trophy. "I have two Super Bowl trophies, asshole," the Tush corrected me, and further amused himself.

But he is no fan of this Boca Raton Resort and Club. Neither are his fellow owners. It will not do, and the head counselor will hear about this. There are too many kids—real kids—making noise amid this great gathering of sportsmen. What use would any titan of great means and legacy have for the Flow Rider Wave Simulator out by the cabanas? It strikes a discordant note with the important business the No Fun League is trying to conduct here.

Ideally, the NFL's winter huddle would take place about an hour to the north. The Breakers in Palm Beach would be everyone's first choice. Boca is okay, and the Resort and Club, a Waldorf property, has its appeal (an ice cream store off the lobby, and who doesn't love ice cream?).

But it's not close enough to the water, the lay-out is strange, and besides, it's hard to be satisfied with anything when you've known the best. As a football potentate, you're in this for the brass ring, and the Breakers—apex of taste, luxury, and convenience—represented the brass ring. About one-quarter of NFL owners have homes within an hour of the premium resort. Built in the 1890s, the Breakers is a playground for this particular kind of tycoon. "After fires in both 1903 and 1925, the hotel reemerged more opulent each time," the Breakers' website reads. The football emperors would hope to say the same someday about their sport; would that their current set of conflagrations end up as only brushfires.

The Breakers is respectable and resilient, just as the league and its patrons believe themselves to be. At any given time, the Breakers' guest register "read[s] like a who's who of early 20th-century America: Rockefellers, Vanderbilts, Astors, Andrew Carnegie and J. P. Morgan, vacationing alongside US presidents and European nobility." Or so says the Breakers' website.

In any event, that is more in line with how NFL owners view themselves. They are not just hobbyists, but more like ministers, or actual figures of history; certainly they've earned the right to be called **philanthropists**, right? With all they've contributed?

They talk a lot about all the "quiet giving" they

do, or have their PR people do it (while mentioning, of course, how "Mr. So-and-So does not like to call attention to himself"). They are rich enough to care about their **legacies.** At the very least the owners fashion themselves as pillars of their communities, although many of them are in fact despised in their hometowns and remain stubbornly out of view. It's hard to dislodge a pillar.

"There is the Breakers and then there's everything else," one of the owners told me as he surveyed the riffraff in the crowded lobby in Boca. He asked that I not reveal his name "because I don't want to come off like a spoiled rich guy."

Not to overstate the gravity of this Boca Raton failure. A subpar resort for the NFL's annual meetings will make no one's roster of "existential" matters that supposedly threaten the league; nothing like the drop in youth-football participation, nor lawsuits, regulatory roadblocks, and disruptions to the broadcast model that the league's modern business has been built on. Nor would it rank among the battery of blows that Commissioner Goodell manages to suffer, or self-inflict, or aggravate, every few months. But it's also of a piece with something being off-kilter with America's beloved blood sport. You hear about "statements" being made in the NFL; as how the Dolphins can "make a statement" to the league by beating the Patriots on a Monday night, or how Adam "Pacman" Jones, the Bengals cornerback with long dreadlocks and a rap sheet to match, can "make a statement" by concussing the Steelers' Antonio Brown with a big hit on a crossing pattern.

NFL meetings also make a statement. They should assert an elegant show of force from a superpower league. The syndicate operates as a drug kingpin of sports and entertainment in a nation packed coast to coast with junkies. Who can't leverage a setup like this? "Hey, even the worst bartender at spring break does pretty well," pooh-poohed Eric Winston, a journeyman offensive lineman, last with the Bengals, belittling Goodell's performance.

Had Peak Football been achieved? As with any empire, there is a sense that for all its riches and popularity, the NFL is never far from some catastrophic demise—or at least might be flying close to the top of the dome.

It was thus vital that this annual meeting convey every confidence at a moment of great prosperity and unease. The owners should feel reassured. Pro football might be played by bulked-up exhibits before tens of millions of viewers, but it's these puffed-up billionaires who own the store. These are the freaks, the club that Trump couldn't crack. They are known in their collective as "the Membership." "The Thirty-two" is an alternative shorthand, or thirty-one if you don't count the shareholder-owned Green Bay Packers (on the other hand, it still totals thirty-two since the

Giants are co-owned by two families, the Tisches and Maras). These members envision themselves as noble stewards of their communities and wield their status with an assumption of permanence—a safe assumption since there are venereal diseases easier to get rid of than, say, the Washington Redskins' owner, Daniel Snyder. Plus, the Membership gets to keep most of the NFL money and none of the brain damage.

Network cameras focus on the bespoke Caligulas in their owner's boxes at least once a game. This is a strange NFL custom. We as viewers must always be favored with reaction shots from the owner's box—their awkward high fives and crestfallen stares. It is as if we could never fully appreciate what we've seen on the field unless we also witness its real-time impact upon the presiding plutocrats. The human toll! Do owners in any other sport receive this much TV time during games? Maybe horse racing. There is something distinctly Roman about this.

THESE LEAGUE CONVOCATIONS ARE HEAVILY anticipated and carefully planned. In the NFL's perennial season of external hype and internal hand-wringing, they are compulsory retreats. Every prime and middling mover from the league is here, though the actual players—with a few scattered exceptions—are not invited. Club executives with team lapel pins cavort with coaches, front-office types, and their hangers-on; agents, "friends of the league" and various appendages, stooges, functionaries from the 345 Park Avenue league headquarters, and TV "insider" types in their perpetual pancake makeup. League meetings are the NFL's Super Bowl without jockstraps.

Boca represented its own special NFL-through-the-looking-glass spectacle for interlopers like me. In the context of today's NFL, there was something elemental about watching the league self-examining and self-celebrating its efforts. The Shield credentialed 310 media members for its 2016 league meeting (compared with 1,711 for the next month's draft), though it seemed like half the people "covering" it either worked for the NFL or one of its team websites or an outlet (ESPN, NBC, Fox, CBS) that paid billions of dollars to the NFL for the rights to televise its games and to be a "valued broadcast partner." Everything feels so perfectly symbiotic.

Perhaps the biggest drawback about Boca is that the grounds get congested. Unlike you-know-where. But apparently the Breakers had decided this year that it could do better charging regular rates during a peak spring break week than by offering the NFL a group package. Insulting! Who said no to the mighty NFL? Was the Breakers making a statement?

League meetings are typically held between the Super Bowl and the NFL Draft. They represent the first official event of the new NFL year, which officially began on March 9 at 4:00 p.m., 345 Park Avenue time. Big Football is such a force that it abides by its own calendar and revolves around its own sun. Execution matters. 345 Park Ave (simply "345" as the entity can be known in shorthand) must demonstrate to its internal audience—particularly the most important internal audience, its thirty-two owner-bosses—that it is vigilant about all threats, foreign and domestic and homemade; that it is capable of striking a proper balance between aristocratic fun and the all-business collusion of gathered mob factions. And this could be such a perfect sunny environment for an existential crisis. So, game faces everyone.

And Shields, many Shields. The grounds were properly decked out with the star-studded, upside-down medallions with a football floating on top. Large golden Shields dominated walls. They were slapped on doors, carved into ice sculptures, and etched into cuff links. The Shield is a symbol of almost mystical power. It stands for big notions, like "Respect," "Resiliency," "Integrity," and "Responsibility to Team" (imprinted in big letters on the glass entrances at 345 Park). Hotel personnel wore tiny Shield pins (valet lady: "They made us wear 'em this week"). The Shield might be a commercial insignia, but at league meetings they also function as icons among the initiated, like Scientology crosses.

It had been a rough few months for the Shield, if not the coffers of those in charge. Fans were craving football more than ever while at the same time finding reason to despise the league. A messy intra-mogul tangle had just culminated over which team, or teams, would win the right to move to Los Angeles, home to the second-biggest TV market in the country (made up of millions of actual people who had seemed perfectly content without an NFL team, let alone two NFL teams, for twenty-one years). Bad feeling would linger between owner factions loyal to the competing stadium projects. Fresh generations of embittered fans were being turned out into the world via the spurned cities of St. Louis and eventually San Diego and Oakland.

The just-completed season began with the Patriots hosting the Steelers in the NFL Kickoff Game, which occurred one week after a federal judge vacated Goodell's four-game suspension of Brady over his alleged role in the Deflategate saga, which still had a whole season left to run. Deflategate was the consummate NFL reality show featuring perfectly unsympathetic perpetrator/victims (the most loathed franchise in the league), as well as an even less sympathetic Keystone Kop (the sanctimonious commissioner) at the controls.

But then (plot twist!) the judge overturned the suspension and the pretty-boy quarterback got to play the entire season and the commissioner was nowhere to be seen at his own NFL Kickoff Game. Robert Kraft strutted before the bloodthirsty crowd on Opening Night and hoisted the Patriots' latest Super Bowl trophy, WWE style.

Joe Thomas, an All-Pro offensive tackle for the Cleveland Browns, compared Goodell with the professional-wrestling impresario Vince McMahon. He called the commissioner's tactics "brilliant." "He's made the NFL relevant 365 [days a year] by having these outrageous, ridiculous witch hunts," Thomas said of Goodell in the midst of Deflategate. "It's made the game more popular than ever, and it's become so much more of an entertainment business, and it's making so much money." He added: "It's almost like the Kim Kardashian factor—that any news is good news when you're in the NFL."

THE NFL IS TOO SELF-SERIOUS TO ACCEPT ANY comparisons with Kim Kardashian or Vince McMahon or Donald Trump. But it's also obvious that even embarrassing episodes—like Deflategate—can provide helpful "entertainment" that diverts from Existential Issue One in football: concussions. Reports of players leaving the game with mangled brains, or prematurely retiring over safety concerns, or the latest retiree discussing how compromised his mind and body are at a young age, have become boilerplate accompaniments to your weekly betting lines, injury reports, and fantasy stats. At what point would fans of the game become rattled? Lawyers, parents, and the media had taken notice. But based on TV ratings and league revenues, customers to this point had proven immune from any repetitive trauma. Denial is itself a powerful shield.

At his Super Bowl "State of the League" press conference the month before, Goodell was asked about a spate of youth football players who had died the previous season. "Tragic," he said, and then touted all that the league is doing to teach safer tackling techniques. "There is risk in life," Goodell concluded. "There is risk in sitting on the couch."

"Roger's couch remark," as it became known, did not go over well among the increasingly vocal set of crippled former players and the surviving family members of dead ones. "These men and their families deserve better," said Tregg Duerson, son of the Bears safety Dave Duerson, who committed suicide in 2011 at age fifty and was later diagnosed with chronic traumatic encephalopathy, or CTE, the degenerative brain disease found in scores of deceased players. Duerson spent eleven seasons on the couch.

Goodell is always touting the league's virtues

as a moral force. "The game has so many elements I think our country admires and respects," he told me. Football provides a belief system at a time when faith in so many community, religious, and family institutions is weakening. "It unites people," Goodell continued. "It gives people a chance to sort of come together and enjoy people around this country today."

League meetings also give people—needy billionaires in this case—a chance to sort of come together. Would they ever choose one another as business partners? Probably not, but that's the nature of a cartel. You don't always get to choose. NFL owners are stuck in a vicious marriage, but no one wants a divorce and why would they?

Really, what signature player of the twenty-first century would not want a piece of the Shield? Put it on TV, and people will watch; stick it on a jersey, they will wear it. The price of television ads during the Super Bowl has increased by more than 75 percent over the last decade.

If greed is ever a topic among owners, the conversation is mostly rhetorical. Is it worth more pie—maybe another billion or two of dollars in annual revenue for a league—for a franchise (say, the Oakland Raiders) to rip the hearts out of some of the most devout fans in the country to grab a much sweeter deal in a city like Las Vegas? Is it the league's problem that Vegas is willing to shell out three-quarters of a billion dollars to build a stadium even though its schools are underfunded and its roads are medieval? Takeaway: Rhetorical quandaries are tiresome. And they can cost you money.

"You guys are cattle and we're the ranchers," the late Dallas Cowboys president Tex Schramm once told Hall of Fame offensive lineman Gene Upshaw during a collective bargaining negotiation. It is an oft-quoted line that encapsulates the whole setup. Players get prodded, milked for all they're worth, sold off, put out to pasture, and slaughtered. Implicit also here is that the cattle's time is fleeting, like Not for Long football careers. "And ranchers can always get more cattle" is how Schramm's quote concludes.

Likewise, the Patriots can always get another defensive lineman, which is why Nick Fairley, a veteran free agent previously of the Rams, was being whisked through the Boca Resort. Fairley is the rare cattle to be seen at this ranchers' convention. Bill Belichick, the head coach, will inspect the livestock here along with the rest of the New England brass. (Fairley wound up signing with the Saints.) Upshaw said he had considered writing a memoir about his union activities—joking that its working title was "The Last Plantation."

2.

THE MONKEY'S ASS

March 20–21, 2016

I arrived at the Boca Resort on a humid Sunday afternoon, a day before the official kickoff to the 2016 meetings. Jerry Jones was the first owner I spotted. He was rounding a corner into the lobby, which set off a brief fight-or-flight commotion in the court of media carnival barkers and nugget seekers. "Nuggets" are vital currency in the NFL's manic information economy. They are the bite-size, lightweight, drive-by, Twitter-ready items about who is being traded, released, signed, suspended, arrested, diagnosed with dementia, etc. They might as well be gold nuggets, given how well the likes of ESPN's Adam Schefter are paid for their maniacal mining.

Normally the brash and rascally King Jerry

would be thrilled to preside for a few moments over the Court of Nuggets. But in this case he quickened his gait. He might have been gun-shy after an encounter he had during a previous league meeting shortly after the Cowboys had signed defensive lineman Greg Hardy, the serial batterer of quarterbacks and women. Jones had a bad hip at the time and had taken a wrong turn that brought him face-to-face with about two dozen media hyenas hungry for Greg Hardy nuggets. Jones was in pain and not in a feeding mood. He tried to pivot away but could only hobble and was quickly cornered (few things are more amusing than watching a wounded billionaire gazelle laboring back to safe haven behind a velvet rope). In another world, one in which Jerral Wayne "Jerry" Jones senior was not a multibillionaire and not the most powerful owner in America's most potent sport, he could have been just another schmuck in a hospital gown with his ass hanging out, making a break for the exits.

There were not enough places to hide in Boca. It could also be loud. This was a problem because owners need hushed conversation spaces. To re-iterate: the Boca venue was suboptimal. Few stigmas are worse in the NFL than a deficient venue. Quality of "venue" represents a kind of arms race among the owners, a marker of their pecking order; and double bonus points if you can get local pols and taxpayers to pony up.

Jones is a venue god. He built AT&T Stadium, the 110,000-capacity pleasure palace in
Arlington, Texas, known as "Jerry's World,"
with its gourmet menus, high-definition video
screen spanning between the 20-yard lines, and
$1.15 billion price tag. It also houses a massive
collection of contemporary art and many, many
big photographs of the owner himself all over the
stadium (there's Jerry watching a Cowboys game
in 1999 with Nelson Mandela—great states-
men, both, one imprisoned by apartheid and the
other by his own need to be closely involved in
football decisions). Since being completed in 2009,
Jerry's World was unmatched around the league
for its size and opulence, though that mantle will
be threatened as soon as the L.A. Rams owner
Stan Kroenke completes his gridiron Xanadu in
Inglewood, California. This was no fair fight.
Kroenke's stadium plans were so grand, Jones had
to concede, they clearly "had been sent to us from
above."

Bringing up the rump end of the stadium parade is Raiders owner Mark Davis, spawn of the
team's outlaw founder, Al Davis. Davis sports a
blond version of a Prince Valiant bowl cut and
looks every bit the misfit cousin at the Membership's Thanksgiving dinner. As a practical matter, the Davis family baggage also includes an
unfortunate preexisting condition—the worst
"venue" in the league. O.co Coliseum, which the

Raiders share with the Oakland A's, exposed Davis to a most lethal contagion within the confederacy: to describe an NFL stadium as being "built for baseball" is like saying it has herpes. Add to that the rowdy occupants of the so-called Black Hole, a hybrid of silver-and-black face-painted biker-Goth–Gangsta Rap–Heavy Metal costumes to honor the marauder identity of Raider Nation, and you have one terrifying assembly. If NFL teams and their home fields are properties on a Monopoly board, think of AT&T Stadium as Boardwalk—and O.co Coliseum as jail.

Davis is fully aware of his runt-of-the-litter standing. His fellow owners find him amiable, though they treat him like their pet rock. But Davis also knows that to own an NFL team is akin to holding a precious lottery ticket. "Everyone thinks I have no money," Davis told me. "But I've got $500 million and a team." Yes he does. And what makes Davis a really Big Man in Boca is that he was, at that point, looking to move his team the hell out of Oakland. He was a free agent and ready to roam—the Raiders were "in play." Davis might frequent Hooters for its all-you-can-eat-wings specials and wear a fanny pack. But don't for a second think he is not royalty in Pigskin America. Davis moved coolly through the lobby in a black and white pin-striped suit, taking questions about his plans.

This was a few months after Davis's fellow owners, in late 2015, had thwarted his attempt to move the Raiders to a new stadium in Los Angeles. The Membership preferred that the St. Louis Rams and eventually the San Diego Chargers go there instead. The league had multiple concerns about the Raiders in L.A., not least of which was making Davis the face of the NFL in the country's second-biggest market. Cue parable: "You get your butt kicked, you get off the ground, you move forward," Davis went on. "That's what you do in life. And you learn that in this business on Sundays."

Football never lacks for parables. Keep moving the ball down the field. Mind your blocking and tackling. Run to Daylight (a gridiron philosophy immortalized by Vince Lombardi). For Davis daylight represented anywhere but Oakland. Las Vegas was very much on the radar, he said. Putting an NFL team in the gambling capital of the world held a certain danger and allure, like the Raiders themselves. In general, there will be no shortage of civic suitors waving their thongs in the faces of NFL owners stuck in bad stadium marriages. (James Carville's line about Bill Clinton's extramarital accusers kept jumping to mind: "Drag a hundred-dollar bill through a trailer park and you never know what you'll find.")

"St. Louis, as you may have noticed, doesn't have a team," a reporter from the just-abandoned home of the Rams was saying to Davis in Boca. "St. Louis would love to have the Raiders," the reporter persisted to Davis, sounding more and more desperate.

"Why aren't you interested in St. Louis?"

Davis said he understood the man's anguish. He assumed a tone of empathy as he let the man down in gentle buzzwords: "The Raider brand is a different brand that St. Louis would not maximize," he explained.

"Would Las Vegas maximize the Raider brand?" another reporter asked.

"I think the Raiders would maximize Las Vegas." The moving gallery behind Davis laughed, except the intrepid St. Louis reporter.

"St. Louis doesn't have enough of a Raiders image?" he said, a little sadly. "It has beautiful land, a nice stadium."

"I don't feel it in my heart," Davis said. "Sorry, man."

THE REST OF THE MEMBERSHIP ROLLED INTO THE resort by Town Car and wheelchair. By league convention, they must always be referred to as "Mr. So-and-So," befitting their status and genders (among the rare female members of the Membership is a widow, the Detroit Lions' then-ninety-year-old Martha Firestone Ford, wife of the team's late owner William Clay Ford; Virginia McCaskey, the then-ninety-three-year-old "Corporate Secretary" of the Bears, is the eldest daughter of the team's late founder, coach, and owner, George Halas). The first batch of arrivals resembled one of those reunions of ancient World War II squadrons, minus the flags and applause. New Orleans Saints owner Tom Benson, then eighty-eight, was wheeled through the front entrance with a big grin on his face belying the battles he has fought with the league over the years (and more recently with his children in court over control of the Saints, among other toys).

Jones, who entered wearing dark aviator glasses, was nearly chop-blocked by a pair of runaway kids. He was holding a tumbler of something—never just a glass with Jerry, always a **tumbler,** even if it's milk, which it rarely is. He loves a "big old time" and can be irresistibly fun, with a big taste for Scotch, a gleam in his icy aqua eyes, and a penchant for circuitous lectures that he will often stumble over but that will still make a strange kind of sense—sometimes.

When I asked Jones why the NFL could hum along despite the perennial crises it faces, Jones launched into something he once heard from a friend who owned a chain of Howard Johnson's restaurants. He asked his friend how HoJo's could keep the tastes and flavors of the food consistent from franchise to franchise. The answer: intensity. "If something is supposed to be cold, make it as cold as hot ice," Jones said. "If it's supposed to be hot, have it burn the roof of their mouth. Intensity covers up a lot of frailty in the taste and preparation." Thus, he concluded, the hot intensity and drama of football can obscure the dangers and degeneracy inherent to the sport.

Next down the virtual red carpet was Patriots owner Robert Kraft, strutting through the front entrance in his Nike customized sneakers ("Air Force 1's") and silvery hair stuck straight up in the wind. If you achieve a status of "influential owner" around the league, as Mr. Kraft has with his multiple Lombardi trophies, sexy young girlfriends, and perceived closeness with Goodell, you get called by enhanced names, or better yet, initials. Mr. Kraft was merely "Bob Kraft" when he bought the team in 1994, but at some point graduated to "Robert Kraft" and then eventually "RKK," at least among certain initiated sectors of Foxborough and 345 Park Ave. You know you're exalted when you achieve initials status. "Brady calls me RKK," I heard Kraft boast to Adam Schefter when they passed each other in the hallway. If RKK is good enough for Brady—"a fellow Michigan man," Schefter pointed out—it's good enough for King Nugget.

Kraft had been making a big show of still being mad at the league over the endless Deflategate saga. He believed Goodell and a group of his bitter rivals are intent on messing with his dynasty, stealing his draft picks, soiling his reputation, and railroading his quarterback. "Jealousy and envy are incurable diseases" had become Kraft's signature refrain.

Woody Johnson, owner of the Jets and heir to the Johnson & Johnson fortune, trailed several paces behind Kraft in the lobby, as he has for years in the AFC East. He wore a white Jets cap and crooked backpack. Kraft would diagnose Robert Wood "Woody" Johnson IV with the "incurable disease." On the day that the league announced its sanctions against the Patriots and Brady, Johnson's wife, Suzanne, tweeted out a smiley face emoji before deleting it. Even worse was when the Wood Man himself "favorited" a tweet calling for his own general manager at the time (John Idzik) to be fired. Johnson apologized and called the move "inadvertent."

There is much about the Membership that is "inadvertent," starting with who gets to join this freakish assembly. They are quite a bunch: old money and new, recovering drug addicts and born-again Christians and Orthodox Jews; sweethearts, criminals, and a fair number of Dirty Old Men. They are tycoons of enlarged ego, delusion, and prostate whose ranks include heir-owners like the Maras, Rooneys, and Hunts, of the Giants, Steelers, and Chiefs, respectively, whose family names conjure league history and muddy fields, sideline fedoras and NFL Films. There is also a truck-stop operator whose company admitted to defrauding its customers in a $92 million judicial settlement, a duo of New Jersey real estate developers who were forced to pay $84.5 million in compensatory damages because, according to a judge, they "used organized crime–type activities" to fleece their business partners, an energy baron who funded an antigay initiative, a real estate giant married to a Walmart heiress, tax evaders, etc. One imagines those black felt pictures from the seventies with dogs playing poker around a table. Trails of ex-wives, litigants, estranged children, and fired coaches populate their histories.

Shopping mall developer Edward John "Eddie" DeBartolo Jr., the beloved 49ers owner who won five Super Bowl championships during his twenty-three-year tenure, was suspended by the league for a year and eventually gave up control of the team to his sister after pleading guilty to his role in a gambling fraud scandal in Louisiana. In an ill-fated effort to get a riverboat gambling license, DeBartolo had agreed to pay Governor Edwin Edwards $400,000 in $100 bills. Somehow "Eddie D" managed to avoid prison and was sentenced instead to the pro football Hall of Fame in 2016.

Membership positions come with no term limits, let alone reelection campaigns. "I own this football team," 49ers CEO Jed York, DeBartolo's nephew, told a group of reporters after firing his general manager and third coach in three years after the 2016–17 season. "You don't dismiss owners," he felt the need to remind everyone. In an otherwise defensive and bumbling performance, this was York's one indisputable line. Technically, York's mother owned the team and she could fire him (as Panthers owner Jerry Richardson once made his sons resign). But his larger point was clear: York served at the pleasure of the roost he then ruled, and so did everyone else.

League meetings offer incidental bits of access at an oligarchic theme park. Normally reclusive and fortified figures favor us with happenstance encounters. Niners cochairman John York happened to be standing next to me in the valet parking line; he is a retired cancer research pathologist and brilliantly credentialed to own an NFL team. How? Because he was smart enough to marry Eddie DeBartolo's sister years before model owner Eddie D became a felon and lost his team. I introduced myself to Mr. York, asked him how the 49ers were looking, and mentioned that I was a reporter, which appeared to stun and terrify him. "We are very excited about our team under Coach Kelly," he said, referring to the team's newly hired coach, Chip Kelly. I wished Mr. York luck in the coming season, by the end of which it would be "former coach Chip Kelly."

AS IT DOES EVERY YEAR, THE LEAGUE KICKED off its annual meeting with a welcome party that was open to all branches of the family. There were splendid buffets, a live band, bright renderings of the Shield in various forms, and even a magician for the kids. Guests balanced cocktails and plates of food around a swimming pool. Everyone was there, Roger and the Membership on down to the lowliest league officials. Even Dr. Elliot Pellman was attending, the notorious former Jets team doctor who went on to become the league's go-to concussion denier for many years. He had chaired the NFL's Mild Traumatic Brain Injury Committee despite turning out to be a rheumatologist who was trained in Guadalajara and had limited expertise in heads. As best anyone could tell, Pellman's chief qualification for the job seemed to be that he was former commissioner Paul Tagliabue's personal physician.

"Is that Elliot Pellman?" I asked a league executive. I recognized Pellman from the various reports I'd watched and read over the years about the league's fumbling of its concussion problem. "Yep, he's still here," the league official said, head shaking. I suggested that maybe the magician could make Dr. Pellman disappear. The executive laughed, but it turns out the league was already on the case. "He's retiring," the NFL's executive vice president for health and safety policy, Jeff Miller, told **USA Today** the very next day.

My main goal for the reception was to eat as much shellfish as possible and to specifically avoid two people. The first was Tony Wyllie, the antagonistic head of communications for the Washington Redskins. He was mad at me because of a story I had written for the **New York Times Magazine** about Goodell a few months earlier. Wyllie had arranged a brief interview for me to discuss Goodell with Redskins owner Dan Snyder. It was a session that essentially amounted to Snyder's telling me about one hundred different ways in fifteen minutes that Goodell "always protects the Shield." Wyllie monitored our interview (as PR guys do), or "babysat," as I described Wyllie's role. Wyllie registered his displeasure to me earlier at being called a "babysitter."

"We're done," Wyllie told me, after also saying that I had no right in the story to mention the issue of the name "Redskins" being offensive to Native Americans. I had indeed mentioned the Redskins name in the story, mostly because Houston Texans owner Bob McNair had weighed in on the issue in a particularly striking fashion. McNair told me he was not offended by the name "Redskins" and explained that he had grown up in North Carolina around many Cherokee Indians. "Everybody respected their courage," McNair said of the Cherokees. "They might not have respected the way they held their whiskey, but . . ." McNair laughed.

This not surprisingly drew criticism from offended Native American groups, anti–Redskins name protesters, and people who can appreciate the irony of headlines like this one, on **Deadspin**: NFL ASSURES FANS THERE'S NO TOLERANCE FOR RACIAL SLURS AT REDSKINS GAMES. But I had been told that McNair was mad since the "Redskins" name was not the designated topic of our interview (the unquestioned greatness of Roger Goodell was said designated topic). As for the commissioner, I had asked the Texans owner whether he was concerned about the volume of criticism Goodell had been receiving. With success comes scrutiny, was how McNair had replied, although once again he said it in a much more excellent way. "It's like the old saying," McNair said. "The higher up the palm tree the monkey climbs, the more of his ass is exposed." McNair laughed. If the commish objected to being compared with a monkey's ass by one of his bosses, he had about 40 million reasons this year to take it like a man.

MCNAIR, THEN SEVENTY-NINE, HAS A BALD OVAL head and a slight resemblance to Mr. Clean. I saw him standing with his wife at the reception looking clean in a pressed white suit. I surveyed the monkey's ass in full. Everyone was dressed for leisure: Kraft in a too-unbuttoned dress shirt and his customized Nikes; Jones in a powder-blue blazer, no tie, and a glass (sorry, tumbler) of something; Ravens chief Steve Bisciotti in beautifully pressed jeans, white shirt with an open collar, and loafers without socks.

49ers coach Chip Kelly elbowed his way up next to me at the paella table. He had been talking to Rex Ryan, who was then coaching the Bills and whom I barely recognized after he had lost considerable weight following a lap band procedure in 2010 (Kelly might consider this). I had, for the record, never seen so much paella in my life. The league does know how to feed itself.

After a few minutes, I gravitated to a mountain of lobster meat, crab, and shrimp. And also to Woody Johnson. I was eager to discuss politics with the Wood Man given his longtime involvement with the Republican Party. He had been the national finance chairman of Jeb Bush's ill-fated presidential campaign until it had been officially euthanized a few weeks earlier. Trump had taunted Johnson via a tweet, saying, "If Woody would've been w/ me, he would've been in the playoffs, at least!" The Jets owner was now slowly warming to Trump.

He gushed to me about how brilliant "build a wall" was as Trump's signature theme. The phrase sent a simple, elegant message of what he stood for and what his campaign was about. Johnson was hopeful that Trump could act in a more restrained and presidential manner going forward—hopeful enough that Johnson would eventually raise nearly $25 million for the future president, much of it from fellow NFL owners.

ESPN's Herm Edwards, the former Eagles defensive back and Jets head coach, came over to say hello to Johnson. "Love you, man," the owner said, greeting his former coach. Johnson had also professed his "love" for Herm following the 2005 season exactly six weeks before "releasing him from his contract" under mysterious circumstances. I excused myself from this discussion, walked about ten feet, and found myself face-to-face with Goodell. "Good to see you," Goodell said to me, and I reminded him I had interviewed him two months earlier for a story he claimed not to read. Suddenly there was a loud pop. I turned my head to see that a kid's balloon had burst and its poor owner had burst into tears. By the time I turned back around the commissioner was gone, escaping behind a wall of owners.

The highlight of the evening came about a half hour later. Cynthia Hogan, then the league's head of public policy and government affairs, walked over and introduced me to Jane Skinner Goodell, Roger's wife. Her Majesty is a former Fox News anchor and the daughter of Samuel Skinner, a former transportation secretary and White House chief of staff under George H. W. Bush. I felt immediately at ease with Mrs. Goodell, though it might have been the booze. I asked her if she could help get the Pats' stolen draft picks back after the Deflategate travesty. She chuckled, and then I asked her how many Shields Roger insisted they display around their estate in Bronxville, New York. "Only one," she said evenly. "It's tattooed on his chest." I had heard rumors that Mrs. Goodell had an actual sense of humor, despite her husband's being the enemy of lightness in any form. This confirmed it. She had a friend in me for life at that point.

"It doesn't sound sexy," Mrs. Goodell elaborated on her husband's Shield tattoo. "But there are times . . ." Her voice trailed off and everyone who was listening laughed. But then she appeared to become nervous. "Okay, the tattoo on the chest is off the record," she insisted to me. No way, I replied, and so the Queen of the Shield doubled down: "I didn't say anything about the tattoo on his ass," she said.

3.

NUGGETS

No less of a genius than Bill Belichick appeared
to be lost. I watched him and ESPN's Trey
Wingo passing each other twice down the same
hallway. They then pivoted and changed directions and passed each other again. Belichick was
wearing flip-flops, cargo shorts, and a trademark
gray hoodie with big sweat blotches on the back.
He also wore his trademark "I hate this fucking
league" scowl, a few notches more grim than his
usual default scowl.

This aloofness goes well beyond Belichick's
well-established commitment to "ignoring the
noise." "Ignore the noise" is one of the many ano-
dyne phrases that get elevated to branded merchandise by the Patriots because it happened to
emanate from the tongues of Mr. Kraft or Coach
Fucking Genius ("one of the most active organi-

zations in sports as far as trademarking phrases goes," ESPN reported. When 345 Park is involved, Belichick has been known to ratchet his contempt to Hall of Fame levels. A few minutes after the Patriots defeated the Seahawks in Super Bowl 49, an NFL flunky assigned to the Patriots coach mentioned a few "league things," like interviews and posing for photos, that were expected of the winning coach. "Fuck the league," Belichick said at this moment of pinnacle triumph. They should trademark that, too, if they haven't already.

The closer one works to a football field, the less use one would have for a league meeting. Conversely, these are crunch-time events for the parasites, support staff, and media eavesdroppers who can get a great deal done here. In the lobby I encountered the perma-tanned Drew Rosenhaus, who pimps himself as "the NFL's Most Ruthless Agent." Rosenhaus stood a few feet away from the NFL's leading media busybody, ESPN's Schefter.

These league powwows are like Adam's bar mitzvah. He knows everyone here. He waves to passing GMs, coaches, and agents in the lobby, holds a phone to his left ear and checks a text on another in his right hand. This is the population that makes up the "per sources" that Schefter cites whenever he tweets out a nugget to his seven million followers. Schefter is the prototype of a sports media subspecies that has gained cachet: the NFL Insider.

"Dannon goes with Cowboys QB Dak Prescott after dropping Cam Newton, per source," Schefter tweeted after the Panthers' quarterback went off on a sexist riff at a press conference, costing him endorsements. Schefter did not specify whether his scoop came per football or yogurt sources. But **take it to the bank** (an insider catchphrase) the man has sources; or even more than sources, he has "relationships," as Schefter described them to me. "There are some that are friends," he said. Schefter mentioned that a head coach had invited him to his son's wedding last summer. "My friends in the sport, they call me for advice, ask what I think," Schefter told me.

But, I asked, isn't the notion of "friend" a bit fraught in the journalism business? Maybe, but the nugget racket is its own distinct subset. The Schefters of the space do not play for the Pulitzer Prizes (the eight-part series and **textured storytelling**). He was named "Most Influential Tweeter in New York" by **New York** magazine is more like it.

Insiders have their own reward system and play by their own rules. I asked Schefter what would happen if he had to report a critical item about one of his "friends" in the business. His tone became slightly defensive. "Hold on," Schefter said. "How often am I writing a critical thing? That's not what I do. My job is trafficking information—who's hired, fired, traded, extended."

Nuggets!

Nuggets aren't "news" necessarily, in the same way that Chicken McNuggets aren't really food. But they have become pleasing, even addictive, components of the fan diet nonetheless. When I was growing up, NFL transactions—like those from the other major leagues—were mostly rendered in agate type in the back of the sports pages. That's where one would learn, for instance, that the NFL fined Steelers safety Mike Mitchell $48,620 for his late hit on Chiefs quarterback Alex Smith, or that the Redskins were signing kicker Nick Rose or that former 49ers linebacker NaVorro Bowman had struck a one-year deal with the Raiders. These items were packaged as the afterthoughts they were. Even among hard-core fans, the privilege of learning that the Colts had placed running back Robert Turbin (elbow) on injured reserve could wait until the morning. These followers did not have fantasy moves pending— because fantasy football did not exist, and neither did the Internet and neither did Adam Schefter in his multiplatform embodiment.

There is no great Big Bang theory to explain how yesterday's agate type became the nugget cosmos that Schefty rules. Or, if there is, he isn't pondering cosmic questions like that. I once asked Schefter whether it bothered him that the half-life of his art form—the nugget—lasted roughly as long as a single dose of Ritalin. "Everything's fleeting," Schefter said, shrugging. He checked his phone as if it were an involuntary brain function, like breathing.

Schefter would be loath to waste a second before discharging some morsel of "breaking news," just as his customers would be loath to learn of a transaction one second later than they had to. With his always-refilling hoard of data snacks, Adam feeds a dynamic market of incremental news in which he is also the chief broker and disseminator.

Schefter is coiffed, suited, and perpetually made up. He cultivates a harried bearing, as if carrying the weight of each follower's information needs. Increasingly, he is feeding their addiction to fantasy leagues. "There's been a shift over time," said Schefter, who joined ESPN in 2009 after five years at the NFL Network and more than fifteen years covering the Broncos for the **Denver Post** and **Rocky Mountain News**. "I am rarely asked how a team is going to do, and I am regularly asked whether I should start this player or that player, draft this player, who's a sleeper, who's a breakout guy." Schefter is, to paraphrase Hair Club for Men president Sy Sperling, not only the Nugget Club for Men president but also a client. He is a devout fantasy owner in his own right. His team is called "Per Sources."

Schefter's full-on life commitment to the hunt for nuggets is his brand animator. He enjoys the fact of his one-dimensional existence—no hobbies, no time for anything besides job, family, and venti soy chai lattes. He sleeps five fitful hours a night ("in bursts, never continuously") and tries to get a date night in with his wife on weekends. He works out Tuesdays, Wednesdays, Fridays, and Saturdays, and never without his phone. A driver takes him the two-to-three-hour distance between ESPN's Bristol, Connecticut, headquarters and his home on Long Island, which allows Schefter to work en route or maybe to steal an extra burst of shut-eye. "I regret to say I am not the most well-rounded individual," he told me. He barely writes anymore beyond firing off a few lines via Twitter and TV. And that's fine. "I'm a hit man," he said. "I hit a story, bounce to the next one." Schefter no longer ventures into locker rooms and attends just one game a year (the Super Bowl). He engages "per sources" almost entirely by phone and text message. This makes these league gatherings a rare opportunity to lay eyes **per** them.

Observing Schefter on his manic routine, I was left to wonder: would there be a day when this fully customized insider will be replaced by some Siri- or Alexa-like oracle? Maybe named "Nuggetia"? (**"Nuggetia, is Adrian Peterson too injured to start on Sunday?"**)

But then you see Schefter working his sources/relationships/friends, and you sense something that approximates human warmth. There is also something earnest, even winning, about how transactional his interactions are. When I interviewed Schefter, he won me over by dismissing my small-talk efforts at the outset. "Okay, you don't have to warm me up, time is of a premium, I got it," Schefter said, directing me to turn on my tape recorder. "I'm going to give you whatever I can. I don't want to waste your time." By that, Schefter meant he did not want to waste his own time, which is almost always better spent hunting his Big Game—trophy nuggets.

On the sidelines before Super Bowl 51, Schefter was actually seen hugging Bill Belichick. This would earn him a personal foul—15 yards—from certain journalism referees. But damn, you kind of marvel. No one hugs Bill Belichick, certainly not reporters. Schefter should go into the Hall of Fame for that alone.

In Boca, I watched Schefter huddle with Berj Najarian, Belichick's longtime consigliere—or director of football/head coach administrator (former Patriots quarterback Drew Bledsoe once had a dozen roses sent to Najarian on Secretary's Day). Berj is a jittery presence generally, but particularly so whenever Belichick is not around, like a St. Bernard displaced from his master. He is just the kind of functionary whose cock-blocking and secret-keeping powers make him an essential, even feared figure inside the league. "How many people talk about the consigliere?" the retired

Patriots linebacker and ESPN analyst Tedy Bruschi said by way of refusing to speak about Najarian when Bruschi was approached on the subject by the **New York Times**. Schefter talks **to** the consigliere, which is all the more impressive. It makes Berj a solid gold source/relationship/friend. Quiet chuckles emanated from the Najarian and Schefter powwow, a sense of a mutual comfort being taken.

Well-barbered ESPN insider Sal Paolantonio stood a few feet away from the duo, also yapping into his phone. "That tanned NFL guy from ESPN" is how an older gentleman in a Chicago Cubs cap described Paolantonio to his wife as they passed by the pack of media busybodies. Paolantonio has a long face and sports suede shoes and a pair of Rick Perry–vintage glasses that make him look cerebral when reporting the latest on whether quarterback Ryan Fitzpatrick will return to the Jets. Like many of his Hair Club for Nuggets cohorts, "Sal Pal," as he is known, is a former print guy. He covered the Eagles for the **Philadelphia Inquirer** in the 1990s. But when you see him working insider quorums such as this, Sal Pal brings the strut of someone who has fully "graduated" to TV "personality," at least tripling or quadrupling his salary along the way. His earpiece might as well be made of gold. "I don't want this to sound the wrong way," he told me, "but I feel like I was born to do this."

Also reporting for nugget duty was another NFL insider, ESPN's John Clayton, who might have been my personal favorite. Slight and unassuming, Clayton looks like a parakeet with glasses, or maybe a math teacher. But he is also a machine, and one of the small victories of my career was to persuade my bosses at the **Times Magazine** to assign a Q and A with Clayton on the eve of the 2013 season. (First question: "You just covered twelve different team practices in the last eleven days. What did you dream about being when you grew up?")

After I summoned the nerve to introduce myself, Clayton confirmed a previous nugget I had extracted from **Sports Illustrated**'s NFL kingfish Peter King: that a woman wearing an I LOVE JOHN CLAYTON T-shirt had traveled to Indianapolis during the NFL Scouting Combine to track Clayton down and announce herself to him as a John Clayton groupie. "Her name was Candy," Clayton told me (of course it was). "The whole groupie thing is definitely a little bit creepy," Clayton added. It's safe to say that Clayton, who would be let go by ESPN a year later, could still walk through any airport in the United States and get hit up for more autographs and photos than the vast majority of NFL players, U.S. senators, and Nobel Prize winners.

Our quadrant of the lobby had by now also come to include **Sports Illustrated**'s King and

Profootballtalk.com's Mike Florio. It made for quite the impressive cluster of NFL media yentas from the Nugget Industrial Complex. If God forbid a bomb went off in here and wiped everyone out, we would suffer an immediate nugget famine, necessitating an emergency airlift to fantasy players. Seeing all of them clustered, waiting to do their "stand-ups"—or "hits"—my mind jumped to the ESPN ad tagline "We Are Men Wearing Makeup Talking About Sports." That is indeed what they are, but it misses how dead serious their rat race is.

Nugget dealers run in a pack, and most do their best to be classy about giving shout-outs where due. ("Bengals Rey Maualuga checking into Betty Ford later this month, according to Adam Schefter," praised **Sports Illustrated**'s Peter King. "Good Nugget." Credit for nugget recognition in this particular case: **Deadspin**'s Drew Magary.) But some do not give proper shout-outs, which can be a sore spot and invite pariah status in the academy. Don't get Schefter started, for instance, on his former employer, NFL Network, and how derelict they can be about giving props. Actually, I did get him started. He was being driven in to work one morning during the season and listening to some NFL show on Sirius Satellite Radio. "They're saying [Bengals tight end] Tyler Eifert is going to have back surgery and be out four to six months. I'm like, 'Really, where did you get that from?' Nothing about ESPN. Nothing! Nothing. If I ever did that to somebody, what is done regularly to ESPN, I would be called on it every time." Not cool!

No doubt, things can get heated inside the kettle of nuggets. Florio, of ProFootballTalk (PFT) and NBC, has developed a devoted following for his aggressive and increasingly combative tone. Several team and league officials told me they check ProFootballTalk—and Florio's Twitter feed—first thing in the morning and several times a day. He can be refreshingly edgy toward subjects and competitors alike—though not everyone finds him refreshing. "He's not a journalist," ESPN nugget-monger Chris Mortensen said dismissively to me about Florio. "He's really not a good person."

Florio has even been accused of being (gasp) unclassy! After the 2018 Super Bowl, Florio went out on a lonely limb to report that Patriots offensive coordinator Josh McDaniels was having second thoughts about becoming the next coach of the Colts—though several outlets had reported his hiring as a done deal. When Schefter reported that McDaniels would be staying in New England after all, Florio made a point of tweeting thus: "Attention everyone who assumed I was making it all up: SUCK IT."

FOR AS FOCUSED AS THEY ARE ON THEIR PHONES and next hits and receiving their just shout-outs, nugget hunters have a sixth sense whenever Big Game enters their perimeter: a head coach or chatty owner, perhaps, or the occasional Moby-Dick himself. As Goodell moved through the summit grounds like a traveling sheikh, a siren might as well have sounded in Insider Village, such was the state of high alert. No one would expect the commissioner to actually feed anybody anything, but still, witness must be borne to the ruddy-faced emperor. The son of the late Republican senator of New York Charles Goodell, the commissioner's politician genes are evident. He is a most prodigious slapper of backs, knower of names, gladder of hands, and toucher of bases. He moved among his constituents in a former jock's ballet of bro hugs and two-handed handgrips and shoulder squeezes punctuated with backslaps. He received guests, laughing easily, maybe for real, or maybe not.

"Good to see you, Coach," Goodell called out to Carolina Panthers headman Ron Rivera in a central patio. Goodell's orange hair looks especially bright and shiny in the sunlit room, as does the Creamsicle hue of his face. "Great season this year," Goodell tells Coach Rivera. Their handshake flowers into a hug. Goodell then sees the Philadelphia Eagles owner Jeffrey Lurie, one of the thirty-two most important bases he has to touch, walking in his direction. He stops and has a word. The commissioner nods and is listening, quite clearly.

This is Roger's element. He looks freshly worked out. It would please him very much to hear me say that. He works out a great deal. And he loves to talk about how he works out a lot (SoulCycle, Pilates), and also mention exactly for how long he worked out that day. Goodell likes to trash-talk colleagues who don't get to the gym at the early hour he does. "Good afternoon," he will taunt them as they straggle in before 7 a.m. He runs an annual 40-yard dash in his work clothes, following up on a gimmick that NFL Network's Rich Eisen performs every year at the Scouting Combine. Before the Super Bowl, Goodell holds a press conference where he typically takes a question planted with a kid reporter who might toss up some puffball about a league public service program, like one that encourages kids to exercise for at least sixty minutes a day— "Play 60," the initiative is called.

"Mr. Commissioner, how do YOU play sixty?" a kid asked Goodell before Super Bowl 49 in Glendale, Arizona. The beast pounced: "I played sixty-five this morning on the elliptical," Goodell preened. I am going to venture that you'll never meet a man in his late fifties with such rock-hard abs.

Goodell also likes to talk about how he used to play The Game himself. He played through high school till he wrecked his knee. But playing football was such a great experience for him. It gave Roger so much camaraderie and instilled so much character. If he had sons, instead of teenage twin daughters, he would by all means encourage them to play football. Other prominent parents have said they would not be so sure—Barack Obama and LeBron James have expressed ambivalence, as well as the actual father of Tom Brady, **knowing what we know now**; Troy Aikman, Terry Bradshaw, too, and a bunch of others. But Goodell says there are no sure things in life, whether you're football playing or couch sitting, and he does his best to make the case.

Goodell is apparently required to say that his first job is to "protect the Shield" **x** number of times a day as a condition of the $111 million in salary and benefits his owner-bosses paid him between 2013 and 2015. The Shield evokes gallant warriors and immovable forces, but it is also a reminder that the enterprise itself requires protection—a shield for the Shield. When Goodell sits at his desk, he gazes upon a large rendering of the Shield on a back wall of his office. "It is a reminder to look out," he says.

"Protecting the Shield" roughly equates to protecting "the integrity of the game," which is another platitude the commissioner throws out all the time. What all of that essentially means is that Goodell's first job is to protect the Membership, and often from itself.

The league, for instance, would prefer it if the Membership left the discussion of brain health to the experts, or at least to Dr. Goodell. It is part of the commissioner's job, after all, to cushion billionaire brain farts on this issue. When health and safety questions are asked of the Membership, as they inevitably are, the moguls are careful to inflict the repetitive sound-bite trauma that the league arms them with ("the game has never been safer"). They then move on as quickly as possible.

But owners can't always help themselves, and at least one of them seems intent on proving this every few months. Colts owner Jim Irsay, for instance, sat in a golf cart in Boca, smoking a cigarette and holding forth with Dan Kaplan of the **SportsBusiness Journal** about the varying side effects of playing the sport. He likened the risks to the possible side effects of taking aspirin. "You take an aspirin, I take an aspirin," Irsay said. "It might give you extreme side effects of illness and your body may reject it, where I would be fine." This caused an Excedrin headache at the annual meeting, which Jerry Jones decided to assuage by brushing aside the rather obvious link between chronic traumatic encephalopathy and football.

"No, that's absurd" was Jerry's take on whether playing football can result in CTE.

Candor can prove as problematic as ignorance. Bills general manager Doug Whaley, for instance, was trying to be philosophical when making the obvious point that football is a dangerous sport and that injuries are inevitable. "It's a violent game," Whaley told WGR 550 radio. It would have been fine if he ended the sentence here. But instead, Whaley ended the sentence with ". . . that I personally don't think humans are supposed to play." And the headline wrote itself.

Bills GM: I "don't think humans are supposed to play" football

This was problematic since football-playing robots had not yet been invented. What's more, Whaley was trying to convince actual human beings to come play for the Buffalo Bills. You can imagine the GM was frog-marched up to the Bills' PR office for cleanup duty. "Clearly I used a poor choice of words," Whaley clarified in a statement the next day. He is human after all.

So are NFL owners, just like us, although their positions grant them superhuman deference and platforms that can be irresistible. That is why league meetings, teeming with media, can be so treacherous. The Membership is forced into the sunlight—when in fact most of them are suited to the shadows. Robert Kraft made himself available to the media for twelve minutes on a back patio. RKK had a message to convey. His audience was about twenty reporters and camera people, most from New England outlets. Kraft said he is proud of all the great things the Patriots have accomplished during his twenty-three years as owner. We know this because he is always saying so and listing all the accomplishments (the Super Bowls, conference championship games, the consecutive sellouts). He does again: "It's nice to step back a little bit and contemplate," he said. But what RKK really wanted to say is that he is still angry over Deflategate. It's important for New England fans to hear that, because they, too, are still angry and probably will be even if Brady wins another ten Super Bowls.

"I want our fans to know that I empathize with the way they feel," Kraft said. (Robert is a mogul of empathy kill!) Not only that, but he has written a letter—a letter!—requesting that the commissioner return the first- and fourth-round draft picks he had docked the Pats over Brady's alleged and horrible crimes. Kraft said the league was derelict in not considering the Ideal Gas Law when determining the team's guilt or innocence (the Ideal Gas Law, as Joey from Quincy and most the rest of Pats Nation could explain much better than me, is an old physics rule explaining why a football might naturally lose air pressure in cold weather without the intervention of, say, a needle administered by a locker room attendant whose nickname is "The Deflator"). You can be certain that Mr. Kraft's letter was a succinct biting missive written in his own hand, perhaps on stationery from the Ritz Paris.

This flaccid protest was Kraft's attempt to pander to New England fans while not losing his seat at the Membership Big Boy table or jeopardizing his still-close relationship with Goodell. He tries to have it both ways, which elicits eyerolls from owners and league officials who are on to him. They call him "Krafty" (behind his back) and "needy Bob Kraft" (longtime **Boston Globe** columnist Dan Shaughnessy).

One nugget-hungry pest in Boca asked Kraft the requisite question about concussions. He parried it with the requisite sound bites about how "the game has never been safer" and how he used to play football himself ("lightweight" football at Columbia, gives him a certain authority). Another reporter pressed him to assess the overall performance of Goodell, who had just completed his tenth season as commissioner. "Putting personal situations aside," Kraft straddled, "I think he's done a very good job."

Translation: forgiveness comes easier when you're making reams of cash.

The Patriots' longtime PR man Stacey James halted the session with a "thanks guys" in time for me to catch Woody Johnson doing a similar gaggle in a nearby conference room. Johnson does not often speak publicly. This is not atypical for hapless franchise bosses who oversee periodic coach and GM shake-ups in big media markets like Woody and the New York J-E-T-S, **JETS JETS JETS!** Johnson also has an amusing gift for knucklehead statements, which makes him a recurring character on **Shit the Membership Says** (a sitcom I plan to develop someday). My favorite Woody wisdom occurred after Schefter had produced a nugget quoting an anonymous Jets assistant coach critical of quarterback Christian Hackenberg. The Jets rookie, according to the coach, "couldn't hit the ocean" with one of his passes. Asked whether he agreed, Johnson said he had indeed seen Schefter's ESPN report, and then tried to defuse the situation with, uh, humor. "I guess it depends on which ocean," Johnson said. "Maybe it was a small ocean." (He makes a fair point.) "The EPA describes that as an ocean. Anyway, no, that's not funny."

Johnson always looks slightly daydreamy and disoriented. He is like an overgrown third-grader who collects toy trains and rotten quarterbacks. His press session in Boca was no different, though he wore the game expression of a kid hopping back on a jumpy horse.

He was immediately asked the evergreen question about the Jets' quarterback situation. What was the Jets' interest in free agent Robert Griffin III, who had visited the team? Johnson was noncommittal but generous enough to describe Griffin as being "very presentable," an innovative construction in the tradition of Very White Men Describing Black Quarterbacks. He also offered a twist on the standard response to the concussion question, saying that he cares passionately about the issue because "I come from a health background." (Being the great-grandson of the Johnson & Johnson cofounder would, I suppose, technically qualify someone for a "health background.") Regardless, the Wood Man was not going any further on the issue. "I'll leave that to the neurologists," he said, presentably.

Johnson had been responding to a question about an attention-grabbing comment that was made a few days earlier by the NFL's senior vice president for health and safety policy, Jeff Miller. Miller, a nonneurologist (lawyer), had been asked by a congresswoman at a roundtable discussion whether "there's a link between football and degenerative brain disorders like CTE." "The answer to that is certainly yes," he replied. Given the volume of scientific evidence and consensus on the matter, the admission carried a certain Is-the-Pope-Catholic obviousness.

But in light of the NFL's past denials and hedging on the subject—including Jerry Jones directly contradicting him almost simultaneously—

Miller's words landed as a stunning confession. They garnered dramatic "Game May Never Be the Same" headlines (in the **New York Times**). They also made the NFL nervous—lawyers and owners especially, even beyond their baseline state of unease that any little thing could topple their fragile dynasty, and possibly impact future litigation.

League officials had always been, at best, cautious about larding their public statements with "potentials," "possibles," "allegeds," and other qualifiers. Owners felt blindsided by Miller's acknowledgment, especially as it signaled a shift in the NFL's official line that there was no definitive link between football and CTE; and now they were all being asked about it at the league meeting. Of Miller's remark, Woody Johnson stuck with "I'm not qualified to agree or disagree," despite his health background.

"WHERE THE HELL IS THAT THING SUPPOSED to be?" Bills coach Rex Ryan asked me on Tuesday morning. He was trying to get to the mandatory AFC coaches' breakfast in which each team's head man must endure a forty-five-minute-or-so tribunal at a table covered with reporters' tape recorders, microphones, and heat-lamped eggs. Ryan appeared not to know where he was going, and I told him I was headed to the same place he was. I was walking with a sense of purpose, which was an act (I have no idea what my purpose was), but enough to win Rex's trust.

He sipped from an iced coffee drink topped off with whipped cream in a Big Gulp–size cup. By way of small talk, I asked him about Heather Locklear, the nineties-era TV goddess known for her work on **Melrose Place**, and who I happen to know is Ryan's favorite "celebrity crush." I picked this nugget up from being one of the few people to read a behind-the-scenes book— **Collision Low Crossers**, by my pal Nicholas Dawidoff—about the Ryan-coached Jets teams from earlier this decade. You can also get a lot done by having one obscure detail at the ready about a famous someone in case an icebreaker is needed. "She's the best," Ryan gushed over Locklear as he walked. Ryan's better-known sexual taste is his well-documented foot fetish (because God forbid a middle-aged football coach's foot fetish not be "well-documented"). New York's tabloids documented the naughty coach's proclivity after an online video surfaced featuring a woman who looked like Ryan's wife showing off her feet while a voice that sounded like Rex's narrated the action. "I'm the only guy in history who gets in a sex scandal with his wife!" Ryan said. Ryan's assistant coaches with the Jets arranged to have an autographed poster of Locklear sent to him. He hung it on his office wall and cherished it except for one thing. "She has her shoes on," Ryan lamented.

Rex was one of the few people I encountered in Boca who seemed curious about who I was or what brought me there. He did not recognize me as a sportswriter. I told him that normally I wrote about politics, which like football had reached a feverish level of fascination as Trump was then in the process of manhandling his way to the GOP nomination. Ryan was a public Trump supporter, but celebrity crushes excited him far more during our short walk. He told me he has added other crushes to his personal fantasy team over the years, Reese Witherspoon being the most recent. "It's important to have some that are totally unattainable," he mused. What's the fun of having something you know you can have? I asked Ryan if he enjoyed these mandatory coaches' breakfasts. "No, of course not," he said. "Does anyone?" They take away from valuable work he needed to be doing for the Bills, for whom the playoffs have also been unattainable for seventeen years.

Coaches took up their stations at assigned tables. Reporters and cameramen positioned themselves to best receive their boilerplate meals. Bengals coach Marvin Lewis vowed to "take each day as it comes," and Steelers coach Mike Tomlin said running back Le'Veon Bell was recovering nicely from his knee injury, and then-Broncos coach Gary Kubiak said he had no time to savor his team's Super Bowl win—or, for that matter, the plate of cold breakfast meats placed before him. Life is hard.

Ravens coach John Harbaugh was sitting a few tables away, announcing that he is "passionate about football." He launched into a defense of the sport. There was a lot of this all week, especially from coaches. You mention concussions enough, and the parents who won't let their kids play and all the damning media portrayals, and it gets them going.

"Half our time here was spent talking about this issue," Harbaugh said of concussions, sounding exasperated in response to a question from Peter King about the future of football. "I see a lot of people out there who are pretty passionate about attacking football," he said. It was time to fight back. He spoke for an empire under siege. "I think it's about time some people are passionate about defending football. And all of us that know what football's about should stand up and do that." King asked Harbaugh what he was running for. He suggested that the Ravens coach be appointed America's "President of Football."

NFL coaches naturally make fervent evangelists for the game. But there has always been a flavor of exceptionalism around the sport, too, that suddenly felt outdated. "Presidents of Football" have long pushed the idea that football, and only football, can instill the character traits that are essential to what makes men Men. "Football requires and develops courage, cooperation, loyalty, obedience and self-sacrifice," the legendary coach Pop Warner himself wrote in his 1927 bible, **Football for Coaches and Players**. "It develops cool-headedness under stress, it promotes clean living and habits." Implicit here is that football promotes such virtues to a degree that basketball, soccer, or tennis never could. But it's also more complicated than it used to be.

THE ONE ESSENTIAL PERFORMANCE AT THE coaches' breakfast was Mr. Personality himself, Belichick. He had managed to skip out on many of the week's other functions, such as the annual group coaches' photo (along with his pal Andy Reid, the Chiefs' coach, apparently to go golfing). But the breakfast was as close to mandatory as it got for the future Hall of Fame headsetter. The cliffhanger to be resolved: How contemptuous could Belichick make himself? What was the minimum he could do to fulfill his obligation?

Breakfast with Belichick has become its own perverse attraction. He is not just his usual smirking, grunting crank, but something more here—a talking halitosis that you could actually see and (barely) hear. He exuded a kind of personality antimatter with its own gravitational pull.

At the previous year's league meeting in Arizona, Belichick had shown up twenty minutes late, and his rudeness had triggered a small tantrum by the **Daily News**' NFL writer Gary Myers (the brunt of which was felt by the Patriots PR shield Stacey James). Whether related or not, Belichick showed up more or less on time in Boca. He wore a light blue Johns Hopkins lacrosse hoodie and mumbled something at the outset in tribute to the just-retired Patriots linebacker Jerod Mayo. "We're happy to add all the players that we've added," Belichick said about some recent addition to the team. He slurped between words. ("When we're out there, we'll see how it goes.") He smacked his lips. A reporter tried to place an NFL Network microphone in front of Belichick, which inspired his pièce de résistance of the morning and a viral video clip for the ages: Belichick moved the NFL Network mic as far as he could reach and then cleared away a bunch of tape recorders in front of him with his forearms.

Belichick's valet Berj Najarian, who had been huddled with Schefter against a nearby wall, walked over at one point and placed a cup of icy water in front of the coach to warm him up. Finally, a Patriots beat reporter, Tom E. Curran of Comcast SportsNet New England, managed to get a small rise out of Belichick by asking where the coach's breakfast rated on his list of favorite things to do. "It's just part of the exciting week that is the NFL owners' meeting," Belichick said in a way that could be described as buoyant for him but dead-pan for anyone else. Curran's Comcast colleague Ray Ratto, a longtime Bay Area sportswriter, observed via Twitter that Belichick could have used his forty minutes more wisely by setting a league employee on fire. "Missed opportunity there," Ratto lamented.

A few minutes later, Belichick stood up, threw his backpack over his right shoulder, latched on to Berj like a teddy bear, and departed the premises.

4.

"TOM BRADY HERE"

July 2014

What to make of Tom Brady?

The Patriots quarterback has been defined by competing narratives for years. Neither is that compelling except in their incompatibility. The first is the familiar against-the-odds construct: Brady as the not-great high school player, up-and-down college quarterback, and 199th pick in the draft who caught stardom out of nowhere. Now over two decades of dominating a league designed to thwart dominance, a second narrative has taken hold: Brady as fairy tale and anti-underdog. He might be the most envied man in America: he dated an actress (Bridget Moynahan, with whom he has a son), married, and had two children with a Brazilian supermodel. His net worth is well into the nine figures and he plays for a team that always wins.

Tom Brokaw, the legendary newsman, tells the story of going through cancer treatments a few years ago and generally feeling like crap. He would, on his daily walks through his Upper East Side neighborhood, pass a bus shelter adorned with Brady's likeness on an ad poster for UGGs. "Fuck you," Brokaw would make a point of saying to the poster. "It was less an attack on him and more a catharsis for me," Brokaw explained, "but Brady was the perfect object."

Being a sports fan, generally speaking, can require a faith both blind and durable. Being a Boston fan has made this easier, in some ways, with our gaudy prosperity of late (ten rings combined this century from the four Boston/New England teams—and yes, we're counting). But the birthright is not without its embarrassments. You love your kids and try to be proud. Yet marrying my sports identity to glum, rude, and possibly devious characters like, say, Belichick can get exhausting. (I know, fuck me, Boston fans are tiresome enough without the self-pity routine.)

Brady's cultivated elegance could also be a bit much. He is "that perfect blend of goofy and handsome that makes you feel simultaneously inadequate and superior," wrote a car blogger named Matt Posky. Posky was disgusted upon learning that Brady had signed a lucrative endorsement

deal with Aston Martin, the British luxury au-
tomaker preferred by **Bond, James Bond.** It is,
apparently, a vehicle held most sacred among car
bloggers (like this guy Matt Posky), and it was not
just any Aston Martin car that Brady was hawking, but a DB11 model that sold for $215,000.
Aston Martin's partnership with Brady would
be long-term, according to the company's press
release, and the campaign would emphasize the
quarterback's "affinity for the love of beautiful."

It went on: "Brady will seek to share visualiza-
tions of where he sees beauty in his sporting moments, what he sees as beautiful in life, and what
continues to compel him to pursue greatness."

By contrast, Eli Manning has a deal with Toy-
ota and Aaron Rodgers is a pitchman for Ford.

Even in his younger, underdog days, Brady was
always a skewed fit with his townie worshippers.
While he managed to exhibit his own kind of
sheepish grace within the parochial madhouse
of Boston sports, Brady could seem as far away as
any athlete I'd ever rooted for. This went beyond
the shout-in-the-canyon remove that investing
emotionally in a pro athlete will always entail. He
was one of those everywhere-but-nowhere people. He would write a celebrity self-help book,
promote exotic diets, and get called the NFL's
answer to Gwyneth Paltrow. Who could identify with a man photographed in **GQ** holding a
baby goat? Brady didn't belong to any world I

would ever know. It seemed unlikely I would get close enough to venture a guess.

Yet here was an email in my inbox. From the Greatest of All Time (GOAT). "Tom Brady here" it said in the subject heading.

This was, in retrospect, where my expedition into the NFL began: New York, July 2, 2014, a few weeks before the Patriots were scheduled to start training camp, relatively innocent days for the NFL Reality Show. Ray Rice had only been suspended two games at that point. No one had accused Brady of cheating, or knew that the air pressure in footballs was something anyone could care about. He had yet to lend his name, at least publicly, to any Aston Martins, TAG Heuers, or Donald Trumps.

I'd been trying to meet and write about Brady for a few years. It was a Hail Mary pursuit, I always figured, but at the very least, trying to get to him had become an occasional side project. About four years earlier, I had struck up a sporadic phone dialogue with Donald Yee, a sports agent in Los Angeles who had represented Brady since he entered the NFL in 2000. Yee had built his NFL clientele in part by signing up lower draft picks with marginal NFL prospects—the football equivalent of penny stocks. In that regard, Brady turned into a payoff for the ages.

Brady remained loyal to Yee through his career while Yee has, not surprisingly, clung to his asset like a toddler to a blankie. He fit no archetype of the hustler agent in the Jerry Maguire mold. And while being full of shit is an occupational hazard among sports agents, I found Yee to be full of shit in such counterintuitive and even refreshing ways that I took a liking to him.

Yee grew up in Sacramento as part of a Chinese American family that emigrated in the 1850s. His ancestors sold herbal medicines. In scouting talent, Yee told me that he looked for less traditional and "more Eastern" qualities in the college players he wished to attract. Those qualities included a mixture of quiet confidence, even temperament, and "outward tranquillity," he said. (A more likely explanation is that Yee's services were not in great demand among first-tier college prospects, so he took a flyer on a bargain-bin QB from the University of Michigan and got lucky as hell.)

I told Yee I was interested in writing about Brady even though I was not a sportswriter. I was aware that Brady almost never did interviews. Yee said Brady preferred talking to people outside his usual field, so that was encouraging. It was also clear to me that Yee wanted me to think that he, himself, was more than just some fast-talking operator. The job of being a sports agent, Yee said in an interview with Sacramento's **Sactown** magazine, allowed him to be "very creative in the sense that it's very fun to try to procure a client that you have a big vision for and then see the client paint the picture." Yee compared his work to "a white canvas" waiting to be realized. "Then I see what I would consider to be a beautiful painting. And then I try to find the person who can paint that." I figured maybe I could humor Yee enough so that he might help me become a speck on the beautiful canvas of Tom Brady's life.

Yee told me to keep in touch. We checked in every year or so. Yee once tried to pitch me on doing a magazine story on another of his clients, an extreme wheelchair athlete I'd never heard of (Aaron "Wheelz" Fotheringham) who I guess is a big deal in "the extreme wheelchair" space. Then, a few days before the Fourth of July weekend in 2014, Yee called out of the blue and asked me if I wanted to grab lunch with Brady in New York the following Wednesday. Uh, sure, I said, I would do my best to be available, maybe move a few things around.

I made reservations at a restaurant in SoHo called The Dutch. Brady approved, via Yee, which I took as an affirmation of my class and refinement. But then Yee went dark and stopped answering my calls and emails for several days. Part of me wondered if I was being pranked. I took a train up to New York from my home in Washington on the night before the appointed Wednesday. Brady's email was waiting for me when I woke up the next morning. He offered robotic pleasantries, as if the email were composed by Siri.

"Good morning," it read. "I hope you're having a good week." We confirmed our lunch. But an hour later, I received another email from Brady. He said he wanted to call "an audible" (audible!) and asked if we could meet at his apartment instead of the restaurant. Sure, sure, I said. Where was that?

Twenty-third and Madison, Brady said.

I was in the cab on the way there when it occurred to me that any number of homes might be found at Twenty-third and Madison. So I emailed Brady back to ask for a more precise address.

"Hahaha, I wish I knew the address," he replied.

Brady didn't know his home address? Another point in favor of the prank theory. At the very least, Brady's casual ignorance of this most basic personal data reinforced the notion that he did not dwell in the pedestrian realm of slobs who must remember street addresses. He wrote back that he lived in the only skyscraper on the block, next to a McDonald's. Rupert Murdoch had apparently paid $57.25 million for four floors in the building.

I admit to having been nervous. In fact, I don't recall being this nervous before interviewing anyone in my entire career—and I've interviewed presidents, a bunch of CEO and celebrity types, and even the guy who used to host **The Apprentice**. Sports pedestals are funny that way.

Athletes often constitute our earliest objects of allegiance. Staying starstruck is an indulgence of our arrested developments, even for jaded middle-aged reporters—sweaty ones, in this case.

This was one of those **de**-luxe apartments in the sky that the elevator opens directly onto and takes up the entire floor (forty-eighth). Brady stood waiting for me. He wore a newsboy cap, tan corduroys, and a V-neck sweater over a T-shirt (in retrospect, the newsboy cap was sort of ridiculous). He is six-foot-four and appears taller in person. That's partly because it's hard to determine a football player's height when he is seen on TV surrounded by other large persons. But Brady also stands tall as a default posture. Nothing about him slouched.

My goal for this visit was to convince Brady to let me check in with him during the season for a magazine profile (and also, if I'm being honest, to become his best friend). His young son and daughter were running around. Brady introduced me to a nanny, whom he addressed as "babe." He calls a lot of people "babe," apparently, both male and female. He said "awesome" a lot.

We moved to a side parlor with a view of Midtown Manhattan. Brady left for a minute and then returned with a plate of almonds and water in two blue bottles. Gisele, I had read, had endorsed the supposed health benefits of spring water kept in blue bottles that are exposed to direct sunlight.

"Yeah, she puts the bottles of water in the sun and it energizes or charges them or something," Brady confirmed. I took a sip and felt myself energized.

We talked about football, about Boston, about the Bay Area, where Brady grew up (where I used to live) and the University of Michigan (which we both attended, ten years apart), and our kids (we both had three). It became evident that Brady and I were the same person and had lived the exact same life.

Brady kept talking about "taking care of my body," "preparing for football," and leading a life that would "optimize" his ability to endure an NFL season at "peak performance." He mentioned "lifestyle choices" that he wanted to promote. He had started a health, fitness, and wellness enterprise—TB12—with his closest friend, personal guru, and "body coach," a guy named Alex Guerrero. "TB12 is a way of life," Brady said, increasingly giving off an infomercial vibe.

He was quite conspicuously pitching a new product—the product being the lifestyle that works for Tom Brady. Not only that, Brady is betting that TB12 would help him play longer and better than anyone else ever has. But this formula need not only be exclusive to superstar quarterbacks. It can work for you, too, whether you're a weekend tennis player, would-be marathon runner, or just someone who's willing to pay to be more like the quarterback for the New England

Patriots. Brady would be the product's chief life-style missionary and poster child.

On the surface, it all sounded straightforward; Brady and his friend Alex were starting a high-end gym and fitness program. But he was also trying to convey something loftier here. He was determined to subvert the expectations of how long a superstar quarterback could play like one.

"The decisions that I make, about what to eat and what to drink and when to sleep, those are choices not everyone wants to make," he said. "They're like, 'Fuck it, I want to go to Shake Shack.' And I'm like 'No problem, but that's going to catch up with you at some point.'" (It was now clear that Brady and I in fact did not live the exact same life.) Brady said he has played with many teammates over the years who are content—thrilled—to have survived ten years before retiring. "They've played ten years eating pizza and drinking beer, that's fine, people have proven you can do that," Brady said. "But I've already played fifteen years, and I want to play longer. I don't know how much, but I want to play over twenty, I know that."

Brady seemed a little shy at first but overall was pleasant and laughed easily. He did say a few things that stuck out to me: professional football players as a group, he observed, tend not to be the most normal and well-adjusted cohort in society. His teammates over the years have included "not that many assholes," on the whole. He also told me a hilarious story about a fellow football player and close college friend, one that involved pizza, a fire in West Quad, and a photo of a bong in a damaged dorm room that ran in **The Michigan Daily**. Relatable!

At one point I gently raised the topic of concussions. Did the growing evidence about their toll give Brady any pause? This is sometimes not the easiest subject to bring up with a football player, especially one you've just met. ("Nice to meet you, Mr. Coalminer, any thoughts about black lung?") Brady kind of shrugged it off. But he also mentioned something about how Guerrero had a "system" and "technique" to help him deal with head trauma. I later learned that Brady had endorsed a dietary supplement that Guerrero had been selling, called NeuroSafe, that had dubiously promoted faster healing from concussions. "There is no other solution on the market that can do what NeuroSafe does," said Brady in a quote attributed to him in 2011 for a NeuroSafe print ad. "It's that extra level of protection that gives me comfort when I'm out on the field." The Federal Trade Commission eventually began an investigation but in the interim took no enforcement action because NeuroSafe sales were discontinued.

After about forty-five minutes, Brady's phone rang. He picked up, and a loud and distinctively accented female voice echoed up from his phone.

GISELE!

Brady addressed her as "G." "Where are you?" I heard her ask. G sounded annoyed. Brady adopted that clipped "I'm with someone, Hon, can't really talk" voice familiar to spouses everywhere. Brady said he'd be finished shortly and would see her at home (**"Love ya, Babe"**). She appeared to end the call without saying good-bye.

I told Brady I wanted to follow him during the season as he tried to defy the NFL actuarial tables. He was trying to "make history," I suggested, or some such bullshit I threw out in an effort to communicate that I **totally** got his elevated purpose. Brady said he would try to carve out pockets of time to get together over the coming months. He allowed, however, that once the season began, he would be on "Belichick Time." In other words, he would be absorbed into the scheduling equivalent of a black hole.

A few minutes later, Brady's then-five-year-old son, Benjamin, and then-two-year-old daughter, Vivian, were released into the room. They served as pediatric two-minute warnings. They both jumped on Brady, and Brady said something to "Benny" in Portuguese while little towheaded Vivian toddled over and looked sternly into my face. "Bye-bye," she said. I took this as a sign it was time to leave.

This was as close as I would get to my new best friend for a while. Brady kept putting me off, by way of Yee. Soon after we met in New York, the quarterback embarked with his family on a pre–training camp vacation in the Bahamas. The trip represented a rare separation between Brady and Guerrero, whose control over Brady's day-to-day regimen was far more powerful than seemingly everything else except possibly "Belichick Time." "Guerrero Time" was more like a New Age lockdown.

The "body coach" label understates Guerrero's reach into Brady's life. Guerrero is his spiritual guide, counselor, pal, nutrition adviser, trainer, massage therapist, business partner, and quasi–family member. He is the godfather of Brady's younger son, Ben. Guerrero works on Brady seven days a week, usually twice a day during the season. These sessions focus on Brady's legs, thighs, and right arm, the one he throws with, which he calls "the moneymaker."

Guerrero also works with Brady's personal chef to put together seasonal diets emphasizing certain foods in winter (lean meats and chicken), raw foods in summer, and a general food intake that is 80 percent alkaline and 20 percent acidic. This has something to do with balancing Brady's metabolic system for reasons I can't even begin to understand, much less explain, or (if I'm being honest) care about. Guerrero also gives Brady special cognitive exercises that help "de-stimulate" his mind so he can fall asleep every night by nine p.m. while wearing the $99.99 biodynamic sleepwear made by Under Armour that Brady would endorse. "If my opponents aren't wearing what I wear, I'm getting the edge on them even while I'm sleeping," Brady wrote in a TB12 manifesto published a few years later. If Brady is the Beatles, Guerrero is his maharishi—although he's also been compared with Yoko, suggesting a potential for disruption, or worse. "Everyone thinks I'm a kook and a charlatan," Guerrero told me, referring to how some traditional trainers view him. He has been called by less flattering names ("scam artist," "snake oil salesman") as well as cited by the FTC for marketing that concussion-prevention drink. And there was another potion that he claimed could cure cancer and heart disease and arthritis, among other things. And the trail of false claims, lawsuits, and broken partnerships in what turned out to be quite a checkered past. A 2015 exposé in **Boston** magazine described sketchy TV infomercials in which a guy calling himself "Dr. Alejandro Guerrero" boasted of having run "clinical studies" in which he helped two hundred patients overcome terminal illnesses through a nutritional supplement called "Supreme Greens."

Guerrero, in various court documents, denied many of the allegations. Brady said he was aware of "most" of Guerrero's troubles, which occurred before they ever met. He chalks it up to a learning experience for his best friend. "That's part of growing up and understanding there are certain things that happen in life that you wish you didn't do," Brady said in a weekly interview he does during the season on one of Boston's sports radio channels, WEEI.

Brady and Guerrero's TB12 center is housed in the shopping center behind the stadium. As with most New England businesses, it's a few doors down from a Dunkin' Donuts. It is difficult to describe what exactly TB12 is—not a gym, not a group practice of personal trainers, not a nutrition or massage-therapy center. Whenever I asked Brady and Guerrero to define TB12, they would speak of "reeducating muscles" and "prehab" (preventing injuries, rather than dealing with them after they happen). To the uninitiated, Guerrero's "bodywork" resembles massage, but Brady told me he does not like the term "massage." He believes that sells short the awesomeness of his body coach's "technique." "It's like giving a chef some flour and eggs and saying, 'Okay, we'll make biscuits,'" Brady says. "Well, sure, everyone is going to make them different. But Alex is perfect at it." Inevitably, Brady and Guerrero would come around to the word "lifestyle." Inevitably, I would still be confused about whatever TB12 is. But Brady's conviction appeared sincere, and the results he could point to from his own career made him a winning infomercial.

Brady is always talking about the importance

of "muscle pliability." After Brady mentioned it for the seven thousandth time, I asked him to elaborate on what "pliability" meant. While traditional football training emphasizes muscle strength, he explained, Brady wants his muscles to achieve maximum sponginess and elasticity—or pliability.

"So how do you keep your muscles soft?" Brady said. "Like when you're a kid, when you squeeze their little butt, and they're soft, and you grab their little cheeks, they don't get hurt. When they fall, they don't get hurt." As a person ages, you lose that. "You lose your collagen. You lose your growth hormone. You lose testosterone, and all of a sudden your muscles become tight and tight muscles start pulling on tendons and ligaments, which create joint issues."

Every morning in the Bahamas, following his pliability workouts, Brady joined his family for a late breakfast that for him consisted mainly of a protein shake that was also high in electrolytes and included greens like kale and collards. "Sometimes we'll go over to Tom and Gisele's house for dinner," Brady's father, also named Tom, told me. "And then I'll say afterward, 'Where are we going for dinner?'"

I MET THE ELDER BRADY IN CALIFORNIA A FEW days after the family returned from the Bahamas.

He could become quite animated on the topic of how disgusting T and G's diets were. "Not only can I not eat that stuff, I can't even look at it," he told me. I instantly loved Tom Senior, who refers to himself as "the Original Tom Brady." He was as emotional as his son was cool, which made him a much easier read. A self-employed insurance salesman specializing in high-net-worth clients, Tom Senior spent seven years in a Catholic seminary before deciding the priesthood was not for him. He and his wife of nearly fifty years, Galynn, still live in the same house in San Mateo where his son grew up. The Bradys had three daughters, who would all become star athletes. "It was a crazy girl environment," Mr. Brady recalled to me. "We'd have periods going on every single week." Tommy came along last, and father and son would become unusually close.

"Tommy was my best friend," said Mr. Brady, who started taking his son on golf outings at the age of three. When Brady chose to go far away for college, to Michigan, his father was devastated. "I had to go into counseling," he said. After a few days, father and son convened in the living room for a tête-à-tête. They held hands. "I was crying like a baby and said, 'Tommy, this is going to change our relationship,'" he recalled. "And he said: 'Dad, I know. It has to.'"

Tom the son also sought professional help when he landed in Ann Arbor. Therapy was hardly the norm in the hypermasculine culture of Michigan football, but Brady sought it out with his father's encouragement. "I went into counseling when I was in seminary for two and a half years because I come from a very dysfunctional alcoholic family," Tom Senior told me. "Galynn and I, when we got married, we did a lot of marriage encounter sessions. It helped a lot. There's a stigma in our society around counseling. I wanted to make sure Tommy wasn't held back by that when he needed it." At Michigan, Tom became close to Greg Harden, a counselor who worked with the university's athletes. "Greg kind of sought me out," Tom said. "I looked like this vulnerable guy that maybe he thought he could have an influence on." Harden operated "outside the system," Brady said. "Those are the people I want to learn from. Now, do I take every nugget of information that someone gives, no, but there's a lot that's applicable to me."

Much of Brady's career as a Wolverine was defined by the oft-told saga of how he was never named the team's starting quarterback. Even as he apparently had earned the job his senior year, head coach Lloyd Carr made him split time with elite recruit Drew Henson. Decades later, Tom Brady Sr. remains quick to anger on the subject of his only son's getting "totally screwed over" by the Michigan coaches. "I have Irish Alzheimer's," Mr. Brady said, not a clinical term. "I forget everything but the grudges." He added that he retains a nagging desire to "punch Lloyd Carr in the nose."

At the end of July, I met Tom and Galynn in Orange County, where they had traveled from their Bay Area home to watch one of their grand-daughters play in a softball tournament. We met in the lobby of the Best Western Hotel at John Wayne Airport in Santa Ana, their base for the weekend. Mr. Brady offered me a platter of fruit, eggs, and bacon that he had piled up from the breakfast buffet. He had a free voucher that he said must not go to waste—so I was a good soldier and cleaned the plate before it was time to head to the softball game.

I would follow Mr. Brady to the field in my rental car. Galynn offered to ride with me. She was raised in rural Browerville, Minnesota, and worked for a time as a flight attendant for TWA back when they were still called "stewardesses." TWA did not allow their flight attendants to be married or to have children, so she eventually had to quit to be wedded to Tom.

Mr. Brady peeled out of the parking lot of the Best Western, leaving me struggling to follow be-hind him. He drove fast and sped up at yellow lights, forcing me to run red ones. It would be really bad if I got into an accident, I kept remind-ing myself—especially with Tom Brady's mom in the car; I would never forgive myself and neither would Tommy, and it might damage our blossoming friendship. I slowed down and stopped trying to follow Mr. Brady, and his still-living wife and I managed to find the field on our own. We arrived without incident to find Mr. Brady waiting for us, having already laid out three lawn chairs next to a cooler of beer at 10:30 a.m.

5.

"BEWARE THE PISSED
OFF PRETTY BOY"

October–November 2014

I have a favorite old quote about Washington, D.C., from Senator Thomas Gore, a progressive Democrat from Oklahoma who served in the 1930s (and was grandfather of the acerbic writer Gore Vidal). With its architectural grandeur, Senator Gore said, our capital would someday "make wonderful ruins." I have similar thoughts sometimes when I approach a gleaming twenty-first-century football stadium. Stadiums constitute the true measure of an NFL owner. Or "stadia," to use the plural form the league will often deploy when discussing "venues." The NFL loves anything that evokes Rome—e.g., Roman numerals for Super Bowls, never mind what happened to Rome.

The vast buildings rise like monuments to a

market legitimized as sufficiently Big League to deserve an NFL franchise. And then you imagine these coliseums abandoned one day, as "wonderful ruins" for anyone studying the passions and priorities of a civilization after it falls. This is not a complete fantasy in certain "markets": the Houston Astrodome, billed as the Eighth Wonder of the World when it opened in 1965, now sits forsaken in the shadow of the Houston Texans' lustrous NRG Stadium; Detroit's 80,000-seat Silverdome opened in 1975, was deserted after it closed in 2006, and has suffered a spectacular public decay ever since (a YouTube video of the trashed fossil in 2014 is a haunting thing to behold).

As I pursued Brady, I made my first ever trip to Gillette Stadium, the Patriots' home since 2002. In week five of the 2014 season, I flew to Boston from D.C. and drove south to Foxborough to see the Patriots host the unbeaten Cincinnati Bengals (4–0) in a **Sunday Night Football** game. Patriot Place, as the larger complex is called, rises along a could-be-anywhere blotch of car dealerships, billboards, and fast-food franchises on Route 1 between Boston and Providence. No one lives at Patriot Place.

Robert Kraft described Gillette to me as a "diversified" stadium, meaning that it offers fans a diversified menu of ways (shopping, dining, game tickets) to be separated from their money. Because football is such a perfect TV sport, in both production and ratings, teams must offer extracurricular attractions to entice ticket buyers; only 7 percent of NFL fans have ever attended a game live.

People outside New England who experience Foxborough as a recurring set of the NFL TV studio might believe the town is a quaint village of greens, Revolutionary War monuments, and assorted Ye Olde tropes. Returning from commercial breaks, networks reinforce this Disneyfied version of New England with stock shots of a steeple, a cider mill, maybe a landmark in Boston, which is a forty-minute drive away. A huge replica of a lighthouse looms over the north end zone, though you're as likely to see a real lighthouse in inland Foxborough as you are an actual Minuteman strolling through Harvard Square. In real life, Gillette Stadium is a concrete football Oz that reeks of merchandise, corporate sponsorships, and winning. Fans of the team have witnessed an astounding run of fifteen consecutive ten-win seasons by the Patriots; the stadium has sold out every game since Kraft bought the team in 1994, including pre- and postseason games. I'd still much rather watch on TV.

I arrived a few days before the game and paid a visit to Guerrero in his TB12 lair at Patriots Place. Guerrero, who was forty-nine at the time, is a practicing Mormon of Argentine descent with a master's degree in Chinese medicine from a college in Los Angeles that is no longer in business. His philosophy is built on three components, he told me: "We work on staying physically fit, emotionally stable, and spiritually sound." Guerrero shared with me a mantra that he and Brady invoke a lot: "Where your concentration goes, your energy flows, and that's what grows."

Brady is always telling his teammates to see Guerrero. It can be a tricky part to play with teammates. The Patriots have their own training, conditioning, and medical program. When I asked Guerrero if the conventional philosophies that govern training and treatment in the NFL ever clash with what he is doing, he said, "Most of the time." I later put the same question to the Patriots' owner, Robert Kraft. "It doesn't come without its challenges," Kraft replied. "It's not a straight line."

Brady barely hides his contempt for many of football's traditional training methods. He told me about one of his teammates, an offensive lineman hampered all year by a bad shoulder. The guy's shoulder was "on fire," Brady said, and he was told to strengthen the area. Brady winces. "I'm, like, the guy presses seven hundred pounds and you need to make him stronger? The guy can lift a fucking car." Brady's tone can edge toward proselytizing.

"The reality is," Brady said, "if you want to live a better life, and you want to live well, you're probably gonna have to take some different steps." He shares with me a word he learned in Sanskrit, **mudita**. "It's, like, fulfillment in seeing other people fulfilled," Brady says.

The Patriots were looking anything but fulfilled on the field. They began the 2014 season 2–2 and had just been destroyed by the Kansas City Chiefs, 41–14, on a Monday night. Brady, who threw two interceptions, was pulled in the fourth quarter and replaced by rookie quarterback Jimmy Garoppolo, a second-round selection out of Eastern Illinois University, and the highest draft pick the team has used on that position since Brady became the starter.

A reporter asked Belichick after the game "if the quarterback position would be evaluated." The coach chuckled, shook his head, and said nothing. He dispatched subsequent questions with "We're on to Cincinnati," a reference to the Pats' next opponent, and he said it enough that it became the catchphrase example of Belichick's tunnel vision and general noncommunicativeness.

Fans and the press across the NFL were drunk on Schadenfreude. The Patriots had become widely resented for reasons that go well beyond jealousy. Fort Belichick is known as a paranoid and joyless place whose inhabitants are not above pushing rules to gain a "competitive edge." Haters prefer the far less euphemistic term "cheating." It's a charge that stemmed from the so-called Spygate incident of 2007, in which a Patriots employee was caught illicitly videotaping the hand signals of opposing coaches. For critics, that episode is like the first Ebola exposure from which everything nefarious about the Patriots can be sourced.

The Patriots would beat the Bengals 43–17, with Brady completing 23 of 35 passes for 292 yards and 2 touchdowns. He performed with urgency and even vengeance. "Trust me when I tell you," the actor Rob Lowe would tweet before halftime, "beware the pissed off pretty boy."

I saw Brady briefly in the winning locker room. He was wrapped in a towel and carrying a toothbrush, exiting a shower room. "Nice seeing you here," he said to me. "You picked a good week." I told him I'd see him soon. "Awesome," he said.

The victory began a seven-game winning streak that left the Patriots tied for the best record in the league, 9–2. I returned to Gillette the Wednesday before Thanksgiving as the Patriots were preparing to play the 8–3 Packers. It was a dreary, sleeting day in Foxborough—a perfect backdrop for a Belichick news conference. The coach looked to be in an especially foul mood, like he was about to vomit. I thought of an **Onion** headline from a few years earlier that seemed apt at this moment: BILL BELICHICK FORGETS ABOUT LOSS BY RELAXING IN BATHTUB FILLED WITH WARM ENTRAILS. Back to live action, when Belichick was asked whether it was an advantage that he had never faced Aaron

Rodgers, the Packers' quarterback, he said: "I mean, it is what it is. Whatever hasn't happened hasn't happened." In response to a question about whether he saw any similarities between Rodgers and Brady, Belichick said, "They both wear number 12," then headed off.

When Belichick was done, Stacey James, the team's longtime head of media relations, opened the Patriots' locker room to reporters for the league-mandated forty-five-minute period. Locker rooms are not comfortable places for people who don't belong there. Reporters are not sanctioned in the sanctuary, only briefly credentialed—and at best tolerated. Unwritten rules govern most interactions. As an outsider among interlopers, I was unfamiliar with most of them. Nearly all of the thirty or so media bull-rushers were from New England outlets. A good number of them carried some food or beverage item from Dunkin' Donuts. Quite a few of them seemed to be named Ryan.

Players walked around in various states of undress. Their eyes were fixed on their phones and headphones were fastened on. Reporters clustered around a few of the more prominent and talkative actors, like defensive back Devin McCourty and tight end Rob Gronkowski. The rest of the media massed in the middle of the room, talking quietly among themselves and reading Twitter—out loud if there was something germane. "Aaron Hernandez murder trial delayed by other Aaron Hernandez murder trial," said one TV reporter, reading a headline on BostonMagazine.com. I laughed, maybe audibly. Bad idea. Hernandez, the homicidal tight end, must never be mentioned in his former team's locker room, let alone chuckled at. Fortunately no one heard me.

Brady walked in wearing a red, white, and blue ski cap. He took a seat at a stool in front of his locker. He was given a wide berth, at least twenty feet in all directions. It is understood that Brady, given his star power, would do his own media sessions from a podium once a week and after games.

Otherwise the King must not be approached. I didn't realize this and walked up and said hello. Stink-eyes were trained my way from some of the Ryans. How dare I address Zeus directly? Brady did not seem to mind, however, or was willing to humor me. We chatted for a minute or so. He wished me a happy Thanksgiving and I headed back to the scrum of Ryans.

Brady returned to what he was doing at his stool, which involved stretching out a pair of gloves—a task he appeared completely locked into. It was as if the rest of the nonfootball bubble did not exist, a place where he would, by necessity, need to transform into a less organic self (i.e., someone who has to make small talk with a clueless locker room invader). He stood up after a few minutes and headed out through a door marked ATHLETIC TRAINING.

"In front of seventy thousand people, I can be who I am," Brady would say in a Facebook documentary, **Tom vs Time**, that came out a few years later. "If I want to scream at somebody I can scream at somebody. I can be who I am in a very authentic way." As Brady says this, it's impossible not to extend the thought a beat—and then he does so himself: "That is hard for me when I walk off the field."

Brady has described the sport as being "synonymous with my being" in a way that nothing else in his life could ever be. He can sit for hours in his den watching game film on his laptop, so fixated on the riddles and subtleties before him that hours can pass without his even noticing. Football for Brady—and I've heard countless other athletes say versions of this—is also the ultimate reprieve from the grind and bullshit of reality. It offers him his best shot at freedom.

JAMES WALKED OVER AND ASKED ME IF I wanted to meet "Mr. Kraft." Deadpan and efficient, James might have the toughest PR job in the league. He is charged with running interference among a competitive group of beat reporters, a mumbling control freak of a head coach, and an image-conscious owner. James, a native of Washington State, grew up rooting for the Seahawks and joined the Patriots in 1993, the year before Kraft bought the team. He adheres to a stubborn and even slightly Baghdad Bob manner of devotion to the so-called Patriot Way.

The Patriot Way is a term of admiration, self-congratulation, or derision, depending on who is using it. To fans and insiders the Patriot Way stands for the selfless, no drama, "Do Your Job" mentality at the core of the team's success—an almost Maoist decree of labor for the collective. "Ignore the Noise" is another Belichick mantra (trademarked, licensed, merchandised) that is often invoked by the Greek chorus of Pats fans who make most of that noise.

"No days off, no days off," Belichick started yelling at one of the team's post–Super Bowl celebrations in front of Boston City Hall. Bizarrely, he would go on to chant the phrase nine times until he was joined by a good portion of the crowd— many of whom had taken days off from work to attend the rally.

To detractors, of course, the Patriot Way reflects a humorless and win-at-all-costs monolith. And while I'm grateful for all the victories Belichick has coached, I'd rather jump into raw sewage than go to work every day for Bunker Bill. In case Coach was thinking about asking me.

The Patriot Way is also—and I say this in the

most respectful possible way—complete bullshit. People use "the Patriot Way" as a catchall to justify all manner of cold decision making. The term is thrown around like it is some secret organizational sauce. When successful institutions rise to the level of having a "way" attached to them (IBM, Goldman Sachs), they are often too good to be true and invite comeuppance: I remember thinking this after baseball's St. Louis Cardinals—they of the "Cardinal Way"—were busted in 2015 for hacking into the computer database of the Houston Astros.

Players who might have previously had "issues" on other teams, or in college, come to New England as damaged goods, often on the cheap. They then, as the story goes, get a taste of the Patriot Way. They adopt the ethic and get contorted into the mold. Upon signing a $40 million contract extension in 2012, Aaron Hernandez talked about how buying into the Patriot Way had changed him. He went from being a talented but troubled young man at the University of Florida—considered a "character risk" and thus lasting until the fourth round of the 2010 draft— to being a Pro Bowl–caliber tight end. "You get changed by the Patriot Way," Hernandez said in an emotional press conference after signing the new deal. He talked about how touched he was that Mr. Kraft would make such a long-term commitment to him. He pledged $50,000 to a charity named for Kraft's late wife, Myra. "I said, 'Aaron, you don't have to do this, you've already got your contract,'" Kraft said at the press conference. "He said, 'No, it makes me feel good and I want to do it.' And that made me feel good."

Even given how Hernandez wound up, Kraft continues to invoke "the Patriot Way," especially the idea that the Patriots are like a family, at least to him (if not to the "family members" that Belichick will jettison for cheaper parts). Kraft, who is now seventy-six, cuts a more rumpled figure in his office than the magnate we see on TV. During games, Kraft will sit in his private box watching the action through binoculars from a raised seat, giving an impression of a king on a highchair. He wears bright suits with expert pocket squares. He is always accompanied by his son Jonathan, and often some celebrity arm candy, like Aerosmith's Steven Tyler, Elton John, or Jon Bon Jovi (as with many fans of the Patriots, they seemed to all peak in the seventies and eighties). Announcers narrate these money shots by praising, in Kraft's case, his stewardship of the dynasty and contributions to the league and, of course, to so many charities.

On this day in his office, Kraft wore a wrinkled and untucked dress shirt, and his hair and desk were a mess. He was sucking hard candy for a dry throat. Multiple TVs were on, and one office wall was filled with game balls and prints and photos, including one of Kraft at the Wailing Wall beside Brady, who is wearing a yarmulke. There are photos of Kraft with every living president back to George H. W. Bush. Kraft is seen dancing with Jackie Kennedy Onassis at some fund-raiser; the Dalai Lama is captured wearing Patriots gear; on a back shelf behind Kraft's desk lay a copy of Gisele's photo book, the one that costs $700 and includes early nudes.

Kraft mentions again that he "used to play the game," which he often does. A lot of owners do this, feeling it lends them tactile credibility, proof they're not just dilettantes. They were **Players**—and still are. (Al Davis used to wear padded suits to make himself look bulkier.) Kraft began purchasing Patriots season tickets in 1971. He would freeze with his sons on the metal bleachers of section 217 in dumpy old Schaefer Stadium, named for the "one beer to have when you're having more than one"—a mantra many stadium-goers took to heart.

Kraft, who made his fortune in the paper and packaging businesses, purchased a tract of land adjacent to Schaefer in the 1980s, and eventually the stadium itself. This gave Kraft the inside track on the team when owner James Orthwein put it up for bid in 1994. Other candidates included Stan Kroenke and perennial NFL suitor Donald Trump. "We went in there and we saw Robert had the lease under the stadium," Kroenke told me. "We figured this out in three days, and then we were gone." It took Trump eleven days to figure this out, Kraft told Kroenke. The new owner paid $172 million for the Patriots, the highest price ever paid for an NFL team at the time.

Kraft, who was raised in an observant Jewish family in Brookline, Massachusetts, speaks with ancestral pride about many of the players who have come through Foxborough. Randy Moss, a former receiver on the team, paid a shiva call to Kraft's house after the owner's wife of nearly fifty years, Myra, died in 2011. Moss signed the guest book "Randy Moss Kraft." On a hot day in Newton at Temple Emanuel, Myra's funeral drew two thousand guests, many of them former Patriots, fellow owners, politicians, Trump (not yet a politician) and his large entourage. The service occurred during the NFL lockout, which created the awkward scenario of the players and owners not being allowed to speak to one another. Brady came by himself and set off paparazzi convulsions outside the synagogue. Kraft has often said that he considers Brady to be like "a fifth son," although he also described Brady's predecessor, former quarterback Drew Bledsoe, as like a "fifth son," as he did former Patriots defensive end Willie McGinest, and probably others, so that dinner table can get crowded.

"I have terrible ADD," Kraft told me a few times. He goes off on tangents and repeats himself. "One of the reasons I wanted to buy the team is because I have ADD. So as I got older, I would be able to have something that I know would be challenging." (Buying an NFL team would be one of those attention-deficit remedies only the super-rich can consider.) Kraft told a lot of stories I had heard him tell before. Like about the time Brady, then a rookie during his first training camp, encountered Kraft at the stadium. He introduced himself and then, in Kraft's telling (and retelling), "looked me in the eye and said, 'I'm the best decision this organization has ever made.'" Kraft's stories often include someone "looking me in the eye." In his testimony at the first Hernandez trial, Kraft described Hernandez "looking me in the eye" and assuring him he did not murder Odin Lloyd, the man he was later found guilty of murdering. Kraft defended Goodell's conduct during the Ray Rice mess, telling a **Wall Street Journal** reporter that he had pointedly asked the commissioner whether he saw the infamous elevator video. And "Roger looked me in the eye and said 'No,'" Kraft said. "I believe him."

I told Kraft that I grew up a Patriots fan and urged him to bring back the team's old helmet logo of a Minuteman hunched over preparing to snap a football. Kraft said a lot of people tell him that, though I was unable to convince him further (maybe if I'd looked him more in the eye). He asked me if my family belonged to a synagogue.

He talked about his long friendship with Israeli prime minister Benjamin Netanyahu, as many Boston Jews love to mention ("Bibi went to MIT, you know"). Kraft always points out to me that he has known the Sulzberger family, owners of the **Times**—my bosses—for years.

Kraft kept saying how much he loves New York. He attended Columbia and built the Kraft Center for Jewish Student Life there (also home of the Sulzberger Lounge, albeit on the second floor). He owns an apartment at the Plaza and keeps an office at NFL headquarters and has become a regular on the Manhattan/Hamptons party circuit. "Boston is a village compared to New York," he told me. At this moment, I thought Stacey James—who had been sitting quietly next to me—was going to have an aneurysm.

"Can we take that comment off the record?" James said, breaking in.

He meant the "Boston is a village" comment, which might be problematic among Patriots fans who—like many Boston-area residents—harbor a bit of a little brother complex about the Big Apple. This was one of those journalistically ambiguous moments where I had a tape recorder running on Kraft's desk, in full view of James, but Kraft apparently did not see it. We were not explicitly off the record, but I told James and Kraft that I would not use the "village" line in the story since I was writing about Brady for the magazine. I didn't say I wouldn't put it in a book someday.

The village sentiment conveys a meaningful part of Kraft's identity. He came to rule the "village" of his hometown and fought his way onto the ultimate big boys' table at the NFL's dinner party. He relishes the elevated national status that being an NFL owner confers on him. But like all of us, Kraft remains a product of his formative environments. He is still the self-conscious Jewish little brother who felt like an outsider in tribal, Catholic-dominated Boston. He has wondered, privately, whether anti-Semitism played a role in the team's failures at navigating the culture of Massachusetts politics in their efforts to build a stadium on the South Boston waterfront for the Patriots in the 1990s, and later for the Kraft-owned New England Revolution, of Major League Soccer. Patriots president Jonathan Kraft, Robert's oldest son, tends to be less diplomatic. "I don't know if it's anti-Semitism, or anti-Kraftism, or anti-football-ism, but it's really strange," Jonathan Kraft told the **Boston Globe**, referring to the stadium situation.

After bouncing from topic to topic, Kraft announced it was time to "do business" and discuss Brady. Kraft spoke of Brady with a hint of protectiveness, not so much that he wanted to protect Brady, but protective of his own asset, as if it could be taken away. After Brady led the

Patriots to his second Super Bowl win, in 2004, Dan Rooney, the revered owner of the Steelers who had deep ties to the Catholic Church, offered to set up a meeting for Brady with Pope John Paul II. Brady, who was raised Catholic and attended Catholic schools growing up, took him up on it. But not before Kraft complained to the league about Rooney's approach to Brady and accused the Steelers' owner of tampering.

Brady is "one of the most amazing human beings I've ever met in my life," Kraft said to commence the kvelling. "Physically he is very handsome, but as a human being he's more beautiful" . . . "like a fifth son to me" . . . "Tommy has such **sechel**"— a Yiddish word—"which has no English translation except it means someone who does the right thing at the right time with no preparation; he just has good instincts and judgment."

Good example: One time, in Israel, Kraft was leading a group of Patriots players that included Brady. "We were in the King David Hotel on a Friday night," Kraft said. "Bibi came to speak to us, we had a Chabad rabbi. Half the room was gentiles. And the rabbi picked one person to get up and speak and do the hora"—the Jewish adaptation of a traditional circle dance. Of course he called on Brady. "So there's Brady on Shabbat eve doing the hora with a Chabadnik rabbi." Kraft gave Brady's hora effort a stellar review—some serious **sechel** going on there.

Kraft added that part of him could identify with Tom Brady. Brady, he said, "did not have a clear path at Michigan." He had to fight for his time on the field and overcome setbacks. "I can relate," Kraft said, "because I was a middle child." Kraft followed an older brother who was a doctor and was followed by a "beautiful young sister." His father wanted him to become a rabbi. Young Bob found himself buried on the family depth chart. "So I had to fend for myself," Kraft said, "sort of like Brady being as talented as he was, but still the last pick in the sixth round."

Kraft also wanted me to know that he was president of his class at Brookline High School and at Columbia.

Finally, I cooled things off by raising the possibility that things could end badly with Brady. They often do for stars around the NFL, with its salary cap, nonguaranteed contracts, and physical toll. The Patriots have a prolonged rap sheet of trading or releasing several of their most accomplished players over the years. "Randy Moss Kraft," for instance, was shipped to Minnesota in the middle of the 2010 season. Fifth son Drew Bledsoe went down with an injury in 2001, lost his job to little brother Tommy, and was sent to Buffalo after the season.

Kraft never answered me about the possibility of a disagreeable ending between the team and Brady. I asked Kraft if Brady ever expressed

displeasure to him over discarded teammates, especially ones he was close to—like safety Lawyer Milloy and wide receiver Wes Welker. Kraft
flashed something between a grin and a smirk.
"Okay, now you're being a good reporter," he patronized, and did not answer beyond that.

I put the "ending badly" question that I had
asked Kraft to Brady's actual father. He did not
hesitate. "It will end badly," Tom Senior said. "It
does end badly. It's a cold business. And for as
much as you want it to be familial, it isn't."

6.

GARISH FIST ORNAMENTS

January 2, 2015

In the back of the sixth-floor lobby of NFL head-quarters on Park Ave, every model of Super Bowl ring from the last half century is displayed in an ascending row. First to last, the rings tell a story of an institution that just keeps growing and becoming more difficult to turn away from.

They begin with a single diamond on a metal band that was awarded to Vince Lombardi's Green Bay Packers, winners of Super Bowl 1 (engraved 1966 WORLD CHAMPIONS). As the baubles progress, like one of those metamorphic diagrams of early humans evolving into supposedly higher life-forms, the finery keeps growing in size and splash. Garish fist ornaments have become the norm. Will there be a point where the rings escape their bounds, like bodies exceeding the mortal rules of a dangerous game?

Robert Kraft in particular has been at the forefront of this arms race. He has commissioned an increasingly large and gaudy collection of Super Bowl rings, nearly the size of golf balls at this point. They are the kinds of over-the-top knuckle ornaments Donald Trump would insist on (and indeed, he received a special one from Kraft).

"This latest Patriots Super Bowl ring is the largest Super Bowl ring ever created," the team's website boasts in an interminable description of the 10-karat white gold rocks that Kraft had made after his team won Super Bowl 51. Its 283 diamonds are more than double what New England had fixed within their rings in 2004 and 2005. More to the point, "283" was no accident. Kraft wanted the rings to commemorate how special this particular feat was, how his "family" overcame a late 28–3 deficit to stun the Falcons in Super Bowl 51. This is how billionaires do endzone dances.

As a pure matter of taste, Coach Lombardi would never be caught wearing one of these modern accessories. By rule, as the decorum zebras would declare, Super Bowl rings do their best work out of sight. It is the **fact** that you won a Super Bowl ring, not the size or glare, that gives them their authority. "Do you have a ring or not?" is the only question that matters. If the answer

is no, there can be a void in an otherwise celebrated career (Dan Marino, Jim Kelly); if yes,
"how many?" is the natural follow-up. Jimmy
Johnson, who coached the Cowboys to two
championships and won a third at the University of Miami, christened his boat **Three Rings**.
Same with Patriots coach Bill Belichick, until he
was "forced" to rename his vessel **Four Rings**,
and then **Five Rings**—and oh, the painting has-
sles he has had to suffer through, maybe the ultimate First World Problem for an NFL coach.

Tom Brady is often asked whether he has a
favorite Super Bowl ring. The question refers not
necessarily to the jewelry, but to the championship itself—whether one stands above the others.
He has a standard duck for the "Which ring?"
question. "The next one" is what Brady says he is
focused on. It was that time of year again.

THE PATRIOTS HAD FINISHED THE SEASON 12–4,
the best record in the AFC, and had earned a playoff bye. Brady had resisted my occasional over-
tures to get together during the season, but the
bye week gave us a window just after New Year's.

Brady sent me an email with the address of
his mansion in Brookline, which he was living in,
though the home was not yet fully realized. But
when I arrived at the address the security booth
was vacant. The gate at the end of the driveway

was locked and nothing happened when I pressed the intercom. My phone rang. A 617 number. Tommy! A second white security gate was not opening, I explained. He told me to press a bunch more buttons and talk into some intercom.

Finally, the gate opened and I maneuvered up his driveway. The quarterback was waiting for me on his front stoop. Brady asked me what happened when I pressed the intercom button. Nothing, I said. He shook his head with the exasperation of someone who still considered himself somewhat in the ballpark of being the regular guy whose front door in San Mateo was readily opened to those who knocked. I grew up a few miles, and tax brackets, from here a few decades ago, when it was not uncommon to see Larry Bird outside his unassuming Brookline home washing his car. Brady's place is a fortress by comparison, not that anyone could blame him in these stalker paparazzi days.

He led me into a den that doubles as a gallery for his photos and mementos. There were no signs of any MVP or Super Bowl trophies. No **Sports Illustrated** Sportsman of the Year awards, no photos of Brady with the presidents and pope he has met. As athletes' personal shrines go, this one was quite lame, which I respected. It's not that Brady does not appreciate souvenirs. He saves end-zone pylons from big games. He kept a ball from his first Super Bowl victory and a pair of cleats from his second. He said he had no idea where they were. His wife took over the decorating after they moved from their brownstone in Back Bay in Boston the previous year and into this 14,000-square-foot manor.

Kraft lives around the corner, less than a five-minute walk. It was Kraft who suggested that Brady consider building in this opulent Chestnut Hill enclave when Brady expressed to him an interest in moving to the suburbs to raise his kids. Brady had preferred the bustle of city living and for years was one of the few members of the Patriots to actually live in Boston, despite the forty-minute commute to Foxborough.

The Brady-Bündchen estate sits on a five-acre plot that once belonged to Pine Manor College, a bucolic campus that used to be a two-year finishing school for rich girls when I was growing up. My understimulated high school friends and I used to try to sneak on campus to crash "college parties" there. As with many women's colleges, the bored and undersexed adolescent boys in the area (e.g., me) were compelled to give the school a sexist nickname. "We used to call this place 'Pine Mattress,'" I informed Brady, who chuckled knowingly enough to make it clear that the name had endured, though the college began admitting men in 2014.

Brady was sporting a brown playoff beard, a beige cardigan sweater, and, on his sockless feet, a new pair of UGGs, the Australian-made sheep-skin boots that he endorses. There was supposedly a bin of UGGs for guests to wear around the house, but I was not so honored. Brady stood at the window and admired the view in the back. "It's really fucking beautiful here, every morning," Brady marveled. "The sun comes up and it's fucking Zen-like." (I could fucking imagine.)

Brady led me into a backyard adjacent to the country club, one of the oldest golf courses in the United States. Much of this 5.2-acre lot used to be a wooded area, so in order to build the estate, many trees had to come down, which broke Gisele's green heart. Brady pointed to a barnlike guesthouse that was being built next to the backyard. "My wife calls that her sanctuary," Brady said. They often repaired there for yoga and meditation.

Brady then turned back to the golf course. "Fucking beautiful," he again declared of the view, and was then nearly chop-blocked by his pit-bull mix, Lua, who charged past him. As we reentered the house, I noticed a big glass menorah displayed on a shelf. Interesting. "What, are you Jewish?" I teased. "We're not Jewish," Brady clarified. "I think we're into everything," he continued. "I don't know what I believe. I think there's a belief system, I'm just not sure what it is." After Brady won his third Super Bowl in 2005, he betrayed a wistful anticlimax in an interview with

Steve Kroft on **60 Minutes**. "Maybe a lot of people would say, 'Hey, man, this is what it is, I've reached my goal,'" he told Kroft. "Me, I think, God, it's got to be more than this." I read this quote back to Brady, nearly ten years and zero Super Bowl victories later, and he laughed at his naïveté. "I got a litany of Bibles sent to me after that," Brady told me. "When I think back on that, what a narrow perspective I had. I'm twenty-seven. I don't know shit."

People throw out numbers and ages: forty-two? forty-five? Brady was sitting in his den and becoming animated as he discussed the recent history of aging quarterbacks. John Elway, the Denver Broncos' Hall of Famer, was then the oldest quarterback ever to win a Super Bowl, at thirty-eight. At forty-one, Brett Favre had a great year with the Vikings. "He threw that interception in the Saints game," Brady said, recalling Favre's mishap in the closing seconds of regulation time during the 2010 NFC Championship Game. Beyond that, there is no precedent for forty-something star quarterbacks. If Brady can perform at a high level until forty-three or forty-four, would he regard that as history making? "I think so, I think so," he said quickly enough to make clear he'd considered this already.

What jumped to my mind was how hard it had been for Favre to let go. That spectacle was tough to watch: Favre's agonizing, his retiring, the public tears and questioning of whether he was "guilty of retiring early"; the unretirement and the different teams (and the concussions and the memory loss and the painkillers and the dick pics). "God only knows the toll" concussions had on his brain, said Favre, who was sacked more times (525) than any quarterback in history.

It's hard to picture Brady becoming a Favre-like spectacle. If Favre is raw and frontal, Brady is refined and reserved. Don Yee had called him "genially subversive." I was fascinated by Brady's resistance to "the system" that underpins the football industrial complex. He was one of the first public figures I'd encountered, and certainly a rare football player, who preached the power of therapy and meditation. He has attacked the junk food staples of so many American diets, made by companies that have spent zillions on advertising with the NFL. He called Coca-Cola "poison for kids" and mocked the notion that Frosted Flakes is "actually a food." "We get brainwashed to believe that these things are just normal food groups," Brady said.

Brady has also been fortunate. NFL referees protect quarterbacks like fine china. Linebackers don't talk about playing into their forties like Brady does. The only one I could name off the top of my head was Junior Seau, and given how he ended up, he is not the best example of a football player "defying age" (Seau committed suicide in 2012, at forty-three, and a posthumous examination of his brain revealed extensive CTE damage).

Perhaps Brady will feel as if he can play forever right up to the moment he can't. "I've been very lucky" was Brady's recurring message to me when I again raised the issue of concussions. I took this to mean he had not had that many in his career, though it's never a clean measurement. "Concussion" is a broad and imprecise term, Brady says, describing a wide range of head trauma. Very few of them ever get detected in the moment, let alone reported to doctors or the public. Brady and (especially) his family are more worried about the impact of head trauma than they let on. After seeing the film **Concussion**, Gisele told Tom he needed to retire. She was half serious, or more than half. But they laughed it off—or Tom did—and the moment passed.

Gisele would later speak out of school during an interview on **CBS This Morning**, claiming that her husband had suffered a concussion the previous season—even though nothing of it had appeared on any injury report. "We don't talk about it," Gisele had said. "But he does have concussions." When Brady was asked later about his concussion history, he shut down the topic. "I really don't think that's anybody's business," he said. Well, yes, except that Brady is building a health and "lifestyle" business around the example of his perfectly pliable self. Also, Brady was about to make his TB12 "brain exercises" available to paying customers.

Privately, Brady has expressed faith in Guerrero's ability to heal his brain. He will rave about his ability to "work" the area that a concussion will disturb—as if some massage technique could treat a brain injury. TB12 also features a customized program of mind and cognition exercises, as if concussions are just another ailment, like a pulled muscle, that can be avoided with the proper "prehab." When Brady speaks of Guerrero, TB12, and their specialized "ways," he can project the faith of a zealot, a sense of invincibility that goes beyond naïve and might veer into hubris.

Brady has compared playing football with "getting into a car crash every Sunday—a scheduled car crash." I've heard players use this image before, and doctors who have treated football injuries. The first time I heard it was in 2001, after the Jets linebacker Mo Lewis smashed into then–starting quarterback Drew Bledsoe with an impact that sheared a blood vessel in Bledsoe's chest, put him in the hospital, and sent Brady onto the field and into football history. Fate does follow its own fickle game plan; it would be hard to think better "prehab" could have saved Bledsoe from Mo Lewis.

I asked Brady if he worried that too much of his life was wrapped up in football. This was an odd question to ask of a football player. But Brady's investment in the game has been so total for so long, I wondered whether his age-defying quest was driven by some fear of how futile it might be to find satisfaction in anything else. Brady ducked my question, except to confirm its premise: that football is pretty much everything to him. No real hobbies. "I'm not a musician, not an artist," he said. "What am I going to do, go scuba diving?"

Football is not merely what he plays and what he does; "football is who he is," Guerrero had told me. Who would Brady be when there was no football? Former players lament how nothing after measures up to its exhilaration and camaraderie. "The longer you play, the more you get used to the lifestyle, and you can lose touch with reality," said Mark Murphy, a former defensive back for the Redskins who is now the CEO of the Packers. "You have to have a purpose in life."

Brady's parents worry about Tommy after football—what could ever fill the void? Brady's answer to the void is to put it off for as long as possible. Why not treat his body and time as more competitions to win, and clocks to race and rings to chase? I tried to draw Brady further out on this, but his attention was audibled to something out the window. Four men were walking down his driveway and approaching his front door, part of a team working to finish work on his house. "Okay, I need to deal with these guys," Brady said, and we were out of time.

7.

BALLGHAZI

January 18, 2015

On a makeshift stage—they're all makeshift—
Brady and the Patriots received their sixth conference championship trophy on the soaked field
turf of Gillette Stadium. They crushed the Colts,
45–7, and were headed to the Super Bowl in Glendale, Arizona. Brady declared it to be a season of
ups and downs. "Right now, we're up, baby," he
said.

"We're up" lasted until the next morning.
Then news broke that the NFL was investigating
something about the Patriots' playing with underinflated footballs. No one ever knew this was a
thing (the underinflation of footballs?) except for
a few coach and front-office types from the Colts,
and league officials who were suddenly treating

this like Watergate. Bob Kravitz, a longtime Indianapolis sports reporter, broke the news in what might be the most famous tweet in NFL history. "Breaking," Kravitz wrote from the Gillette Stadium press box in a tweet stamped "12:55 a.m. Jan 19, 2015." "A league source tells me the NFL is investigating the possibility the Patriots deflated footballs Sunday Night. More to come." That last sentence might also go down as the biggest understatement in NFL history.

Brady called the ball-tampering charges "ridiculous" when asked about them the next morning on WEEI radio. The hosts took a lighthearted approach to the curious little story, but their questions were on point. "Are you aware of the story about deflating footballs?" began the conversation. "No, I don't," Brady said. This was the first he had heard of this matter, Brady added. "Care to tell me if you were deflating footballs?" one of the hosts followed up. "I have no idea," Brady replied. "Did you get the sense that you were able to grip the ball better than the Colts last night?" Long laughs. "I think I've heard it all at this point," Brady said. Listening to the interview now, it's striking how deflective and askew the sleepy-voiced superstar's answers were. "Oh God, it's the last of my worries," Brady concluded. "I don't ever respond to stuff like this."

Within thirty-six hours, "stuff like this" would be leading all of the network and cable newscasts.

ESPN's nugget-monger Chris Mortensen sent the freak-out meter to 11 with yet another tweet. "NFL has found that 11 of the Patriots footballs used in Sunday's AFC title game were under-inflated by 2 lbs each, per league sources." This was the nugget that would launch a million hot takes. America, meet Deflategate.

The Mortensen report also turned out to be wrong. According to a subsequent ESPN.com cleanup, "additional reporting clarified that 11 of the 12 balls were 'significantly underinflated,'" as opposed to "under-inflated by 2 lbs each." Never mind that a subsequent multi-million-dollar in-vestigation by the league found the balls weren't even "significantly deflated." Or that the NFL's vice president of officiating admitted that week that the pounds per square inch (PSI) of the foot-balls before the game was not recorded by the ref-erees, thus making it impossible to know exactly how much air pressure would have been lost in the balls used by both teams.

Or that if I read (or write) another sentence about football air pressure and PSI variations in cold weather, I'm going to jump out the window.

Mortensen was one of the league's most au-thoritative and plugged-in "insiders." No one had any reason to doubt him, but even if anyone did, this was still a fascinating story whose ultimate untruth made it no less irresistible in the moment. Bottom line: even though no one knew anything about air pressure, this sounded kind of bad. Was New England caught cheating again—this time in the midst of the biggest pregame media circus of the sports calendar?

Brady has long prided himself on the fact that he has succeeded despite not being the most gifted or talented athlete. This is a classic trope of star athletes, who use self-deprecation to disguise self-congratulation for their superior work ethic and mental prowess. "I'm always a thinker—I've got to outthink them," Brady told me, referring to his competitors. He talked a lot about flouting conventional wisdom. Does that extend to flouting rules? At the very least, Brady had some explaining to do. But he wasn't really talking in public at that point, well, except to me.

We had a phone call scheduled for that Wednesday morning to do some final follow-ups and fact-checks for the magazine story I was working on. Brady called me at the appointed time from his home. He said he was immersed in studying film and in full "ignore the noise" mode. When I started asking questions about deflated footballs, I became noise.

It was time to lose my quasi-fan shtick. "You're in the news," I said. Brady chuckled, but was suddenly displaying an uncharacteristic shakiness—the verbal equivalent of happy feet. I asked Brady whether he preferred a harder, fully inflated football or a softer, less inflated one. He took another indirect route to the ball. "I get a chance to pick 'em out every week," he said of the footballs. His evasive construction jumped out: why respond in the present tense when this was about something three days ago?

"Whatever the balls are at, that's how I like 'em," Brady continued. So I asked again, How **does** he like them, softer or harder? "I've been at it for fifteen years, we break them in." (In a 2011 interview with WEEI, he had, in fact, expressed a preference for "the deflated ball.") Brady then told me that other people had more information than he did. Not really, I said. He had far more contact with the balls in question than anyone besides the Patriots' center and possibly the official who spots the ball. "Truthfully, the balls feel the same to me," he told me. "We pick them out, and that's what we go play with." Nothing felt unusual about the footballs in the Indianapolis game, he said. "I've got so many things to focus on in the next ten days," Brady said, ending the discussion. "And this is not one of them."

Not for long. Twenty-four hours later, Brady was the main attraction at an insane news conference, carried live by CNN(!). He wore a goofy Patriots ski hat adorned with the throwback Minuteman logo. He discussed the size and firmness of footballs for nearly thirty minutes. While a nation reeled, Brady tried to reassure: "This isn't

ISIS," he said in one of his more notable moments. "You know, no one's dying."

Well, except for Brady. He delivered a rather terrified performance—though in fairness, the press conference wasn't his idea, and he (like the rest of the world) had no idea Mortensen's numbers were so wrong. "He was a lamb to slaughter," Brady's father said of his son's production. "How the league could make him face a firing squad of reporters and not allow him to know what the actual readings of the balls were, it's absolutely downright evil." QB Tom would suffer stress-related canker sores during the peak days of the firestorm. Outside the bunker, public opinion was running against my pernicious Pats. There was a sense, at the news conference, of the lions seizing on a rare moment of vulnerability for the GOAT. Brady makes an even more perfect villain than hero. The press conference offered a thrilling spectacle of pretty-boy comeuppance. He seemed to embody what Alfred, Lord Tennyson called the "divine stupidity of a hero." And of course, there's an **Onion** headline for everything: TOM BRADY KEEPS REFERRING TO SELF AS "GOLDEN BOY" WHILE DENYING CHEATING ALLEGATIONS.

A few of the lions took it upon themselves to elicit public submission from the accused. "Is this a moment to just say 'I'm sorry' to the fans?" one asked. "I think it's disappointing that a situation like this happens," Brady said. Another inquisitor tried. "For the fans that are watching and looking into that camera, what do you say?" The question hung like a wounded duck as the betrayed children of New England awaited their closure. Brady seemed confused.

"What would you like me to say?" he said, finally. This struck me as the appropriate response.

In what might have been my favorite moment of the fiasco, former NFL quarterback Mark Brunell actually choked up when discussing Brady's press conference performance on an ESPN **NFL Live** segment afterward. "I just didn't believe what Tom Brady had to say," he said, his voice breaking. Brunell started 151 games in seventeen NFL seasons and the only thing I will now remember about this clown is that he nearly cried on national television over barely deflated footballs.

Brady would appear the next morning on the cover of the **New York Post**, standing with Gisele; "Tommy, why did your balls go soft?" read the bubble over her head. Sometimes you just have to stand back, put matters big and small aside, and tip your helmet to America.

A WEEK AND A HALF LATER, BRADY WENT OFF to win the Super Bowl. Terms like "vindicated" were thrown around. A new hero, Malcolm Butler, was born, and it was safe for me to be a fan again. My story ran in the **Times Magazine** on Super Bowl Sunday, with Brady on the cover, as if we had planned this all along. The detail that Brady had a menorah in his kitchen received a great deal of pickup in Israel the day after the game. WHY DOES TOM BRADY KEEP A MENORAH IN HIS HOUSE? was the big headline in the **Jerusalem Post**. (Subheadline: PATRIOTS BEAT SEAHAWKS.)

Sometimes the people you root for please you, sometimes not. Athletes are like your children that way: win or lose, you're pretty much stuck with them. You tailor your views and biases, for better or worse. After going off on an extended ridicule of Brady on **The Daily Show** in the middle of Deflategate, Jon Stewart spoke to this blind loyalty with the following disclaimer: "If you think I would not chastise you if you had committed these acts while in my team, the New York Giants', uniform, that would be correct." We like our confirmation biases served undiluted.

After a while, a certain "much ado about nothing" consensus set in about Deflategate. As many pointed out, not only did Brady perform better in the second half of the AFC title game after the alleged ball deflations were discovered, but he also was the MVP of the Super Bowl two weeks later—a game whose footballs were presumably more closely scrutinized for air pressure irregularity than in any in NFL history.

Belichick went on David Letterman the

week after the Super Bowl. Deflategate came up, of course. Both characters were in their perfect elements—Letterman the bemused wiseass, Belichick the deadpan killjoy. "I know you know exactly what happened," Letterman said. "It was some kind of horseplay, am I right?"

"No," Belichick replied. The host, an Indy native and Colts fan, then mentioned a Patriots equipment assistant—John Jastremski—who was seen on a security camera before the game carrying the footballs into a Gillette Stadium bathroom. Press reports referred hilariously to the employee as a "person of interest" in the NFL's investigation. The alleged evildoer was seen on camera leaving the bathroom about a minute and a half later. Jastremski claimed he just had to take a leak, which set off many side debates over how long urination should actually take a healthy man in his thirties (accounting for possible hand washing, or ball-adjustment activities, depending on whose side you're on here).

"I can't remember the last time I took a leak in ninety seconds," Letterman said. "Are you at the age where you have this problem?" Belichick smiled and grunted and suggested that Letterman come in to testify before NFL investigators. "I'm ready, swear me in," Letterman said, "I'm ready to go!"

Belichick seemed to be enjoying his off-season as much as he does anything, except possibly killing puppies. He became an oddly peripheral character in the Deflategate saga. Not only did he successfully shift suspicion to his quarterback (**"Tom's personal preferences on his footballs are something that he can talk about"**), he also delivered the greatest podium performance of his career holding forth on the subject. He was the first to posit, for instance, the explanation that the footballs lost air pressure due to weather conditions and constant rubbing, not horseplay. "Bill Belichick, the Science Guy," he was dubbed on a **Good Morning America** report, which then cut to an arch rebuttal from Bill Nye himself, PBS's original "science guy." "What he said didn't make any sense," Nye said.

The coach was quick to acknowledge, "I am not a scientist . . . I am not an expert in football measurements, I'm just telling you what I know." He could have left it there, but was good enough to throw in this keepsake for the ages. "I would not say I'm Mona Lisa Vito of the football world," Belichick said, "as she was in the car-expertise area." This was an adroit reference to the character played by Marisa Tomei in **My Cousin Vinny**, which (who knew?) turned out to be Belichick's all-time-favorite movie. "He was definitely, you know, dead-on balls accurate" was Tomei's postgame assessment of Belichick's presser. Yes, Marisa Tomei was being interviewed before the Super Bowl discussing Bill Belichick and a twenty-three-year-old movie—on the NFL Network. Bill Nye could not be reached for comment. And again, American greatness was fully achieved, thanks to football.

I WENT TO THE WHITE HOUSE IN APRIL TO watch the president's customary Rose Garden reception for the Super Bowl champs. Brady was a last-minute no-show, citing a "prior family commitment," though I'd heard from a friend of Brady's that he was protesting a months-old wisecrack from White House press secretary Josh Earnest who had disparaged Brady's GOAT-to-slaughter press conference a few days after the Deflategate game. Brady was sighted at Gillette Stadium on the day of the White House visit, according to ESPN.

In the Rose Garden, President Obama hailed the Patriots' fifteen-year dominance behind Brady and Belichick. "They have set a standard of excellence that we may not see again for a very long time," Obama said. But then Obama couldn't help but get in on the fun himself. "I usually tell a bunch of jokes at these events," the president added. "But with the Patriots in town, I worried that eleven of the twelve would fall flat." A mix of polite laughter, groans, boos—and a thumbs-down from Belichick. This, at the highest level, epitomized how the Patriots' success had become intertwined with derision.

The Rose Garden was packed with the transplants from New England who are never shy about making themselves, uh, heard. They also always seem to travel in swarms. This included seemingly every elected football "fan" from New England (Vermont baller Bernie Sanders), a bunch of high-level appointees (Secretary of State John Kerry, reporting for duty), and an inordinate number of Pats fans on the White House staff, as Obama mentioned. "Maybe I need to do a better job screening," he said in his remarks. After the event, I was nearly trampled by a group of Massholes trying to get selfies with Super Bowl hero "Malcolm Butlah." I recovered in time to witness Belichick introducing himself to Elizabeth Warren, or maybe it was the other way around. I wondered if they would keep in touch.

Belichick stuck around D.C. for a couple of days to attend the annual White House Correspondents' Dinner. I spotted him at a big fancy after-party at the French ambassador's residence. It was after one a.m., I was standing in a side parlor when who should walk in but the sullen sideline sage himself. He wore a tux (no hood) and brought along his much-younger girlfriend. John Henry, the owner of the Red Sox and **Boston Globe**, was with him, along with his much-younger wife. Belichick looked somewhat out of place and wore the shell-shocked expression of someone who had been blindfolded and kidnapped straight out of his film room. But he also wore an endearingly awkward grin, which I took as a signal that it was okay to approach. I made a beeline for the Death Star.

I congratulated Belichick, told the coach I was from New England and a Pats fan and he smiled, no doubt impressed by my icebreaker. I mentioned that I had written a story on Brady and the Pats for the **Times Magazine** that was published on Super Bowl Sunday. I spoke with a cocktail-driven self-assurance that Belichick would be instantly familiar with my work.

"Yeah, I was busy that day," Belichick said dryly, and then made his own beeline, for the bar. I figured this was something for us to build on.

8.

CHEATER

May–September 2015

The thought of returning to politics made my head hurt. I had gotten a peek behind the Shield and I wanted to keep looking. There was an inevitability about this. For years I'd resisted sports as anything but a walled-off object of my mental energy—toys to play with on the side of all the serious. I used to get mad at myself for investing so much emotion in these figurines on the other side of the screen. Why grant them power to disturb my moods?

After a while, you learn to accept the addiction. The players and teams you root for become part of a shared birthright, seasonal pieces of our thought sceneries. In my case, even though I haven't lived there for a while, I will always belong to the Boston/New England chapter of fans. We are one of but several wings in a big loud mental ward.

People have asked me over the years why I did not just become a sportswriter. My answer, more flip than anything else, was that I did not want to pollute the joys of being a fan with professional stress. As soon as sports became a job, part of my love for it would die.

Between the sidelines, NFL football is for the most part a clean meritocracy, with some exceptions (one being an otherwise employable quarterback who kneels in protest during the national anthem). This is why any suggestion of cheating—of skirting rules or fixing games or using banned substances—can be such fighting words. That is why the word "integrity" might be the single most important tool in the league's propaganda kit. "Integrity" is etched onto the NFL's most hallowed walls, embedded into its mission statements and everywhere in the commissioner's declarations. Goodell invokes the "integrity of the game" with the same righteousness as a Fox News anchor asserts that the network is "Fair and Balanced." Say it enough and it becomes part of the Shield.

Everyone is expected, at the very least, to be on the level. Now Tom Brady was a cheater. Again. Deflategate had subsided in the months after the Super Bowl but made a sudden comeback May 6. The league released its report on the matter from its special Deflategate detective, attorney Ted Wells. Clinically titled "Investigative Report Concerning Footballs Used During the AFC Championship Game on January 18, 2015," the report landed as I was downing a Chinese lunch near my D.C. office. I emerged from the restaurant to find a distended inbox of emails and texts on my phone.

The subject lines were filled with headings such as "Cheater" and "Brady" and "Wow."

The Wells Report had been hanging out there for months. Why was it taking so long? Personally I had interpreted the absence of news as a sign that Wells had found nothing; that Deflategate was fizzling into the goofy afterthought it should have been from the start. Bad read.

The Wells Report dropped like a ton of cement on the village. It turned out to be a flawed but plenty damning document for Tom Brady, the Patriots, and leapers-of-faith like me. That was my takeaway from an initial read of the 243 pages of lawyer porn that was the Wells Report. The overriding impression was that the Patriots were, to say the least, difficult to deal with. No upset there.

It sounded like the Patriots dealt with league investigators with the same arrogance and hyperregulation that they have with much of the outside world during the Belichick years. While

most parties on the other side of this treatment—
say, the media—have little choice but to swallow
it, the league does not. This was per the authority
vested in the commissioner by the NFL's collective bargaining agreement and Goodell's own zest
for being the Man in Charge. The commissioner
enjoys full disciplinary authority over his thirty-
two bosses and their teams. What's unusual about
this arrangement is that he also serves at the pleasure of the thirty-two owners and carries out their
wishes—except when he is fining them and taking away their draft picks and damaging their
reputations.

Brady was fingered as the main perpetrator in
the report even though Wells's evidence was cir-
cumstantial and his conclusion heavily caveated:
"It is more probable than not" that Jim McNally
and John Jastremski participated in a deliberate
effort to release air from the Patriots game balls
after the balls were examined by the referee, the
report said, referring to the locker-room lackey-
accomplices. It also concluded (kind of, sort of,
maybe, perhaps) that it was "more probable than not
that Tom Brady . . . was at least generally aware
of the inappropriate activities of McNally and
Jastremski."

At worst, whatever more-likely-than-not offense this was would seem classifiable as an
"equipment violation." Using an illegal Stickum-

like substance on a towel or uniform might also be listed as such, which the Chargers were caught doing in 2012. The league fined them $20,000 for not cooperating with the game official who noticed the infraction (this was later overturned on appeal). You could dwell on some version of the "everyone-does-it" explanation and find examples of NFL quarterbacks (Aaron Rodgers, Peyton Manning, among others) voicing preferences for having their essential professional tool— a football—prepared in a certain way. I guess you could compare this to Yo-Yo Ma liking his cello tuned in a certain way, albeit without a pack of three-hundred-pound rival cellists trying to behead him while he performed. (Fun fact: Yo-Yo is a Pats fan, I think I heard that somewhere.)

At the very least, this smacked of selective enforcement, involving the NFL's most successful and resented team and star. This was also not the first time the Patriots had been called to the principal's office. In 2007, the newly named Commissioner Goodell docked the Patriots a first-round draft pick after the aforementioned team official was caught videotaping Jets coaches sending in plays via hand signals—"Spygate." That revelation also triggered talk of asterisks and poisoned achievements and freighted legacies.

I admit the "cheater" rap bothered me. It messed with my irrational but powerful fan's belief that I was on the side of the righteous winners, if not the angels. That was my stab at a higher cause.

The inflated scandals also disturbed the creed of the Patriot Way, whose mythos I liked to believe incorporated an adherence to fair play. Were the Patriots' victories a sham? Were the Super Bowls tainted? Was **I** tainted? Maybe the Patriots' success was always too good to be true. Maybe they were all impostors, like me. Sports can trigger all kinds of psychological demons.

It has never been clear to me how big of a deal Spygate was. No one ever gave a good answer about why it would be so wrong for a team official to videotape opposing coaches from the field but okay for anyone—even that same team official—to buy a ticket and videotape the same coaches from the stands. Belichick made this point during his post-Deflategate/Mona Lisa Vito tutorial in January in response to a reporter's question that referenced the then-seven-year-old videotaping matter. "The guy's giving signals in front of eighty thousand people, okay?" Belichick said. "So we filmed him making signals out in front of eighty thousand people like there were a lot of other teams doing at the time, too."

I asked Kraft about Spygate, which he has pinned on Belichick over the years while insisting that he knew nothing about the team's taping practices. He shrugged, assumed a reflexively pained look, and proceeded to tell me a story. After the Pats were busted in 2007, Kraft asked Belichick how much competitive benefit the taping had gained him on a scale of one to one hundred—especially in light of the penalties and embarrassment the team suffered after getting caught. About a 1 percent benefit, Belichick replied to his boss (no doubt looking him in the eye). "Then you're a schmuck," Kraft told Belichick.

Kraft relayed this conversation to me in a quiet and oddly conspiratorial way, as if he were taking me into his confidence by sharing it. In fact he has recounted this "schmuck" exchange many times over the years. It is a go-to sound bite from Kraft's Spygate repertoire. And I've always been puzzled over why Kraft is so fond of this explanation, other than his seizing the opportunity to use a naughty Yiddish word ("schmuck"), which I can respect. The explanation raised more questions than answers. Kraft seemed to be saying, in essence, that the minuscule payoff the Patriots might have gained had not been worth the trouble.

But what if Belichick's answer had come back higher, say 10 or 15 percent? Would that make the cheating kosher?

Kraft had no comparable "you're a schmuck" story for Deflategate other than saying Brady had assured him he had had nothing to do with removing any air from footballs. Brady was suspended four games for his more-probable-than-not/ at-least-generally-aware link to the alleged caper.

I could relitigate Deflategate up and down, which I am not proud of and won't bore anyone further with. It was, in retrospect, a dark period in my annals of time management. Several times a day I would refresh the various sports websites for fresh nuggets and to see if justice was any closer to prevailing. It was like watching a playoff game in progress with the stadium lights off. I read the Wells Report three times (729 pages in total), and then (at least twice) the Patriots' rebuttal to the Wells Report titled "The Wells Report in Context" (another catchy title), which still resides online. I could give tutorials on the Ideal Gas Law and how the league scorched Brady's reputation over nothing.

I listened a lot to Boston's sports radio stations online. It always makes me feel so smart and well informed, to a point where I can now probably teach a college course on the PSI saga, except that a law professor at the University of New Hampshire, Michael McCann, beat me to it (INCO 460: "Deflategate: The intersection of sports, law and journalism"). The Boston sports media was almost comically in synch with its outraged customers.

One exception was Michael Felger, a former **Boston Herald** football writer who grew up in Wisconsin and went on to become a contrarian fixture on "The Sports Hub," one of the city's two radio sports outlets. I was driving around Boston one day while visiting my mother and happened to catch a heated back-and-forth between Felger and a cohost. The cohost kept imploring "Felgie" to, for just one second, "try to put yourself in the position of the average Patriots fan." To which Felger calmly replied: "But that would require a frontal lobotomy." I considered that to be a valid point.

Boston fans were fluent in the nuances of this rolling injustice. What was especially galling was how the original narrative was set in motion. Someone, almost certainly employed at league headquarters, had given the bad air pressure numbers to Chris Mortensen a few days after the AFC Championship Game. ESPN (a valued NFL broadcast partner) went months without correcting the record even after it learned the information was wrong. In other words, the NFL was complicit in creating the outrage, stoking it, and then declining to kill it, even after the league knew it was wrong. It's hard to think this was not part of some NFL-driven PR campaign, if not to persecute the Patriots per se, to propel the story in a direction the league wanted. Damn, I feel myself getting worked up again, about fucking air pressure. In footballs.

Whatever.

"I have never been involved in a national story

that transcended all common sense like this," said Bob Kravitz, the Indianapolis sports commentator whose tweet a few hours after the AFC title game started the whole thing—making him the Johnny Appleseed of the Deflategate media forest. "Not only do you have an eighteen-month clusterfuck that ends up in federal court, I've had an entire city threatening my well-being."

ESPN's Mortensen received a similar pelting even after he was diagnosed with throat cancer and off the air for a stretch. "People for the most part feel free to say anything they want to on social media," he told me. That included in Mortensen's case a series of death threats. "Listen, I'm a big boy, I really am," Mortensen said. His concern was for his wife, who he said was shaken by the barrage and whom he urged to avoid New England—not easy since her husband has to spend a lot of time in Connecticut, where ESPN is based.

Certainly Mortensen screwed up, but I've always respected him for not burning his source, no matter how badly the source burned him. He told me Robert and Jonathan Kraft had been nothing but gracious to him in the aftermath. What was more relevant to me was that the league seemed very much to be driving an agenda here.

The main target of New England ire was Goodell, serving as the heat shield for the Shield—or, more to the point, heat shield for the thirty-one non-Kraft owners. "A lot of the reason Roger is paid a lot of money is that Roger takes a lot of fucking arrows for a lot of owners," Falcons owner Arthur Blank told me.

Or bullets, figuratively speaking—so one would hope. A Boston sports radio host called for Goodell to be murdered (he claimed to be kidding) while effigies of the commissioner were being burned across New England and another faux-Roger was being tied up to be burned at the stake as part of some clever fan's Halloween display—so puritanical! Special police protection was provided to Goodell's summer home in Maine. Sports fans are not known for benevolent impulses. But then, they were fighting for a cause bigger than themselves: their football team.

9.

NO ONE BUYS TICKETS
TO WATCH A MORALITY PLAY

October 19, 2015

Somewhere along the way, mere "stories" were deemed insufficient. They had to be inflated. Or deflated. They had to become "storylines," or "backstories," or if the storytellers were feeling really literary, "narratives."

In October, the reality show caught itself a nice storyline in Indianapolis, where the Colts would be hosting the Patriots in a Sunday night rematch of the AFC Championship Game, billed "the Deflategate Bowl." NBC had at its disposal one of the world's most time honored of storylines: revenge. The network did not disappoint. Neither did the two fan **bases** (as what used to just be "fans" are now called). Even then–Indiana governor Mike Pence got in on the fun, posting a totally original tweet of a deflated football sitting on his desk. Apparently Pence was always a laugh riot.

Indy's autumn air was spiced with the scent of payback. Not only did the Colts dime out the Pats over their alleged air pressure antics the previous January, they had set in motion this whole interminable saga that rained asterisks down upon the enemy helmets. "I'd like to see them put 60 points on the board," Tom Brady Sr. had told the New York **Daily News** a few days earlier, "and I'd love to see Tom throw for 500 yards and eight touchdowns."

Not to belabor this, but—oh, let's belabor this: the Colts had it coming.

They were the worst kinds of snitches: self-righteous ones. Ryan Grigson, then the Colts' general manager, had written a beaut of an email to the NFL operations department before the AFC Championship Game, urging the league to be on the lookout for funny business by the Pats. The Colts' equipment manager had heard through the grapevine that the Patriots preferred playing with smaller footballs. They had been known to fiddle with their pigskins after the referees had inspected them. "All the Indianapolis Colts want is a completely level playing field," Grigson wrote. "Thank you for being vigilant stewards of that not only for us but for the shield and overall integrity of our game."

The Colts couldn't just take their 38-point beating in the AFC Championship Game like men; they had to also become the league's leading-edge bitches and the first to cry "cheater" over air pressure. Of course, everyone on both teams had to refrain from saying anything that might provide "bulletin board" fodder for the opposition. By the anesthetic norms of football-speak, they would treat NE @ IND on Week 6 as **just any other regular season game**.

And it was just any other regular season game—except for all the people walking through downtown Indy with deflated footballs on their heads.

The festive mood around Lucas Oil Stadium was nations removed from the "bitter celebration" that Cris Collinsworth described in Foxborough a few weeks before at the Patriots' latest banner-raising ceremony. While it is no vibrant megalopolis, Indianapolis was no longer the bleak picture that native son David Letterman would compare with "a minimum-security prison with a racetrack." Friendly and well-liquored Hoosiers paraded toward the stadium past the various Deflategate-themed displays that were set up inside the tailgating area at the corner of Meridian and South streets. A local bakery was selling limited-edition cakes in the shape of sagging footballs; one buffet featured a centerpiece of Brady on a box of Wheaties defaced to say "Cheaties." Fun!

Well, except for oversensitive Pats fans. Even casual ones could become prickly at being called cheaters, to say nothing of people close to Brady, the no-longer-stainless signal caller. Tom Senior and Galynn took the ordeal hard. They absorbed all the noise their son was adept at sealing off. They stopped attending Tom's away games, which they had done without fail every season of his college and pro careers. The taunts and abuse and CHEATERS LOOK UP signs—which became a fixture of enemy stadia—made them quick to anger. "It's just not worth it," Tom Senior told me. "Life's too short." One afternoon, Tom Senior was driving around the Bay Area when he heard a radio host refer to his son as a liar and cheater. He pulled his car over and called in to KGO, the San Francisco radio station whose host—Chip Franklin—made the charge. The producer put Mr. Brady right on the air.

"You are full of crap," he began, his voice jumping from agitation to full-on rage. In an epic five-minute rant, Mr. Brady would refer to the whole investigation as "a kangaroo court," dismiss the NFL's "propaganda," and denounce Goodell as a "flaming liar."

All things being equal, it's probably a good thing the Brady Bunch was not in Indy. Tom Senior might not have been able to control himself, and could have gotten up in the face of Wayne Gainey, a goateed Chevy dealer in Noblesville, Indiana, who was showing off a display of a dummy dressed in Brady's #12 reposed in a coffin. "You got one life, you might as well live it up," Gainey rhapsodized to me, deploying for me his personal motto (and vanity plate: LIVITUP).

A WHITE VAN WITH RHODE ISLAND PLATES pulled into the tailgating lot. Face-painted Pats fans, about half a dozen of them, filed out into the enemy throng. No great commotion ensued: lighthearted taunts were exchanged—something about Brady's balls. Bratwursts were offered and consumed by Pats fans, and cans of Miller Lite were touched in fellowship. While it's been said before, tailgating is one of the truly great remnants of American unity, creativity, and appetite in an otherwise barbaric realm. This was football in America at its happiest—with refreshments and before kickoff.

"Eli Lilly is around here, so maybe they put fucking Prozac in the fucking drinking water or something," Bob Kravitz was theorizing to me in a bar. Kravitz is a longtime Indy sportswriter best known for his charter status on the Deflategate Enemies List. We met a few hours before kickoff at the Claddagh Irish Pub & Restaurant up Meridian Street, where the early games were being shown on TV. I sought out Kravitz because he embodies a modern phenomenon of media notoriety:

he is a longtime print hack self-transformed into a TV, web, and Twitter bulwark; a local Indy fixture who has exploded nationally with the suddenness of an early-morning tweet about football air pressure. It is almost impossible in this day and age for any reporter to not become a cause célèbre after breaking a controversial story that goes national.

Kravitz says he has read the Wells Report four times, including once on the beach in the Bahamas. He has haunted press boxes and locker rooms over a thirty-five-year career for the Bergen **Record**, **San Diego Union-Tribune**, Cleveland **Plain Dealer**, and **Indianapolis Star**, among other outlets. He chews tobacco, can barely move his neck from an old hockey injury, and projects the endearing jadedness of an ink-stained journeyman. He couldn't care less who wins and who loses, on most days. Today is not one of those days.

"After eight months of horrible abuse from Patriots fans, not only towards me but towards my wife and towards my daughters, I would love nothing more than to see the Colts shove it up their ass," Kravitz told me. I took this to mean he did not care for my people.

He handed me his phone to reveal the up-to-the-minute greetings he had been receiving that afternoon via Twitter from his New England friends—unspeakable things, about unspeakable acts. He kept interrupting himself to point out something transpiring on nearby TVs. "I'm fifty-five and this is the first time I can remember giving a shit about the outcome of a game," Kravitz said ("Wow, Cincinnati is kicking the shit out of Buffalo"). "I've been abused by so many miserable people in New England that if they are just a little more miserable tonight or tomorrow, it would make my day just a little bit brighter" ("Chicago beat Detroit, wow").

Kravitz goes on for a few more minutes before pivoting to a more philosophical take. He calls it "the sports fan pathology." He is not the first to identify this phenomenon, but clearly has more direct experience with it than pretty much anyone. Social media has afforded the world's bravest cowards a flea market for their artistry. "I kind of miss when people actually had to get an envelope and stamp and put pen to paper," Kravitz said, "or crayon to paper, in some cases."

The bar kept erupting in cheers and oohs as the early slate of games wound down. Everyone in the place seemed to be wearing some officially licensed NFL merchandise, mostly blue-and-white Colts jerseys. It is no longer enough for NFL customers to merely root for their teams; they must also dress exactly like the players. "Fans now actually think they're playing in the game," Kravitz said.

Notions of "vicarious" keep shrinking. The action is right here, fans inhabiting this intimate crush via high definition. Many of them "own" teams and players in fantasy leagues. A Colts fan devastated when Peyton Manning departed the Colts in 2012 can still profit from his success via fantasy. "People are so isolated in their gadgets and desperate to be part of something bigger than themselves," said Kravitz ("Oh, that was one killer hit in the Browns game!"). The prickly sportswriter was now going full Philosopher King. "We don't put trust or faith in any institution, really," Kravitz said. "But strangely enough, we choose to put trust and faith in the one institution that gives us CTE and painkiller addiction and things like that."

Playing his final season for the Broncos and looking as if he could barely move his arms, Manning threw a bad interception up on the TV. Crushed again, the man in a #11 Colts jersey keeled over in disappointment ("Oh, Peyton"). Every sports bar in the nation is at this moment incubating a similar stew of emotion. Do this many Americans go to church on any given Sunday? Peyton might prove a humble mortal next to God, but my money says he puts up bigger numbers.

In other news, I still needed a ticket to the game.

I LEFT KRAVITZ AT THE CLADDAGH AND HEADED south on Meridian toward the stadium. A few blocks down, I struck up a conversation with Juan Collier, a gap-toothed African American gentleman from Cincinnati whom I found standing in front of a bar called the Slippery Noodle Inn. He was high-fiving anyone who was dressed in New England gear, and while I was not, I introduced myself to him as family.

Collier told me he'd been a Patriots fan since Drew Bledsoe was drafted first overall by the team in 1993. "You never know how these rooting things start, you know?" he said. One day, the Pats were just a terrible, anonymous team. Few people outside of New England ever thought about them. (Brady's dad once told me that before the Patriots drafted his son, they might as well have been the Jacksonville Jaguars.) Then New England drafted Bledsoe, eight-year-old Juan decided he liked the rocket-armed quarterback, and the Patriots became his team. And here he was in front of the Slippery Noodle two decades later taunting strangers in Colts jerseys.

One of Collier's tauntees had an extra ticket to the game, which he sold to me for $100. It was on the 20-yard line and the guy assured me I could see the entire field from the seat. This was technically true, in the same way that you can see the entire city block below from the top of the Empire State Building. But whatever, if you're going to go to a football game, chances are you're not going to improve on the TV view no matter where you sit. You just embrace the being there.

The stadium roof was closed and the crowd's Sensurround roar made it seem as if we were inside a massive sound studio. We effectively were, all of us extras in the weekly TV extravaganza that, per usual, would be the most watched show in America that week. I carried a cheeseburger plate to my seat.

The Colts mascot—a giant stuffed animal of undetermined breed named "Blue"—delivered a theatrical pummeling of a Pats mascot facsimile in the end zone. It fired up the crowd, in a kind of pro forma way. A CHEATERS LOOK UP sign greeted Brady as he ran out of the tunnel. Frank Sinatra Jr. sang "The Star-Spangled Banner" in a Colts sweatshirt; quarterback Andrew Luck appeared on the Jumbotron to remind everyone to refrain from using abusive language. Another PSA urged fans to wash their hands to avoid the spread of germs.

As kickoff approached, a video montage came on featuring highlights from the Colts' thirty-one-year history in Indianapolis. It began with a brief shot of the Mayflower moving trucks pulling out of Baltimore on a snowy night in 1984. This is an iconic image in the history of the NFL, and not in a good way. The Mayflowers represent the heartlessness of NFL oligarchs at their worst: in this infamous case, they signified the nerve of the late, loathed owner of the Colts, Robert "Tiger" Irsay, who uprooted the team from its longtime home under cover of darkness. This act of betrayal remains remarkable for its audacity and cowardice over three decades later. Even more remarkable was that Irsay's caper would be included in a testimonial to the Colts in their current residence, the city that inherited the team—or "stole" the team, as they still say in Baltimore.

The flight of the Colts illustrates both the best and worst facets of the NFL. Except for maybe Green Bay, no community in America was identified more closely with its football franchise than Baltimore was with its Colts. No community embraced its team harder and no population saw its identity more proudly reflected on its home field. When any serious fan considers the glory days of the NFL, the period when the league gained its foothold as the most popular sport in America in the 1950s and 1960s, it is impossible not to think of those vintage Baltimore teams of Johnny Unitas, Raymond Berry, and the Sudden Death NFL Championship Game of 1958 at Yankee Stadium. It was won by Unitas's Colts over Frank Gifford's Giants, 23–17, in what came to be known as the "Greatest Game Ever Played."

Sadly, Baltimore would also become the exemplar of how one terrible owner can wreck an idyllic football marriage. The reign of Tiger Irsay was a circus from the start. It was marked by the leading clown's flamboyant need to flaunt his ability to move the Colts at his whim. He flirted with cities like Memphis and Jacksonville because why shouldn't he? The team is "my candy store and I can move it wherever I want to," he would say. Commissioner Pete Rozelle believed he had persuaded Irsay to stay in Baltimore. But then off went the Mayflowers bound for Indy, an image that will endure in permanent infamy in Baltimore.

Baltimore wound up getting another team in 1995 after the Browns' (late, loathed) owner Art Modell pulled an Irsay on the city of Cleveland and moved his team to Baltimore. Modell's escapade rivaled Irsay's in terms of pure chutzpah, not only because the Browns also had a long connection with Cleveland and their home fans, but also because Modell had been a vocal critic of NFL franchise relocations. "We can't hopscotch franchises around the country," Modell said. "We have built this business on the trust of fans. If we treat that as if it doesn't count, it isn't going to wash."

Modell never set foot again in Cleveland after the Browns bolted. Smart move. "It was the worst feeling I've ever had other than when Kennedy was killed," said Browns legend Jim Brown of the team's leaving Cleveland. The newly renamed Baltimore Ravens found more success on the field than the Browns had in Cleveland in several decades (the Ravens won the franchise's first Super Bowl in 2000); likewise, the league granted Cleveland a replacement Browns franchise, which started up again in 1999. The sparkling new Cleveland Browns Stadium was just the kind of gridiron palace that Modell had been craving for years but that the city of Cleveland would never build until he was gone.

You could make the point that all's well that ends well. Baltimore and Cleveland were both eventually made whole by the league. NFL teams have after all been moving around the country since the league's inception (Cleveland was home to the Rams until the team moved to Los Angeles in 1946, before it left again—in 1995—for St. Louis). And we all understand that football is big business and that the NFL didn't fatten into this most golden of geese by being hung up on sentiment. "Relocation is always a painful process," I've heard Goodell say about a million times. He affirms this in that frigid, doctorlike way of his, as if he were describing the passage of a kidney stone.

Growing up in the seventies, I always liked the Baltimore Colts. They were in the Pats' division back then, but unlike our other AFC East rivals (mainly the Dolphins and the Jets), I found them charming, even venerable in their stately blue-and-white jerseys. My favorite non-Patriots player was

Bert Jones, Unitas's heir apparent with the Colts. He was the MVP of the league in 1976 and, a few years later, became the first quarterback in NFL history ever to be sacked twelve times in a single game (the record still stands).

The Indy incarnation of the Colts has enjoyed its share of success, most of it during Peyton Manning's time. Jim Irsay, a recovering addict and an eclectic figure inside the league, is by no means a model owner but still an upgrade over his late father. Indianapolis has fine fans and hosts a perfectly serviceable NFL experience. The Colts won a Super Bowl in 2007 and hosted one in 2012.

But as a notion, the Indianapolis Colts have never sat right. There is a remote white-noise quality to them, as if the team with the iconic horseshoe helmets doesn't really play anywhere. Once they left Baltimore, where they belonged, they might as well have been dropped on San Antonio or Columbus or Sacramento and it wouldn't have mattered. Indianapolis merely spent itself into being the most opportunistic landing spot for NFL's next studio. And more power to Indy, if not its taxpayers.

The Indianapolis Colts are one of a handful of NFL teams like the Jacksonville Jaguars or Tennessee Titans that could vaporize tomorrow and few people outside of those places would miss them. They are, in the spreadsheet calculus of the NFL, second-tier markets. But I was still struck that the Colts would actually show the May-flower trucks pulling out of Baltimore. The image was thrown up as the drive-by origin story for this Indian–**no place** chapter of the Colts. Few people in the stadium seemed to give this karmic spike a second thought, or appeared troubled that the team they've been rooting for all these years might be an ill-gotten gain. Is our mercenary, transient nature so baked into the fan experience that one city's heartbreak can so easily be shrunk down into another's Jumbotron fodder?

Or maybe I'm overthinking this. No one buys tickets to watch a morality play.

10.

DINGS?

Thanksgiving 2015

Enduring this twenty-week colonoscopy of a season was one long "painful process." Not only was the league reeling from Ray Rice, Deflategate, and other player discipline/court messes involving child and domestic abusers (Adrian Peterson, Greg Hardy, respectively); it was also facing the quandary of having three owners desperate to move their teams into the same "market"—or alleged "super-market," in this case, Los Angeles.

On the eve of one of football's High Holidays, Thanksgiving, the family of Hall of Famer Frank Gifford, who died the previous August, announced that Gifford had experienced "first hand symptoms" associated with CTE. Raiders quarterback Ken "The Snake" Stabler, who died in July, was elected posthumously into the Hall of Fame just days after a front-page **New York Times** story by John Branch described the rapid decline in Stabler's cognitive function—the severe headaches, lost sense of direction, his torture at loud noises. "I think Kenny's head rattled for about 10 years," Stabler's longtime partner Kim Bush said.

Concussion was set to be released a few weeks later, just in time to rattle the league for Christmas. The league feared that the Sony Pictures film, starring Will Smith, would be a blockbuster that furthered the impression that football was an unsafe and amoral spectacle—and also that the NFL had been shielding the game's true dangers for decades. Smith played Dr. Bennet Omalu, the Nigerian-born forensic neuropathologist in Pittsburgh who performed the autopsy of the great Steelers center Mike Webster in 2002. Webster, the gap-toothed battering ram who epitomized the Pittsburgh dynasty of the seventies, died at fifty after suffering from dementia and depression and falling into a gruesome spiral of homelessness and addiction. In studying Webster's brain, Omalu discovered the distinct tangles of tau protein that were consistent with what would become known as CTE. Suddenly Webster went from being an archetype of old-school football to the broken face of its toll.

Concussion was less of an exposé than it was

a big-budget dramatization of football's most elemental problem: that it was becoming harder to ignore the game's inherent danger. Whether or not the game really has "never been safer," as the league is always saying, the volume of new research, laments from gimpy retirees, increase in former players willing to donate their posthumous brains to research, and stories like Webster's kept pounding home the inescapable follow-up question: If the game has never been safer—safer than what exactly? And was the NFL, with its souped-up performers, ever going to be safe at any speed?

There is an oft-quoted line from the film in which a doctor (played by Albert Brooks) warns Dr. Omalu about the dangers of taking on "a corporation that has twenty million people on a weekly basis craving their product." The NFL "owns a day of the week," he said. "The same day the church used to own." The NFL has proven durable and won again and again.

The NFL was concerned enough about **Concussion**'s impact that it convened a series of focus groups to gauge how it should react. Based on the market research, the league concluded that it should mention the movie as little as possible, if **at all**; that any kind of response would make it look defensive and appear as if it were hiding something. A team of PR specialists addressed the league's December meeting in Dallas to rearm the owners with some proper sound bites (all the different ways to communicate that the game has never been safer and that the league had given tons of money to research on brain health). Earlier in the season, the **Times**'s Ken Belson had reported that in internal emails revealed in a hack of Sony's computers, executives and filmmakers had discussed altering the movie and its marketing plan to avoid antagonizing the league. One email from August 2014 stated that "unflattering moments for the NFL" were deleted or altered; another email from the previous month claimed that a Sony lawyer had taken "most of the bite" out of the film "for legal reasons with the NFL."

Jerry Jones believed the league's preoccupation with **Concussion** was overstated—both the movie and the real-life hazard on the field. "This is a pimple on a baby's ass," Jones said at a previous owners' meeting, according to an account in **ESPN The Magazine**. Even so, the league's apparatus was in place to soften the film's impact. At the very least, NFL authorities were learning to talk a good game about concussions, even if that contradicted the actual message the game sends its players. Nate Jackson, the former Broncos tight end and author of the football memoir **Slow Getting Up**, said that for all of the league's evangelism about making the game safer, back in the locker room it's always the same conversation. "Hit them as hard as you fucking can," Jackson told me. If you ask most players what they love about football, none of them will tout how safe the game is.

"Literally, if I had a perfect place to die, I would die on the field," said Jamal Adams, a young safety for the Jets in response to a question about his level of concern over CTE. Adams was appearing alongside Goodell at an event for about 150 Jets season ticket holders, who applauded his remark. "I would be at peace," he added of his final breaths on the gridiron. The gladiatorial fatalism of Adams's words drew stark headlines and a follow-up question to Goodell after the session. "I think what he was really making the point of is how much he loves the game and how passionate he is for the game," the commissioner said. "It's just something that means a great deal to him."

On the eve of **Concussion**'s release, one of the league's brightest young stars, the Giants' Odell Beckham Jr., decided that a late-season game against Carolina would be the perfect time to build up a 20-yard head of steam and hurl himself into the helmet of Panthers cornerback Josh Norman, with whom he had been in a trash-talking war all afternoon. Beckham's running launch could have knocked Norman unconscious or who knows what else. It would earn Beckham the first of three unnecessary roughness fouls and lead to a series of wild fights between Beckham and Norman that afternoon that would dominate the week's highlight packages. Eventually, Beckham would earn a one-game suspension for initiating "forcible contact" with the head of a defenseless player and trying to injure Norman.

Whatever Sony might have done to tone down **Concussion**, the film still packed a wallop. Reviews were largely positive, including from active and retired NFL players, many of whom reported that the film left them shaken and angry. Nonetheless, **Concussion** bombed at the box office as spectacularly as the NFL kept dominating TV ratings.

At around the time of the Beckham-Norman melee, quarterback Case Keenum, then of the Rams, suffered a concussion late in a game against the Ravens. Keenum was thrown down by the Baltimore defender and had his head snap back violently against the turf. He grabbed his helmet and writhed on the ground for several seconds before being helped to his feet by teammates. It was clear to anyone watching that Keenum was concussed (a diagnosis confirmed after the game). But the action on the field barely stopped. Keenum was not checked for a concussion, as he should have been according to the league's new "protocols." He wobbled back to the Rams huddle and ran two plays before fumbling away the game to the Ravens, whose kicker won it for them, 16–13, with a last-second field goal.

The video of the Keenum incident would be

played and replayed as a companion to the weekend's montage of tiptoe catches, breakaway runs, and touchdown dances. This mishap was so damning because it was so blatant, as opposed to the concussions that transpire on any given Sunday that are never self-reported, diagnosed, or noticed. Both the NFL and NFL Players Association opened investigations. Four months later, the NFL's vice president of football operations, Troy Vincent, announced the obvious—that the Keenum affair was "a system failure across the board." Blame was parceled among the referees (who did not stop the game), the Rams training staff (who did not check Keenum for a concussion), and the NFL's designated injury "spotter" at the game (who is supposed to stop the game upon detecting a woozy player).

But the more potent enabler of these sequences is the most basic of football instincts: the hunger to compete, keep your job, and win a game. Players and coaches share in it, and so implicitly do the fans. Even fans who, like me, watched the Keenum event with reflexive contempt for the league's continued ability to generate fiascos. I exhaled my obligatory umbrage. I sniffed disgust at the Keystone Kops of Park Ave and spouted off (I'm sure) about how the NFL does not really care about player safety. They run a football league, not a humanity business.

If I'm being honest, though—and I always

am honest, being a Pats fan—watching Keenum stumble around was an almost academic outrage. I had zero stake in the game, either team, or in Keenum's livelihood. He was a middling quarterback playing in a meaningless game for a team going nowhere. But there was also a similar scenario that had occurred ten months earlier, involving a team and game I did have a stake in.

The Patriots were trailing Seattle by ten with just under eleven minutes left in the Super Bowl. They faced a third and 14 from their own 28. Brady then completed a 21-yard pass over the middle to receiver Julian Edelman, who was whacked so hard by Seahawks safety Kam Chancellor that NBC announcer Cris Collinsworth let out a sickened moan at the second of impact. Edelman somehow hung on to the ball. He sprang to his feet in one punch-drunk motion and ran another 10 yards down the field even though he was ruled down and the whistle had blown. He seemed disoriented. It should have been evident to anyone watching, and apparently was to the game's concussion "spotter," who had been overheard by reporters radioing down to the Patriots sideline in a frantic effort to communicate that Edelman did not look right and needed to be examined.

But the Patriots, desperate to get back into the game, were running a hurry-up offense. Their drive continued. Two plays later, Edelman caught another pass over the middle to the 3-yard line and, in a strange motion, crawled a few yards forward on his stomach before struggling to his feet (Al Michaels observed that Edelman was "a little slow getting up" and pointed out that he had been bothered by a hip injury). Brady threw a touchdown pass to Danny Amendola on the next play that cut the deficit to 24–21. Edelman was finally examined when he arrived back on the sideline and was cleared to return.

The incident was also studied by the league and led to the creation of the so-called Julian Edelman Rule. Starting the following season, booth spotters would be empowered to contact referees directly to stop the game. The player they suspected might be concussed would have to miss at least one play while doctors looked him over. Credit the league, I suppose, for being responsive and taking corrective action following another televised misadventure.

But maybe the larger takeaway here was what I remember thinking as I watched the sequence unfold. I remember explicitly saying to myself, if not to the fellow Pats fans I was watching with, "Please get the hell up, Julian Edelman." Or "Please don't have a concussion, we need you." I also remember thinking (or saying) something to the effect of, "I really hope no referee just saw the little stagger-stumble I saw." If they did, they might stop the game. It would not surprise me at all if Edelman, Brady, the Patriots on the sideline, everyone in the coaches' booth and owner's box were all thinking the same. "Get the hell up, we need you."

Implicit in this exhortation was that even if Edelman felt dazed, this was no time for high-minded concussion protocols. Even if he was concussed, he must not act concussed. He needed to do everything in his power to hide the effects. Sure, safety is important—**nothing** is more important than a player's safety, we hear this time and time again, so it must be true. Certainly we all care about #11's well-being, caring and empathic people that we are. More important, though (if I'm being honest), this was a desperate moment in the Super Bowl. Edelman was Brady's favorite receiver and essential to the Patriots' coming back and winning that game. They did, with Edelman catching the decisive touchdown pass from Brady three minutes later. It was a great Super Bowl, epic ending, and 114.5 million viewers tuned in for what would at the time be the most watched TV broadcast in United States history.

Edelman caught no heat, at least that I saw, for playing through a possible concussion. And if the Patriots were criticized for not identifying signs of trauma in him, it was mild heat at best—certainly nothing compared with the scrutiny and sanction the team would endure for its sins involving matters of football deflation. Edelman in fact was celebrated for his toughness and clutch performance. He embodied the old-school mentality that allows a player to keep **grinding** no matter how badly he had "got dinged," as head injuries used to be called in football. "Getting dinged" always had such a lighthearted connotation, as if the experience were like getting a little queasy on a Ferris wheel, all part of the fun. That was before everyone started using more serious words, like "concussion," or ominous abbreviations ("CTE").

"Dinged" is safe because it implies something confined in a moment. It's something that will wear off, something to power through, as Edelman did. And good for Jules, I say. But then I'm not related to him, except by flatscreen.

11.
WHUPPINGS

December 1, 2015

Before the day the Ray Rice video popped up on TMZ, the roughest episode of Goodell's commissionership took place in 2009 at a House Judiciary Committee hearing on concussions. He had been called to testify at a time of growing evidence linking football with an array of cognitive maladies. The session was a bloodbath for the NFL. It was marked by unrelenting criticism of the Shield—namely the owners' human Shield, or commissioner. Goodell came in badly underarmed. He gave stilted answers and referred questions to doctors who were not in the room.

"The NFL sort of has this blanket denial or minimizing of the fact that there may be this link," Representative Linda T. Sánchez, Democrat of California, said to Mr. Goodell in what would become the indelible moment from that day. "And it sort of reminds me of the tobacco companies pre-nineties when they kept saying, 'Oh, there's no link between smoking and damage to your health.'"

The tableau drew comparisons to the iconic image associated with Big Tobacco's death by hubris: top executives from seven tobacco companies standing side by side, right hands raised, while being sworn in before a congressional hearing in 1994. They would then assert, once again, that nicotine was not addictive. The NFL recoiled from any correlation to an industry whose trajectory haunted them. Almost from the day Goodell suffered this inquisition at the Capitol, the league had moved to beef up its legal and lobbying efforts in Washington. In a letter to the **New York Times,** a lawyer for the NFL described the cigarette industry as "perhaps the most odious industry in American history." And the league resists any suggestion that it has taken cues from Big Tobacco in how best to deal with legal challenges and government regulation. But the parallels between the two industries' courses—and certain tactics— are unmistakable. Like pro football, tobacco operated for decades as an unstoppable force. If the NFL owned a day of the week, tobacco was so basic to American life that it was part of the air we breathed. The industry pushed hard against research and news accounts that exposed its dangers. It discredited scientists and researchers as being "alarmists" driven by "agendas." It denied for years any link between cigarettes and cancer, just as the NFL refused until recently to acknowledge any causal relationship between football and CTE. It blamed the media for caring more about the perils of cigarettes than about the preferences of "real people"; Paul Tagliabue in 1994 dismissed concussions in the NFL as "one of those pack journalism issues."

The tobacco industry was fully aware of smoking's dangers but worked to hide or obscure damning evidence. It touted questionable science and research studies to bolster its case. It spent a fortune on lawyers, marketing gurus, and lobbyists—some of whom would go on to do work for the NFL. After a dirge of testimonials from longtime smokers and their survivors, awareness about the dangers of smoking reached critical mass. Attitudes had shifted. Lawsuits and regulations came in rapid fire. The industry still hummed along for a while, fostering an impression that maybe tobacco could survive as some version of the behemoth it once was—scaled down but a behemoth nonetheless.

But the plummet continued. The fall from grace felt sudden, even though the spiral had begun decades before. Smoking was now gross and cancerous. It had become a private shame. The industry shriveled.

There were years—decades—where it felt like the NFL would just hum along forever. Pete Rozelle would always be there, smoking Marlboros and drinking Rusty Nails, working it out. He was too big to fail, and so was his league. Rozelle was the first, and only, sports executive to ever be named Sportsman of the Year by **Sports Illustrated.** No one knew what CTE was, or TMZ, or CBAs.

Not that the NFL was without crises under Rozelle, or did not fret over things that could spoil the whole banquet. But Rozelle also had the luxury to operate in a much simpler field. In April 1963, after the Packers had won their second consecutive NFL title, Rozelle had concluded that two of the game's biggest stars—Green Bay running back Paul "Golden Boy" Hornung and Detroit's defensive tackle Alex Karras—had bet extensively on NFL games, including ones that they had played in. Rozelle ordered a full investigation that uncovered proof of what would become pro football's biggest scandal in decades. Would this be the mess too toxic for the NFL to clean up and survive?

Consider how a similar situation might play out today if two of the game's seminal performers—say Aaron Rodgers and J. J. Watt—were busted like that. No question it would result in massive litigation, haggling with the union, and endless appeals. It would yield enough hot-take tonnage to melt a hundred more ozone layers. And that was before the president even started tweeting about it.

But in 1963, Rozelle merely summoned Hornung's coach, Vince Lombardi, to his office in New York. He handed Lombardi a brief laying out his conclusions. Rozelle told Lombardi he planned to suspend the players for a season. "You have no choice," Lombardi agreed. "Let's go get a drink and lunch."

Early on in his commissionership, Goodell staked his public brand on being a tough disciplinarian. He was big into the whole "new sheriff in town" model of leadership, which followed on the more remote and cerebral style of Paul Tagliabue.

A brilliant lawyer, Tagliabue had worn out his welcome with the Membership over his seventeen years as commissioner. The feeling was somewhat mutual. Unlike Goodell, the senator's son, Tagliabue lacked the political gene that would have made him more attentive to the needs and neediness of his most important constituency, the owners. He cared less about his public image than Goodell did. But compared with Goodell, Tagliabue had a particular gift for avoiding the high-profile and self-inflicted fiascos. "Paul had an expression, 'All's well that ends,'" said Joe Browne, the NFL's longtime head of public relations and a top deputy and confidant of the former commissioner. Tagliabue was less interested in making big disciplinary splashes.

Goodell by contrast presented himself as the righteous arbiter of all things precious in pro football. Tough disciplinary measures were basic to safeguarding "the integrity of the game" and "protecting the Shield" and all that. In some of his initial moves as commissioner, Goodell issued splashy rulings against a pair of recidivist player-criminals, Pacman Jones, then of Tennessee (suspended for the 2007 season), and Chris Henry, then of the Bengals (eight games). "We must protect the integrity of the NFL," Goodell said in a statement at the time. And protect other things.

"There was a great deal of sensitivity and attention paid to 'How does this play?' 'How does this reflect on our image?'" Ray Anderson, the NFL's vice president of football operations at the time, told me. Sheriff Goodell made for an effective persona for a few years, culminating with a 2012 **Time** magazine story in which Goodell was lionized on the cover as "The Enforcer." "They essentially had him as a king, on a throne with a sword," said Anderson, who left the NFL after the 2013 season and is now the athletic director at Arizona State University. "They depicted him as all-powerful. And that wasn't by accident. In my view, that was part of the mistake in terms of the image they were trying to portray. It translated into more of a dictatorship rather than something more collaborative or a partnership. Roger definitely had more of a singular leadership mentality."

Goodell was wielding the baton and restoring order at a time of eroding confidence in American institutions. George W. Bush's second term was becoming a disaster, the Iraq War was spiraling, Congress had suffered a wave of corruption and sex scandals, and the economy was about to collapse. Yet somehow football kept enduring as the rare point of civic connectedness in so many communities. And at least there was a tough guy in charge of our cultural hunger games.

In 2011, Goodell helped negotiate a collective bargaining agreement at terms judged favorable to the owners. The deal ensured ten more years of relative labor peace. Goodell's highest-profile punishments—handing down long suspensions to Atlanta quarterback Michael Vick for his role in running an illegal dog-fighting ring and to the participants in the New Orleans "Bountygate" case—were met with initial approval from fans. They seemed commensurate with the outrage stirred by both cases.

But the Bountygate suspensions were overturned by an independent arbitrator—none other than Paul Tagliabue himself, one of the many "mentors" Goodell had cultivated during his quarter-century climb up the greasy pole of the NFL hierarchy. This was an embarrassing cockblock of the Enforcer. It also ushered in a losing streak of botched disciplinary cases, court decisions, and a growing disrespect for Goodell from players and an overall tarnishing of the Shield and the sheriff's badge.

Nothing epitomized the sense of a flailing Park Avenue better than the case of Ray Rice. A quickie refresher: 1) The role model running back beats up his fiancée (troubling). 2) A security video shows Rice dragging his fiancée's limp body out of the elevator (more troubling). 3) Commissioner suspends Rice for two games; Rice shows remorse (kind of). 4) But then another video surfaces, this one from inside the elevator, courtesy of TMZ (brutal). The video hit early on a Monday and was flooding the nation's screens by mid-morning. 5) Hell breaks loose.

Oh, the hell. NFL officials claimed they never saw the video. "I would have loved to have seen that tape," Goodell said in a press conference in which he apologized for his handling of the case. The commissioner was responding to a question from a TMZ reporter, who pointed out that the tabloid video site had obtained the tape by making a single phone call. "You guys have a whole legal department," the reporter asked. "Can you explain that?" Goodell said he could not. As John Oliver pointed out on his HBO show, "You know things are not going well when you lose the moral high ground to a TMZ reporter."

Reeling, the league adopted a standard damage-control playbook. Goodell was serially apologetic. His PR team pushed a three-pronged message asserting that 1) the commissioner **gets** that he blew it; 2) he recognizes the **seriousness** of domestic violence; and 3) he is committed to doing better (and to prove it, watch him revamp the league's personal conduct policy). A SWAT team of in-house and outside flacks "worked with" sympathetic reporters to "message" the league's resolve. The highlight (or lowlight) came in a front-page **Wall Street Journal** story portraying a most remorseful Roger in his full **hands-on-and-fully-engaged-in-a-time-of-crisis** mode. NFL'S ROGER GOODELL SEEKS TO RIGHT PAST WRONGS was the headline.

Generous behind-the-scenes access was granted the reporter, Monica Langley. "I blew it," Goodell was quoted about a dozen different ways. "Our penalties didn't fit the crime." Langley portrayed Goodell as the "face of the league" and well known to fans ("he is often stopped for fist bumps . . . and photos and has his own bobble-head doll"). She showed him **really listening** in a variety of settings, soliciting advice on how best to deal with domestic violence from a cross section of leaders (police, military, corporate). She described how Goodell had convened eleven former NFL players to collect their input—and then brought home the high drama. "Former Chicago Bears star Mike Singletary slapped his hand on the NFL shield in the middle of Mr. Goodell's conference table and said: 'This means excellence. If a player isn't living up to that standard, he shouldn't be part of the NFL brand.'"

But the pinnacle moment involved a killer anecdote, one for which this article should always be identified: "the cold pizza story." Scene: a late-night meeting at 345 Park Ave. Goodell had called his team together to brainstorm about how best to convince people they were not covering up for Ray Rice, for the Ravens, or for their own incompetence. Pizza was ordered and brought into the meeting room. Langley then delivers the rest from here. "No slice was taken until Mr. Goodell ate," she wrote. "He never did, and the slices turned cold in the box." Anyone who overlooks Roger's zeal to erase the scourge of domestic violence need only recall that cold pizza. It should be frozen and sent to Canton! (One league executive who was in the room disputed the account to me, insisting that he himself ate a few slices of the four pizzas—two cheese, two pepperoni—which he claimed were still warm and depleted by meeting's end. An additional pizza-related nugget: Goodell does not in fact care for pizza himself. He was turned off to cheese in general at an early age after he accidently bit into an individually wrapped piece of American cheese that still had the plastic wrap on it. It disgusted little Rog and apparently soured him on the pleasures of cheese forever. And this explains everything about everything—or perhaps nothing at all.)

Regardless, no one was buying it. Confidence in Goodell was in a free fall. There were calls for him to resign. He was in a funk for much of that season, eager to regain credibility but uncertain how. With some exceptions (cold pizza!), the glowing press coverage Goodell had once enjoyed had flipped. "Roger Goodell uses his office as if he's a blackjack-wielding tough from the 1920s with a crank-starting car," Sally Jenkins wrote in the **Washington Post**.

Even the talking heads of the Nugget Industrial Complex were becoming cranky. ESPN's Adam Schefter called the Rice breakdown "arguably the biggest black eye the league has ever had." (Before the second video surfaced, Schefter had wondered whether Rice's two-game suspension was "lenient enough.")

When you've lost Schefter, you know it's big trouble—we're talking Cronkite Speaking Out Against Vietnam–level trouble! The diminished commissioner needed a lifeline. Enter Deflategate.

Brady and the Patriots were set up as perfect bull's-eyes. Goodell went to work. He slapped the league's biggest star and "model owner" over such an amazingly stupid story—among the most ridiculous sports "scandals" in history. But more amazing still was that the story simply would not end, no matter how trivial it became.

Goodell's decision played well across his NFL nation-states. He was not exactly tackling an important cultural issue, like domestic violence, but in this case Goodell had done something even more important in the eyes of most NFL players, team officials, and fans: he did something to hurt an opposing team.

And not just any opposing team: the Borg. Fans lapped up the Patriots' pain, which was the point: the delicious nothingness of Deflategate, a pleasing snack to follow the heavy indigestion of Ray Rice.

I was in Foxborough for the last game before the innocence died, almost a year earlier; the Pats had defeated the Ravens, 35–31, in the divisional play-offs, after twice overcoming double-touchdown deficits. The game became memorable for a few reasons. One, the Patriots' offense deployed an exotic formation in the third quarter that confused the Ravens (and the referees) about which players were eligible to catch passes. While the Patriots' scheme was determined to be within the rules, Ravens coach John Harbaugh was furious after the game, accusing the Pats of "deception" and calling the formations "an illegal type of a thing." This led Brady to counter smugly that "maybe those guys gotta study the rule book," which naturally pissed Harbaugh off further, and, depending on your interpretation of the reality show, might have triggered the events that led to Deflategate. (Harbaugh was suspected of tipping off the coach of the Patriots' next opponent, the Colts, his former assistant Chuck Pagano, that Brady and Co. might have been messing with the air pressure in their footballs.)

Late in the first quarter, I headed to the men's room where I caught a few minutes of the NBC broadcast of the game on a press box TV. NBC cameras happened to be trained at that moment on Commissioner Goodell and Her Majesty, Jane, who were sitting in the Gillette Stadium stands. This would be the last time Goodell would set foot in Foxborough for thirty-three months, fearing Deflategate-generated vigilante justice from Pats fans.

But no one knew that at the time. And what struck me as I watched the telecast were NBC announcers Al Michaels and Cris Collinsworth discussing the Ray Rice episode that had consumed much of that season. A few days before the game, the former FBI director, Robert Mueller, had issued a report commissioned by the league that described several deficiencies in the league's handling of the Rice affair. Michaels, whose network pays billions of dollars to be a "broadcast partner" of the NFL, went on to praise how thorough

the investigation was and how transparent the
league had made itself to Mueller. The acclaimed
announcer then landed on a note that absolved
Goodell from knowing anything about the security footage of Rice assaulting his fiancée on the
elevator. "The report concluded that there was no
evidence that Goodell or anyone else in the league
had received or seen the tape prior to it going public," Michaels said. "Cris, not a lot of good came
out of this. Obviously, the whole situation, at least
it made it part of the national conversation, and
that was good."

When in doubt, always salute your bungling
patron for making it "part of the national conversation." And give kudos to the league for helping
us look so hard at ourselves, and for sprinkling its
football customers with the fairy dust of "awareness." Normally Michaels and Collinsworth are
an excellent duo. But this was, well, something—
at best, a reminder that the league leaders have a
broad and powerful collection of enablers at their
disposal, even ostensibly independent (if not journalistic) megaphones.

And then Collinsworth got started. "The decision to suspend, initially, Ray Rice for two games
was a mistake," the former Bengals wide receiver
began. "Roger Goodell has admitted that." This
would have been a good place to leave it, which
meant Collinsworth did not. "But I never once

in all my dealings with the commissioner ever doubted his integrity," Collinsworth said, "and I think that came out in the report as well."

"It did," Michaels affirmed.

This was not the prevailing view among the football populace. Goodell has been America's most loathed sports commissioner this decade, easily. In a February 2016 poll of football fans, only 28 percent of respondents approved of the job he was doing. But the sport nonetheless appeared insulated from the contempt fans held for the people in charge. To reiterate: we compartmentalize well.

Whatever, soon all anyone would be talking about were Ideal Gas Laws, football air pressure, and equipment managers in the men's room. You can't help but wonder whether the league concocts these things. "What I have facetiously (I think) referred to as the Deflategate Marketing Plan has worked splendidly," wrote the **Sports Illustrated** business columnist Andrew Brandt, a former Packers executive.

Jerry Jones told me he worried that the threat of Deflategate bleeding into another season could be "a downer" for the league. He feared that it might depress fan interest. He was wrong. "It shot up interest," Jones marveled with a slightly devious smile (as all Jerry smiles tend to be devious). "Now, please don't interpret this as me trying to drum up negative attention. But make no mistake about it, legitimate negative criticism does not diminish interest. There is a lot to be said for that. Deflategate was on CNN. It was just all over the place."

The previous summer, after Goodell had denied Tom Brady's appeal of his four-game suspension and the quarterback's legal team was trying to get the ruling overturned in U.S. district court, I stopped by the TB12 offices in Foxborough and visited briefly with Guerrero. He said Brady had been in a funk over Deflategate and wondering if the whole thing was worth it—that maybe he should just retire. It had taken Brady much of that off-season to get "back to center," Guerrero said.

Brady had become miffed at Kraft that spring. Despite the owner's grousing about how "unfathomable" and "incomprehensible" the league's punishment of his star quarterback was, he stood down and did not challenge the commissioner's ruling in court—as many around the league feared, and many in the Brady camp were hoping. Kraft opted for his business partners over his "fifth son."

Kraft had sound reasons for not contesting the league's ruling. "You can't sue the league," Kraft told me, and then invoked the example of Al Davis, the rogue owner who did during his checkered Raiders reign. Kraft wants to be liked and considered statesmanlike inside the NFL.

As a practical matter, Kraft learned quickly that his grievance over the punishments had little support among his fellow owners. Ever the pragmatist, he concluded this would be a lonely and pointless fight. Kraft also believed that if he did not contest the original punishment, Goodell would reward him with good soldier points and knock down Brady's suspension on appeal.

But Kraft's fighting words in support of Brady and against the league gave the impression he was ready to go to war. When Kraft announced at the league meetings in San Francisco that he would not contest the punishment, Brady was devastated. "Crestfallen" and "betrayed" was how someone who was with Brady at his home on that day described him. Brady had not spoken publicly on the matter. His new team of NFLPA lawyers, led by Jeffrey Kessler, a celebrated union attorney with an impressive track record of beating the league in court, had urged Brady to go dark. He was also careful not to voice any public displeasure with the Krafts. Whenever Brady would complain to Guerrero, Guerrero would remind him that he'd worked with players on all thirty-two teams, and there is no real difference between the teams. It's always about business and bottom lines.

After a while, Brady concluded that Deflategate had very little to do with him per se. He was superstar collateral damage caught up in a long-running Game of Thrones that involved many kingdoms and agendas. Brady had effectively become a political football.

Several owners and team officials across the league were eager to see Goodell wallop the Pats. They were weary of Kraft's sanctimony, jealous of his success, and resentful of what they considered his too-close relationship with Goodell. They cheekily dubbed Kraft "the assistant commissioner." Conjecture also burned over whether the puzzling severity of Goodell's Deflategate penalties might have been a case of the commissioner trying to appease owners who believed he had gone easy on them during Spygate. "A makeup call," one owner described the cause-effect of the two scandals to **ESPN The Magazine**'s Don Van Natta Jr. and Seth Wickersham in an exhaustive report that September.

The owner most vocal in support of Goodell's whacking the Pats was Jerry Jones, probably Kraft's closest rival for first among equal status within the Membership. Jones had been through his own tangles with Goodell over team discipline. In 2012, Goodell docked the Cowboys $10 million in salary cap space for what the league determined to be an improper restructuring of receiver Miles Austin's contract two years earlier. Jones was apoplectic over that ruling, but elected not to sue the league and has remained mostly steadfast in his public support of the commissioner. "I think he's doing a great job and I'm a big supporter of his,"

Jones said of Goodell that summer when asked about the Deflategate sanctions.

When I spoke to Jones a few weeks later, he said that Goodell's role as the singular arbiter of discipline lent drama and clarity to the reality show. In this regard, Jones recalled the whuppings he would endure from his own father. If young Jerry had the nerve to question the verdict, his daddy would have none of it. "You know why and I know why I'm doing this, I don't even need to tell you," his father would say. "Now bend over." Jones told me this with a wink, clearly enjoying the specter of Bob Kraft bent over Daddy Roger's knee.

12.

"WE PAY HIM DAMN
WELL TO BE NEUTRAL"

December 2, 2015

No matter where the league was headed, the swagger of Roger Goodell's "new sheriff in town" days was long gone. By the end of the 2015 regular season, one in which the number of reported concussions jumped 58 percent over the previous season, the difference in the commissioner was unmistakable. His face broadcast the burdens of his job. "I think he's highly sensitive," Jones observed to me about Goodell that November. "He wears his challenges, there's no question." Giants co-owner John Mara said the stresses of recent years have "definitely scarred him a bit." Whereas he once enjoyed the give-and-take with fans and media, Goodell effectively shut down. He went a full 578 days without tweeting. On the increasingly rare occasions when he would speak publicly, Goodell would swaddle himself in talking points. "We'd like to see him more relaxed and smiling and answering the questions," Houston Texans owner Bob McNair told me. "You know, he's got all these legal advisers telling him you can't say this or you can't say that." Another owner compared Goodell, especially in public, with a team that is playing "not to lose." He became jittery, overcautious about making a mistake, which can become self-fulfilling.

I met McNair at an NFL owners' meeting held in Dallas in early December. We met under a Christmas tree in the lobby bar of the Four Seasons overlooking a lit-up swimming pool. McNair, who was raised in the foothills of western North Carolina, is a born-again Christian who had recently been criticized for contributing $10,000 to help repeal a Houston ballot initiative that protected gays and lesbians from discrimination. (McNair later withdrew the donation, but not before Chris Kluwe, a former Vikings punter-turned-progressive-NFL-gadfly, accused McNair of holding "clearly outdated ideals and bigotry and intolerance" and describing the Texans owner as "a pants-on-head, cow-humping glue-huffer.") I asked McNair what he thought of having his team featured the previous summer on the HBO reality show **Hard Knocks** about life at an NFL training camp. He said it was a net plus overall but added that he was distraught and embarrassed over how profane certain Texans personnel were on camera. He addressed this afterward with head coach Bill O'Brien, who himself had used fourteen forms of "fuck" in the first installment alone (O'Brien had already heard from his mother on this). McNair said he suggested to O'Brien that he introduce a "cuss jar" in the locker room to discourage future swearing. He agreed, with proceeds going to charity. This actually happened.

McNair, who sold his energy company to Enron in 1999, is often referred to around Houston as a "billionaire philanthropist." His name adorns numerous buildings, fields, wings, and causes. "I tell my fellow owners all the time that all of our value is in intangible assets," McNair told me. "We have the game, but that's intangible. Most of the stadiums are owned by the cities and counties. Even the players, we don't own them, we rent them." Given what became of Enron, McNair said, he has an acute sense of how ephemeral success can be for even the most invincible-seeming enterprise. The end can come fast and from out of nowhere. He has seen a bounty of intangible value vanish. "The market lost confidence" in Enron, McNair said. "The banks lost confidence and they shut off the lines of credit, and they were out of business, virtually overnight."

McNair brought the Texans into existence in 2002 after the Houston Oilers departed for Tennessee in 1997. He has seen his influence around the league grow despite having survived multiple battles with cancer and employing some of the most inept and overpaid quarterbacks ever to stain the Shield (see Osweiler, Brock). He is considered one of the sharper and more outspoken businessmen in the game, happy to weigh in on dicey issues like Goodell's paycheck (way too high) and Deflategate ("a mountain out of a molehill"). He is also prone to saying things that most owners might believe but would never express out loud.

When I met with McNair for the first time, he was being consumed by the same issue that was then consuming the rest of the league—the three-team battle for the right to move to Los Angeles. As a member of the committee overseeing relocation, McNair held outsized say in the fates of three established franchises (the Rams, Chargers, and Raiders), not to mention a market that the league had been obsessed with reoccupying since the Rams left for St. Louis and the Raiders left for Oakland in 1995. My **New York Times** colleague Ken Belson, who joined us at the bar, asked McNair for his view on the three owners seeking to move—Stan Kroenke of the Rams, Dean Spanos of the Chargers, and Mark Davis of the Raiders. "Oakland gets nothing," McNair said. Why? McNair immediately invoked Davis's late father, the black sheep owner Al Davis, who was at constant war with the Shield. "Al used to sue us all the time," McNair explained, waving the back of his hand (I quoted McNair saying this in the **Times**; since then, every time I've spoken to Mark Davis, he's urged me to be sure to "keep the tape" of that McNair interview—spoken like a man with litigation in his genes).

A little earlier at the Four Seasons, Goodell was the picture of sculpted arrogance as he administered a brief press conference. The requisite Shield logo was affixed before him—the NFL podium version of the presidential seal. In brief remarks, Goodell expressed the proper "thoughts and prayers to San Bernardino," where fourteen people had been killed in a terrorist shooting that day. He volleyed a question about a recent spate of high-profile referee screwups ("when we talk about the integrity of the game, we strive for perfection"). He was then invited by a reporter to weigh in on "a bit of good news": newly released statistics showing that NFL players were getting arrested at lower rates than they had been in 2011 and 2012.

"Well, you have to give credit to the players," the commissioner said generously. This made me chuckle. "Credit to the players . . ." **for getting arrested less?** Funny construction! I chuckled too conspicuously and felt the glare of the very-serious nugget seekers who had been trying to hang on the Supreme Leader's every word. This was my first commissioner's press conference and I had not fully appreciated its gravity.

The exercise of covering an owners' meeting reminded me of covering the United States Senate: a bunch of reporters waiting around for a bunch of rich white dudes, many of them elderly, to emerge from endless meetings. As with senators, NFL owners mostly adhere to a Membership code that forbids disparagement of one another, at least on the record. They reveal very little and leave their chroniclers to overinterpret body language and facial expressions and attempt to eavesdrop.

When I first arrived at the Four Seasons, I saw Goodell and Falcons owner Arthur Blank locked in an intense discussion outside a lobby elevator. Blank, a founder of Home Depot, is the chairman of the owners' "compensation committee." This meant that he was the man most responsible for determining how many tens of millions more dollars the owners would fork over to Goodell for performing his primary function (i.e., making the owners billions more dollars). Goodell's astronomical pay had become its own cause célèbre and received more attention than that of any sports commissioner in history. It was marveled upon at the highest levels of society. "I cannot believe the commissioner of football gets paid $44 million a year," President Barack Obama said in a **GQ** interview with Bill Simmons, who had asked him which professional league he would most like to run.

For his part, Blank seemed to relish his work on the compensation committee as he would a hernia. "Well, it's not more trouble than it's worth," he told me. "But it's definitely a lot of trouble." Now a decade into Goodell's tenure, there was a debate among owners about whether Goodell should be paid like the head of a large entertainment firm, media group, or merely a sports league. And that's before you consider the polarizing figure Goodell has become, and his own ego. Goodell would almost never dare say anything about his salary, certainly not publicly. But it was important to Goodell that he be paid more than any other commissioner of a major American sport, especially former Major League Baseball commissioner Bud Selig. Selig was privately derided among NFL owners and executives as a weak and incompetent boob.

But it was not lost on the NFL Membership—and certainly not Goodell—that Selig was paid a reported $18.4 million a year in 2011, almost twice what Goodell was then making. Goodell mentioned this imbalance in negotiating his new deal, and with good effect. On the rare occasion Goodell would talk about his new salary to anyone during that period, it was to point out that he was being paid much more than Bud Selig was.

The reason anyone even knew about Goodell's

compensation to begin with was because the NFL had improbably been given the status of a tax-exempt trade association going back to the 1960s. It required the NFL to file a 990 form every year with the IRS that listed its top paid executives. The press became more interested in the commissioner's number after it shot up to $44.2 million in 2012—a whopping figure on its own, but especially compared with what the chief executives of other nonprofit trade groups make: the CEO of the American Petroleum Institute, by comparison, was paid $5.6 million that year. Even the head of the nation's largest private for-profit employer, Walmart, was paid "only" $20 million a year. These stories became so annoying to the NFL that it finally decided to start declaring itself a for-profit operation in 2015. That seemed fair since the NFL had been profiting outrageously for decades. It would cost the owners millions of dollars in accounting and legal fees, and millions more in future taxes. But such would be the price of Goodell's getting to reap his tens of millions every year in relative privacy.

Outside the lobby elevator, Goodell listened to Blank with a solemn countenance that made him look deeply preoccupied, even stricken. The Falcons' monarch mirrored the commissioner's grave expression, though that tends to be his default visage to begin with—Blank's heavy-hooded eyes, thin mustache, and bespoke suits lend him the sinister air of a comic book villain or undertaker or art thief (he's also kind of a dead ringer for Grandpa from **The Munsters**). Goodell was nodding slowly at Blank as if he'd just received a bad diagnosis. I imagined this could be the fateful discussion, right there in front of me at the lobby elevators, where Blank might be informing the commissioner whether 2015 would be a $30 million season for him or a $40 million season—and the Goodells could then determine their family budget for the year because, let's face it, all those private SoulCycle and Pilates classes are not free.

Later, during a break, Goodell darted past a bank of reporters and into a men's room. Robert Kraft followed behind him like a beagle. A security guard stationed himself outside the door, temporarily restricting the lavatory to Membership only. Oh to be a fly on the soap dispenser for this toilet tête-à-tête. Not only was the onetime "assistant commissioner Kraft" still supposedly furious at Goodell's actions over Deflategate, but the league had just kept amplifying its malevolent characterizations of Tom Brady's "scheme" to remove air from footballs. NFL lawyers had a few weeks earlier filed a brief in the league's appeal of Judge Richard Berman's ruling that stayed Brady's four-game suspension. In its brief, the league had compared whatever air pressure shenanigans had gone on in Foxborough with the Black Sox scandal of a century earlier—arguably the most infamous calumny in sports history in which eight Chicago White Sox players, including the great Shoeless Joe Jackson, were accused of taking money from gamblers in exchange for throwing World Series games. The NFL likening Deflategate to the Black Sox occurred a few months after Goodell had compared the "more probable than not" behavior of Shoeless Tom Brady with a player using steroids.

Kraft and Goodell remained inside the sanctum for about a minute and a half—roughly the amount of time that the former Patriots equipment man and Deflategate "Person of Interest" had inhabited the Gillette Stadium men's room with his allegedly dirty bag of balls. Arthur Blank came in, too, after a certain point, and then Rams owner Stan Kroenke, the megabillionaire who at the moment was holding a post position in the race for L.A. gold. Here was a convergence of four pivotal figures with big money and legacies at stake, all holding their dicks.

Finally Kraft and Goodell walked out of the Four Seasons john together, laughing.

Goodell is clearly gifted at working the Members. He makes them feel important and heard. And he is especially good at gratifying the older members, whom he cultivates as mentors, even quasi–father figures. Goodell was the middle of five boys born in seven years to Jean and Charles

Goodell. His father was a moderate Republican congressman from New York who was appointed to succeed Senator Robert F. Kennedy after Kennedy's assassination in 1968. He was known as cerebral and somewhat removed, with a custom of reading the dictionary each night before bed in order to enhance his vocabulary. Charles Goodell was a favorite of President Richard M. Nixon's until he turned against the Vietnam War and introduced a bill to end it. The White House then turned against Goodell and worked to defeat him in the 1970 election.

Roger, only a boy, followed his father everywhere on the campaign trail. From this, the commissioner says he learned the value of making tough and principled decisions. He keeps a copy of his father's Vietnam Disengagement Act on the wall of his office. "If there is one thing I want to accomplish in my life besides becoming commissioner of the N.F.L.," the young Goodell wrote in a letter to his father while in high school, "it is to make you proud of me."

When you hear Goodell speak around his owner-bosses, he can evince a similar tone of an approval-seeking son. He leans on authority-figure words, such as "proud" and "disappointed." He is prone to assessing character and deeds in binary, parental terms. "I no longer wanted to disappoint my mom and dad," Goodell said, explaining that he had been an underachieving student in high school before getting serious at Washington & Jefferson College in western Pennsylvania.

Charles and Jean Goodell divorced when Roger was a teenager. By the time their middle son graduated from college, Jean Goodell was dying of breast cancer. Roger moved in with and cared for her during her final years, as he began work at the NFL, the only workplace he would ever know.

Goodell attached himself to Pete Rozelle, the legendary commissioner who had been his idol going back to his teenage years. What football-loving kid grows up idolizing a sports commissioner? He did not dream of being Johnny Unitas or Bart Starr, but Pete Rozelle? ("Probably a little odd," Goodell conceded to me.) But Rozelle was also a giant, maybe the most transformational commissioner in the history of American sports. His mix of personal charm, toughness, business foresight, and political touch steered the league through a remarkable period of growth, prosperity, and turmoil in the 1960s, '70s, and '80s. He was a buoyant, chain-smoking, and cocktail-sipping PR man who exuded confidence. He made himself so synonymous with the modern juggernaut that it became impossible to imagine the NFL without Rozelle.

"Can he dare retire?" Frank Deford pondered in a **Sports Illustrated** profile of Rozelle from

1980. "Surely, if Rozelle ever leaves the NFL, it will turn back into the Decatur Staleys and the Frankford Yellow Jackets, and Sundays will revert back to God, Monday nights to bowling."

Goodell arrived at the league in 1982 as an administrative intern, and Rozelle would remain commissioner through the decade. This allowed plenty of time for Goodell to ingratiate himself and absorb Rozelle's lessons. One of them, which Goodell no doubt internalized—if not then, certainly now—was the credo, "No one is cheering for the commissioner." This has not been a problem for Goodell.

Fans love football, their favorite players and teams, Rozelle would say. But they never love the guy in charge. Goodell was undeterred. He volunteered to be Rozelle's driver at the Super Bowl in New Orleans in 1983.

"I'd do anything," Goodell told **Time** in 2012. "I wanted any opportunity that would keep me around. I practically lived with him." He said he wanted Rozelle to see "how I managed people, managed situations."

Goodell comes off as adept at and attentive to impressing older men. He clearly spent much of his childhood in adult company. This has proved to be useful given that most of the "key owners" during Goodell's tenure have been in their seventies and eighties (Blank, Kraft, Jones, McNair, Richardson, and Dan Rooney of the Steelers, until his death in 2017). Four different owners told me that Goodell has at one time or another referred to them as mentors. Whether or not Goodell is being genuine, or if he's just showing a knack for flattery and seduction, the move is clearly effective. His owner-bosses become stakeholders in his career. "I will work tirelessly to make you proud of me" is how Goodell closed a letter to Arthur Blank in 2011, echoing the exact words Goodell wrote in the letter to his father from college. Blank still keeps the letter displayed on the wall of his office.

When I began reporting on Goodell, his various publicists wanted to stress that for as much of a strict disciplinarian as the commissioner is, he had also built important bonds with some of the people he had previously disciplined. They offered up Michael Vick, the former star quarterback whom Goodell had suspended indefinitely without pay in August 2007 after he pleaded guilty to federal charges for his role in a dog-fighting ring. Vick spent twenty-one months in federal prison and was jettisoned by the Atlanta Falcons; after his release from prison, Vick applied for and was granted reinstatement from the league. He signed with the Eagles in 2009 and played a few more productive years before officially retiring in 2017.

When I reached him, via the league, Vick was playing out the final days of his career as a backup for the Steelers. It was a strange and awkward conversation. Vick did not really have much to say. He did not seem to know why the league had asked him to talk to me at all. After a few minutes, I wondered the same. Vick said that from time to time, Goodell would check in with him. Vick managed to stay out of trouble following his reinstatement with the exception of a 2010 incident in which a codefendant in Vick's dog-fighting case was shot outside a restaurant where Vick had been present (no charges were filed, and Goodell said Vick would not be disciplined).

"He says he's proud of me," Vick said of Goodell.

A key to being a good politician is an ability to prioritize constituencies. Goodell keeps a call sheet at his desk with the names of all the team owners. He checks in with the Members at least once a month. "You have to be able to deal with and get along with thirty-two different personalities," New York Giants co-owner John Mara told me. "We range from people like me who were born in a family business, and people who are self-made billionaires who think they know everything about everything." Goodell is solicitous and attentive, identifies quirks and peeves. He learns what issues are important to each owner, as a good legislative leader would do with his caucus. He humors them over the phone, in meetings, or at urinals. "The job is like attending 10 weddings at the same time," Kraft once said, "and making every bride and groom feel like they're the ones."

Goodell's mentor viewed the commissioner's job as a hybrid between being the executive director of a big corporation and the director of a trade association. "I inherited a strong constitution and an office that held respect," Rozelle said. "But the whole thing, no matter what the constitution says, is getting the confidence of the owners."

In public statements, Goodell will sometimes suggest that he works on behalf of the entire league—players, fans, and all of the virtues and entities that the Shield embodies. "Roger sees his constituencies as plural, more than just the owners," Steelers owner Art Rooney II assured me. The conceit is nonsense, but the claim is nothing new. NFL commissioners have been proffering this lie of even-handedness for decades. Rozelle used to always go on about how he was a "neutral" broker between management and players. Former NFLPA head Ed Garvey complained endlessly to Rozelle about this, insisting that in fact the commissioner works for only one entity and one entity only, the owners. The commissioner serves at the pleasure of the Membership and is quite literally bought and paid for—and paid extremely well—by the owners.

"Dammit, don't be telling us Rozelle's not neutral," one owner complained to Garvey. "We pay him damn well to be neutral."

In 2010, Goodell made a series of training camp visits during a tense period that preceded a player lockout. One meeting, with the Colts, became hostile enough that the team's player representative, center Jeff Saturday, had to escort the commissioner off the premises. "What offended them is that he told them he was neutral and he actually thought they'd believe it," NFL Players Association chief DeMaurice Smith told ESPN's Don Van Natta Jr. a few years after the incident.

"He's the face of the owners," said Jacksonville Jaguars defensive lineman Jared Odrick of the commissioner. "He gets paid, what, $40 million a year just to take the heat and speak so the owners can remain faceless. Is it smart? Hell yeah, it's smart. I'll take $40 million a year to be NFL commissioner and be a politician."

13.

NO BROKE DICKS

January 12, 2016

Goodell's political skills were taxed to the extreme by the Los Angeles decision. It is one thing to perpetrate an illusion of neutrality when working in the collective interests of the owners; but it's quite another when the quagmire pits owner against owner against owner. Goodell really did have to stay nonpartisan, or at least finesse it in a way that would not alienate any of his thirty-two bosses.

L.A. was a classic example of how NFL football might conjure images of dirt-streaked tough guys, but the business orbits around the delicate axes of billionaire egos. Owners tend to think of themselves as the geniuses behind the magic. They are the ones who build the stadiums, lead the committees, spend their own money, and then see their egos tossed up and down on a scoreboard every week.

"This is our deal, it belongs to us," Jerry Jones told me. By "our" he meant the Membership, which he was juxtaposing against the overpaid worrywarts they hire to "run our deal" in New York. By "it," Jones meant the league. And that's what owners do: they **own**. Everyone else works for them.

Owners can pay astronomical prices for their membership, not just financial. They are, quite often, abused by their fans, which they're reminded of if they ever have occasion to venture onto the field. "There are only two times the owner is not going to get booed," John Mara told me. "One is when you're holding the championship trophy, and two is when you're dead and they're carrying your body out. And there's no guarantee on number two."

Owners tend to explain their pariah status as the price of doing business. They are versed in all the self-aggrandizing rationalizations that marginal leaders like to delude themselves with (they are paying for the price of being Men in the ARENA!). But damn right they should be recognized as the Men in Charge, from Park Ave on down to their own palaces. When you arrive, for instance, at "Jerry's World" in Dallas, you are greeted by the Voice of God himself, Mr. Jones, welcoming you via loudspeaker to AT&T Stadium. Stroll into the consumer arcadia that is the New England Patriots Pro Shop at Gillette Stadium and you are soothed by the grandiloquence of benefactor Robert K. Kraft delivering his nasally gratitude on the field while accepting the Patriots' third Super Bowl trophy in 2005.

Because his team keeps winning championships this century, Kraft has had occasion to give several acceptance speeches upon receiving conference and Super Bowl trophies in front of the biggest television audiences of the year. Those remarks tend to be self-satisfied and somewhat unbearable, especially for non–Patriots fans. I have heard two NFL owners imitate Kraft's slow, Boston-accented delivery; Roger Goodell himself has been known to affect a Kraftian cadence in private when quoting something RKK had said.

But the Patriots organization dutifully treats Kraft's post–Super Bowl addresses as if they were pearls from Gettysburg. "At this time in our country . . . we are all Patriots," Kraft shouted upon receiving his first Super Bowl trophy in February 2002, just a few months after the September 11 attacks, as red, white, and blue confetti rained down on the field. WE ARE ALL PATRIOTS is rendered in big letters on the wall near the entrance to the reception area outside his office. The term is also trademarked (goes without saying) with merchandise bearing WE ARE ALL PATRIOTS sold all over the stadium and on the team web-site. "Oh yeah, we're all Patriots—until Belichick finds someone cheaper," said one former player, no-longer-a-Patriot (and not wanting to be named so not to offend the easily offended Mr. Kraft).

At NFL headquarters in New York, big photo collages adorn the walls of the front hallway to celebrate the illustrious patrons of each team—because no one thinks of, say, Joe Namath when they think of the New York Jets. They think of Woody Johnson, right? There has been a semi-legitimate mythology in the league that owners are guardians of a public trust who subvert their own interests for the "good of the game." Ex-amples of this selfless, league-first thinking have abounded through the history of the game. It in-volves its founding fathers (the Maras, Rooneys, and Halases) and fabled commissioners (Pete Rozelle and his pioneering predecessor, Bert Bell) at critical junctures managing to put aside competitive agendas and personal resentments to forge a business model rooted in competitive par-ity and a quasi-socialist form of revenue sharing. Their attentiveness to the greater health and fu-ture of the Shield has been credited with mak-ing pro football the megapopular and profitable sports enterprise it is today.

But when you talk to most NFL owners of the twenty-first century, the "greater good of the game" has the ring of lip service. What animates them most is self-interest—namely the fortunes of their team, on the field and on the balance sheet. Rivalries and petty grudges can play out among the Members in league meetings, but the real face-offs happen by proxy on Sunday. I talked by phone that January to Mark Wilf, co-owner of the Minnesota Vikings, a few days after the Vikings were defeated by the Seattle Seahawks in the first round of the playoffs. The game ended with the Vikings' kicker, Blair Walsh, missing a 27-yard field goal in the final seconds (and later sobbing at his locker). Wilf grew up a Giants fan in New Jersey and used to take losses hard, he said. He remembered his father telling him, "It could be worse. You could be the owner."

I had watched the final seconds of that Vikings-Seahawks game on a TV in the concourse of FedExField in suburban Maryland, where the Washington Redskins were hosting the Packers in the day's other first-round game. I have always been fascinated by Daniel M. Snyder, the Redskins' owner. There are few such pure, straight-ahead villains as Snyder. Contempt for him represents a rare point of agreement among Democrats and Republicans in the capital. He has been pilloried on a variety of issues, from running off accomplished coaches, abusing underlings, meddling in football decisions, and refusing to change the team's name and logo, which offends many Native Americans. Snyder, who made his fortune in various marketing ventures, is known for the aggressive revenue initiatives he has pursued, at one point even charging fans to watch his team practice in training camp.

In 2000, not long after Snyder purchased the Redskins, he appeared at a "Major League Entrepreneurs" forum along with Dallas Mavericks owner Mark Cuban at the Kellogg School of Management at Northwestern. He was asked by moderator Jeff Greenfield to reveal how he was able to make so much money in marketing. Snyder went on to explain that he held weekly meetings at his company, Snyder Communications, where they would discuss potential market niches. "We were looking at trend lines," Snyder said. "We saw that the aging baby boomer demographics were coming on strong. That meant there's going to be a lot more diabetic patients, a lot more cancer patients, et cetera. How do we capture those market segments?" One person's heartache, in others words, could just as easily become a fat "market segment" for Danny Snyder. This might have come off as a little, uh, cold. But it was just the kind of ingenuity that allowed Snyder to buy his beloved hometown team and make it into one of the NFL's most potent revenue machines.

I met Snyder for the first time a few days after the Packers had ended the Redskins' season, 35–18, in the wild card game. We were in Houston at the time, during another owners' meeting. I told

Snyder, by way of an icebreaker, that I lived in Washington and he immediately asked if I was a Redskins fan. Not really, I said, and told him I grew up in New England and, well . . . the Pats.

What I didn't mention to Snyder was that in addition to rooting for the Patriots, I root almost as hard for whatever team happens to be playing against the fucking Redskins. Generally speaking, I have never been able to adopt pro teams in the places outside of New England where I have lived—Detroit, the Bay Area, and D.C. My rationale is that it is not enough that my own teams should win, I always feel better if every fan around me in my adopted hometown is miserable—because that's just the kind of big-hearted sports fan I am (okay, I'm not proud of this).

But my joy in seeing the local football team lose has been exponentially greater since I moved to Washington twenty years ago. And this has almost nothing to do with the fact that Detroit, San Francisco, and Oakland did not have teams with racist nicknames. Largely, it is because of Snyder. He purchased the Redskins for $800 million in 1999, two years after I arrived in D.C. He ushered in a period of consistent losing and fiasco that has coincided with my time here. It has been deliciously fun to watch this play out in the same way that it never gets old to see the pro wrestling heel get his tights pulled down over and over again. If

Vince McMahon ran the NFL, he would have to invent a Dan Snyder.

Snyder is not well liked by his fellow owners, either, though he earns big respect for his ability to squeeze revenue out of the Redskins. His one BFF among the Membership—maybe his only FF among the Membership—is Jerry Jones, Snyder's NFC East rival. Jones must have ascertained my look of surprise when he told me that he and Snyder actually take vacations together. "Yes, yes he is," Jones said when I asked if Snyder would be characterized as "fun." "I think a lot of him," Jones said. "I'm crazy about his family. Dan puts up with my frailties, I put up with his frailties."

Snyder was hardly charismatic, though in the brief time we were together in Houston, he did not appear to be the monster he'd been portrayed as. I found him more jittery and vulnerable than anything else; trying to make a good impression but struggling to keep eye contact. What struck me most about Snyder was the devastation that came over him when he brought up his team's loss to the Packers—which he did six separate times in fifteen minutes.

"I can't even talk about it," Snyder said, shaking his head, and then talking about it. "I thought we were going to win that game, man." He marveled over how great Packers quarterback Aaron Rodgers played. "God almighty, this is just terrible," he said. "This really, really hurts." He said he grows jealous of other owners whose teams are still playing. I asked Snyder how long it would take him to recover from a loss like this. It appeared for a second that he might actually cry. "I'll probably start to feel better after the Super Bowl," Snyder said after a pause, "when all the teams are unbeaten again."

Though Goodell would never admit this publicly, certain members of the Membership are more influential than others. Paul Allen, a Microsoft founder and the owner of the Seahawks, is almost never seen or heard from by the league. Neither is the Lions' matriarch, Martha Firestone Ford, although she did browbeat Goodell at an owners' meeting in 2015 over lousy officiating. Ravens owner Steve Bisciotti held lingering resentment over how the NFL handled the case involving his star running back, Ray Rice, and has basically taken his ball and gone home on his league involvement. But when the agenda moves to big and sensitive matters, like L.A., the debate tends to be dominated by the affected parties and the usual centers of influence.

Los Angeles was an unprecedented circumstance. Never had there been three business partners vying to occupy the same Promised Land, albeit a Promised Land that had gotten along fine since the Rams and Raiders fled from there over two decades earlier. This particular Game of Thrones came down to two competing stadium projects: one in Carson, California, about twenty miles south of L.A., was being pushed by a tag team of legacy owners, the Raiders' Mark Davis and Chargers' Dean Spanos; and another in Inglewood, a "transformational" complex envisioned by Rams owner Stan Kroenke. After the matter remained unresolved following the November confab in Dallas, Goodell reconvened the Membership in January for a special session in Houston. For pure owner intrigue, this was once-in-a-generation. When I mentioned later to Goodell that "the Membership" might be a good name for a reality-TV series (also for a Mafia movie), he assured me: "Oh, you could have a real good reality-TV show in our owners' meetings."

Unfortunately, I was not allowed inside during the L.A. finale, and neither were any of the two hundred or so media types locked in for this season finale in Houston. Citizens of the fan kingdoms massed at various points in the lobby and outside of the Westin Houston, Memorial City hotel. I befriended a group of Oakland Raiders diehards clustered on the sidewalk. They had traveled here, many from Northern California, to display a giant black-and-silver flag and show support for their team's staying in Oakland. They were joined, in smaller numbers, by advocates of the Chargers' staying in San Diego and the Rams in St. Louis.

"The Raiders are bigger than football," a college student named Ray Perez told me. They are certainly synonymous with Oakland, and to a remarkable degree. Even when the Raiders moved to Los Angeles for twelve years, many people were still calling them "the Oakland Raiders." Oakland native Tom Hanks has said that when he travels the world and tells people where he's from, the first thing they ask is "Is that where the Raiders play?" Unlike the more glamorous San Francisco, Oakland views itself—rightly—as the tougher and grittier champion, whose identity has been so colorfully (or menacingly) expressed by the Silver and Black. Oakland might be doomed to be associated with the Gertrude Stein line "There is no there there" (she claimed to be referring to the razed Oakland neighborhood of her childhood, not the whole city), but Stein did not live to see the Raiders in Oakland. At least the Raiders were "there" in Oakland, no matter what else the city was struggling with. But now the city's futility in building a new stadium for the Raiders was leading Davis to the exits.

Perez, who calls himself "Dr. Death," was plaintive and sincere, though I was distracted by the frizzy black wig he was wearing under a silver helmet lined with a Mohawk of daggers. He relayed to me an important lesson that his Raider Nation mentor, "Raider Jerry," had once imparted. Being a part of this brotherhood involves much more than being a sports fan. It is a form of giving back. Raider Nation is not a club, it's a movement. "And it is a people-driven movement," Dr. Death added. "We show the power of people coming together for something that we love and believe in."

The people's power was limited here. The Membership ground through their day of private deliberations. They debated the merits of the Chargers-Raiders complex in Carson, and Stan Kroenke's extravaganza in Inglewood on a 298-acre tract near Hollywood Park. Late in the day, Jerry Jones announced to the commissioner that if discussions went on much longer, he would have no choice but to escape to the bar with his Lioness, Martha Ford (beer and wine were brought into the meeting room). The Seahawks' Paul Allen, who never attends league meetings, showed up for the first time in five years and, according to one owner afterward, "didn't shut up."

Reports trickled out that momentum had shifted in the direction of Kroenke and Inglewood. This was a minor upset since the Carson project, which was backed by Walt Disney CEO Robert Iger, had been endorsed by a 5–1 vote by the relocation committee. Goodell was cautious about not getting between factions. Passions were high on both sides. "Roger did not want to get involved in the abortion debate," Jaguars owner Shad Khan said.

Kevin Demoff, the chief operating officer of

the Rams, presented on behalf of Kroenke, the Missouri native-son-turned-pariah. By most accounts inside the room, Demoff blew away the Carson pitch, which changed the scent of the bake-off. Demoff took aim at what Jerry Jones called "the Big Wow Factor." He stressed the "transformational" nature of "Stan's vision." The project would be less of a stadium than a spectacle. It would not be merely the home of one or two teams, but the league's West Coast capital— a prospective home of the NFL Network, NFL.com, and many of the league's sprawling collection of ventures. "We could host Super Bowls, Final Fours, the college football playoffs, the opening and closing ceremonies of the Olympics," Demoff said. He imagined an iconic dwelling, a destination site, and a must-see landmark for fliers to locate from the air when coming in and out of LAX.

"L.A. has always been where fantasy becomes reality and where dreams come true," Demoff told me. This was the kind of "big vision" that had eluded the NFL in its twenty-one-year sabbatical from La-La Land. And the stadium would be set to open by 2020, in time for the NFL's one hundredth birthday. "The Inglewood thing was more like a massive art exhibit than a stadium proposal," one owner said, comparing the presentation with a Hollywood production with special effects. "You know, we're pretty good at some things, and one of them is real estate development," Kroenke told me. "We went ahead and showed the committee, and I think there were members of the committee, no matter how they ended up voting, when they saw what we had, they went 'Whoa.' And I think that spread around the league a little bit."

Owners felt free to contemplate the possibilities beyond the less ambitious alternative in Carson. "It was like the Arab Spring," said Khan, a native of Pakistan, in the lobby of the Westin afterward. (Khan, who purchased the Jaguars in 2011, is the first member of an ethnic minority to own an NFL team.)

Falcons owner Arthur Blank describes a dynamic in meetings where a few powerful owners—he mentioned McNair, Mara, and Rooney—tend to remain quiet for long stretches, but carry a great deal of influence when they finally do speak. "That's the E. F. Hutton," Blank said. "When they stand, people listen." He contrasts that with a certain blustering baron from the NFC East, Jerry Jones. Blank did not seem to mean this in a nice way. In recent years, a few owners have complained that Jones has become increasingly given to long-winded speeches that have set more than a few billionaire eyes a-roll. Even so, none of the thirty-two would downplay Jones as a force inside the room.

Kroenke and Demoff had succeeded in getting Jones fantasizing. This, the fantasy space, can be a danger for Jerral Wayne Jones. But he is also a powerful ally. "Look, you pay attention to Jerry," Kroenke said. "Jerry has done something unique in this league. He built the biggest stadium. I know it's [Dallas] a tremendously important market, and he had executed and delivered revenues at a level that people had to take notice."

Jones became the Inglewood project's prime mover and carnival barker. In his seventy-five years, he has sold everything from shoes to insurance policies to pizza. He considers himself a connoisseur of the American hustle.

Jones's father and hero, J. W. "Pat" Jones, owned a grocery store in North Little Rock, Arkansas. He was an audacious seller himself. He put on talent shows and built a bandstand in the middle of Pat's Supermarket to create a wow factor around the store. Jerry learned at his knee. "There's always got to be a little bit of scheme to it," Jones told me. Once, he was riding around with his dad and happened to mention that a certain company was worth five million dollars. His father was aghast. "Jerry, don't ever say 'million dollars' like it's casual," he scolded. "'You always say it very slowly. **One. Million. Dollars.** Honor it. Respect it. Let it roll. **One. Million. Dollars.**' It might take him the whole ride from Springfield to St. Louis for 'one million' to come off the tongue."

Jones is a sucker for big swings. In the last category, the Rams' Inglewood project delivered in both price ($3 billion) and the bandleader's wallet (Kroenke was worth $8 billion in 2016, per **Forbes**). He explained his thinking to me about L.A. with a dizzying triple backflip of mixed metaphor: "It's one thing to be an arm waver," Jones said. "It's another thing to be a dreamer. But when you put meat on the bone, they know you mean business."

This was one of those instances where Jerry Logic can stagger his audience straight into the concussion protocol. And yet as he keeps going, you find yourself hypnotized into something that approaches comprehension, if not lucidity. Certain owners, Jones said, resent the wave of stunning new stadiums being built around the league. They get up in the meetings, these small-thinking owners do, and complain about the arms race mentality. They feel pressured to keep up with the biggest and grandest new venues that their partners are building in other cities. Why is it necessary to spend so much on stadiums when the league derives 60 percent of its revenue from TV rights? "But I get up and I say, 'But stadiums **are** about television rights,'" Jones said. "Do you think these networks pay these rights fees to broke dicks? With their ass hanging out?"

"?????" I wrote in my notebook.

I contemplated Jerry's words. **"Networks . . . broke dicks with their ass hanging out."** I honored his words. Respected them. Let them roll. Finally, clarity dawned: What I think Jones meant is that the class and grandeur of these gladiator palaces reflect what the NFL should be selling: bold dreams. Since AT&T Stadium opened in 2009, Jones set the standard for shock and awe. He offered the freshest of sushi and the highest definition of scoreboards and even a stunning collection of modern art. There is nothing half hearted about Jerry's World, no broke dicks. It feeds a leaguewide aura that should scream **WOW**, loud enough to come through the TV.

But on a more tangible level, big swinging projects like AT&T, and what Kroenke was imagining in L.A., bring the NFL closer to another magical number: twenty-five billion. As in, the number of dollars in gross revenue that Goodell said the league aspires to by 2027. The frequency with which NFL executives and owners mention the "twenty-five billion" target suggests a Holy Grail. You could conclude this goal represents a greater preoccupation than the priorities they swear by publicly, like health and safety. When these priorities collide, as they inevitably do, Team Revenue comes in as a heavy favorite.

By 2016, the league was about halfway to $25 billion. Stan's Plan would bring it closer than anything Kroenke could ever erect in a broke-dick town like St. Louis. The venture would involve, certainly, a bigger risk. Who knows if anyone can pull off a project of this ambition? Or whether

Los Angeles, despite its market's size and cachet, could support it? The scale of the effort itself becomes a subset of the reality show. Can this all possibly work?

"I love ambiguity," Jones told me. He was talking about his own bent for thrill seeking, the importance of "going balls out." Jones made his fortune, originally, in petroleum. "Only God knows whether there's oil under the ground," he said. So ambiguous! Eighty-five percent of everything he does in oil and gas will lose money. It has made Jones less fearful of failure, he said. He's seen sky-highs and also felt "about as low as a crippled cricket's ass," as Jones once described his mood after former Cowboys quarterback Tony Romo got hurt. "You don't have to spend a lot of time going over and kind of circumcising the mosquito," Jones added, in the vein of how he does not like to overthink decisions.

Jones hailed Kroenke as being "manna from heaven" for the possibilities of Los Angeles. While the people of eastern Missouri had less generous descriptions, Kroenke had moved on. He and Demoff had captured the only room that mattered, the Membership. There were powerful exceptions. Panthers owner Jerry Richardson had been vocal and stubborn in his support for the Carson project, in keeping with the preference of the relocation committee. He believed St. Louis had done its part to build a sufficient new home for the Rams. "When this is all over, I'd sure love to know what I did to piss off Jerry Richardson," Kroenke told a small cluster of owners as the meeting dragged on.

In general, Kroenke's ambitious project appealed to the newer guard of owners who had paid large sums for their franchises and were eager to see more aggressive revenue initiatives to recoup their investments. By contrast, older-line "establishment" owners—such as the Maras, Hunts, and Rooneys—had inherited teams that had been in their families for generations. They also were predisposed to a measure of loyalty to the Carson project, especially given that the Chargers had been in Dean Spanos's family for more than three decades.

The Membership was united on one particular objective: to wrap up the meeting in one day, rather than the scheduled two. This was a crowded time of year in which many owners and executives were planning for postseason games or were in the process of hiring new coaches. Goodell called a vote at about six p.m. It was determined that the vote be by secret ballot, a measure typically reserved for matters such as the awarding of Super Bowl host cities or the electing of a new commissioner. This fostered a stronger consensus for the Rams since some owners had felt obligated to support Spanos. The secret ballot afforded owners a mask, Jones said, important when sensitive and personal matters are being decided. "When you are voting to remove the king, and the king can cut your head off, then I think it can help," Jones said.

The Membership voted 30–2 to make Stan Kroenke king of L.A.—or at least the kingdom of undetermined size that still cared about football. By nightfall, the tired tycoons began coursing through the lobby en route to limos that would take them to private jets and the hell out of Houston. Jones held forth nursing a tumbler of Scotch, calling this "a cornerstone decision." The Jets' owner, Woody Johnson, strolled past wearing his trademark JanSport knapsack over both shoulders. He appeared agitated, little eyes quickly scanning the room like he was looking for a lost teddy bear.

"Everybody wins in this deal," the Miami Dolphins' owner, Stephen M. Ross, declared to a bank of reporters as he trailed the Wood Man out the door.

"What about the fans of St. Louis?" someone in the gallery cracked. Ross shrugged. "Well, somebody has to lose," he said.

Goodell convened a hurried press conference upstairs. He emphasized that the Rams would be "returning" to L.A., as if they'd merely decamped to a temporary condo somewhere in the Midwest for twenty-one years. As part of the agreement, Goodell said, Spanos would have a one-year option to move the Chargers to Inglewood as the Rams' tenant.

The commissioner was flanked by Kroenke and his two bridesmaids, Spanos and Davis. Roger kicked things off with an important reminder: "Relocation is a painful process," he said, "painful for the fans, communities, the teams, and the league in general." Goodell then pivoted to a grand promise of what could be in store in a future of limitless possibility: "A project that we think is going to change not just NFL stadiums and NFL complexes, but I think sports complexes around the world," Goodell said. He ended on a more solemn note, dubbing this "a bittersweet moment."

By the faces at the podium, the moment looked more bitter than sweet, even for the winner. Kroenke, the real estate magnate with a charm quotient as meager as the Rams' win totals of the previous years, stared at the floor. Kroenke (rhymes with "donkey") has a pale and jowly countenance, an unruly comb-over, and a seventies-porn mustache. He rarely speaks to the media—and you can see why. "We spend a lot of resources trying to make sure that we stay relevant," Kroenke told the assembled press in a monotone mumble. Ray Ratto, a Bay Area sportswriter, observed via Twitter that Kroenke looked as if he were "overdue for his next baby wombat blood injection."

Mark Davis looked about due for a swig of Drano. He tried to put on a good face but failed. He tried to be philosophical. "The good news is we came in third place," Davis said of the owners' vote. "The bad news is that it was a three-horse race."

League people often delineate between "pioneers" and "settlers." "Pioneers" are the owners who actually buy their teams while "settlers" inherit them. Like Davis, Spanos inherited his team from his father, Alex Spanos. He is generally well liked by his partners around the league, but no one would mistake him for a visionary or even that significant of a force. He seemed to engender greater sympathy than respect from his fellow owners, as if he were a hapless little brother. "Dino," they call him. He generally kept his nose clean (well, except for that one unfortunate time back in 1990 when he reportedly got busted for padding his handicap at Pebble Beach—"sandbagging," as the practice is known, a huge sin in Fat Cat golfer circles; Dino was not invited back to Pebble Beach the next year—just as the Chargers were not being invited to L.A. right now). While Goodell spoke, delivering the verdict, Spanos stared at a back wall, appearing shell-shocked.

There was, as always, a technocratic remove about the commissioner. Goodell tried to sell this as an "exciting day" for the National Football

League. "We have a facility that is going to be absolutely extraordinary in the Los Angeles market that I think the fans are going to absolutely love," he said. "We're very proud and we're very excited about the potential for Stan and the Rams in Los Angeles."

By the time this painful process broke up, most of the Membership had fled the premises. I repaired to a bar downstairs at the Westin that had been taken over by a petting zoo of relieved Raiders fans. Lingering reporters filled their notebooks with quotes from Doctor Death and Co. about how the Raiders' "destiny" had been respected on that day, meaning that the team would be staying in Oakland for the time being.

After a few minutes, who should walk into the bar but Mark Davis. He leaned against a couch and within a few minutes was holding court for a group of Black Hole transplants. Davis's trademark bowl of a haircut had achieved a perfectly straight line across his forehead. He had changed into a powder-blue sweatshirt and black-and-white sneakers and wore a relaxed air of resignation. He might have been sedated.

Davis posed for photos and signed autographs with some of the same Raider Nation commandos who only a few hours before had threatened many unpleasant things about Al Davis's kid. This temporary stay from losing their team had brightened their moods and refreshed their outlooks. The bartenders appeared to play significant roles in this, too.

I asked Davis, who does not drink, whether he was mad at Goodell. "Nah, I call Roger the pope," Davis told me. I wondered why. "I like to bust his chops." He bought another round of drinks for the Raider diehards, whom he remained very much committed to disowning.

Next door at an Italian steakhouse called Vallone's, Jerry Jones and Stan Kroenke had reassembled with their families for a celebratory dinner. They drank red wine and looked pleased with themselves, the winning fat cats who swallowed the $3 billion canary. Bills owners Terry and Kim Pegula were there, too. They all kept toasting "to the Los Angeles Rams," over and over like a mantra, honoring the words, respecting them.

14.

ROGER AND ME

January 19, 2016

Propaganda runs thick at world headquarters. Every corporate office celebrates itself to some degree but 345 Park Ave overwhelms, like you've entered a megachurch marrying NFL Films with Scientology. Shields show up everywhere, etched into desks and iced onto cookies and carved in a massive conference table shaped like a football. NFL Network resounds on a theater-size screen behind the reception desk. Hall of Famer Michael Irvin is screaming a sermon via the house organ on how "Victory is such an important thing! It soothes the soul! It lifts the spirit!"

Victory!

Beyond the slap of propaganda, paranoia also strikes immediately. On my first visit to NFL headquarters, late in the 2015–16 season, I had the strange feeling that I was being watched, or videotaped. People smile without making eye contact. They look at the floor and move quickly. You half expect that everyone should be wearing a uniform, something like Bolivian military fatigues.

Greg Aiello, the league's longtime communications director, greeted me in the front waiting area when I arrived. Lanky and serene, Aiello worked as the head of PR for the Dallas Cowboys in the 1980s (and yes, he married a cheerleader). He had a slightly checked-out manner about him as he was about to be replaced as the Shield's top flak catcher by Joe Lockhart, the former White House press secretary during the Monica-era Clinton years. He walked me through the nerve center, pointing out photos of various Patriots on the wall (Kraft, Brady). I had told Aiello before that I was a New England fan and convinced that the league had it in for us. "See, there's Kraft again," Aiello said, pointing to a photo on a wall—more proof that the Shield would **never** discriminate, that integrity is blind.

I noted the disproportionate number of Jets fans—based on desk decorations—who seemed to work in this place.

We ended up in the cafeteria, known as the Huddle. Aiello bought me an iced tea. He sat me down and told me good stuff about the commissioner, good things about the league, big and heady numbers—record ratings, rising revenues, flack things. He handed me positive fact sheets and articles and then, unprompted, summed up what was clearly the message of his campaign: "Roger wins."

During another visit to the Huddle, I met Tod Leiweke, a former Seattle Seahawks CEO who had been hired as the league's chief operating officer the previous summer. Leiweke has brushed-back white hair and a beak nose that bore him a slight resemblance to an actual sea hawk. He first got to know Goodell during a climb up Mount Rainier with other executives for a United Way campaign Leiweke was chairing at the time. Over lunch, Leiweke unleashed on me an avalanche of mountain metaphors, one after another, by way of explaining his new mission on behalf of the Shield.

"There are challenges to running the most successful league in the world," he told me. "It's like clouds on Rainier. Not everything's perfect, but you fight through it." He continued: "The league is trying to climb new mountains of its own."

Leiweke was hired in part to raise morale at 345 Park. Goodell had grown agitated and impatient with many of his deputies. He could become testy in meetings, challenging underlings, complaining in open settings that they made too much money—a glass-houses critique if there ever was one from a commissioner who had amassed more than $300 million in salary and bonuses during his decade in charge.

Goodell had a tendency to micromanage. His plummeting public image, a growing number of owners believed, was becoming a drag on the NFL brand. Several long-serving league officials were either leaving or seeking exit strategies. Leiweke told me his goal was to help lighten Goodell's workload and brighten the mood at the place—including that of the increasingly downcast commissioner. Top executives who had been reporting directly to Goodell—Brian Rolapp, the CEO of NFL Network and executive VP of media, for example—would now be reporting to Leiweke. Some of these top executives were not happy about this (Brian Rolapp, for example), but Leiweke is a self-styled "people person" who believes he can make things work. He is also unthreatening, at least to Goodell, which was one of the main qualities that appealed to the commissioner in picking his number two. To have an understudy too strong is to tempt discussion that he or she is the heir apparent. "Roger wanted no part of having his replacement working directly under him," one top league official told me, a theme echoed around the league.

Upon first meeting him, it is clear that Leiweke is a different bird. He had a sunny and even New Agey presence, like a proselytizing leader. "I have a unique perspective of management," Leiweke told me. "I think of it as 'servitude management,' 'servitude leadership.'" What does this mean? "I work for all the people in this room," Leiweke told me, gesturing to the rest of the Huddle, which was now filling up for lunch.

"I have this ambition that they're going to have better lives," he went on, "and they're going to feel even more proud to be part of the NFL." Leiweke clenched his hands into two fists, demonstrating resolve. He patted the chest of his beige sweater that was embroidered with a big shield. "Together, we're going to better serve the owners, the fans, and the players," Leiweke vowed. "And it's a beautiful thing."

I remember making a note to myself that this guy wouldn't last a year. (He wound up lasting two and a half.)

Leiweke kept describing Goodell to me as "convicted." By this he appeared to mean the commissioner had strong convictions. "Roger is hardworking, dedicated, convicted, tenacious," Leiweke said. "He is an amazing, convicted guy." Leiweke closed by reinforcing the message of the day about the commissioner. "He's a winner."

Reports of Goodell's frustration with his staff were echoed to me by certain owners. One critique was that the commissioner needed a stronger team around him. This was a bit of a shield for Goodell, as it absolved him of responsibility for the serial public relations, legal, and football operations messes the league has suffered, or exacerbated, in recent years. It also overlooks that Goodell hired most of these people himself or gave them their authority. "I think it's been proven out over the past few years that maybe Roger didn't listen to some folks as much as he should," said Ray Anderson, the NFL's former vice president of football operations. "Especially folks who didn't tell him what he wanted to hear. Goodell's top deputy-piñata is Jeff Pash, a longtime league executive and general counsel who was criticized by several owners for the league's "excessive tendency to lawyer up over everything," as one club executive put it. After Goodell, Pash is the NFL's second-highest-paid executive—he took home $7.5 million in 2014 and $6.5 million in 2015. Pash also was believed to have had the top job in his sights seemingly from the day he entered the league twenty years ago. He vied for the commissioner's post when it last came open, in 2006, as did the league's current executive vice president, Eric Grubman, a former partner at Goldman Sachs. Both were viewed as strong internal candidates to replace Paul Tagliabue but neither made it to the final round. In the end, Goodell, who was then the league's chief operating officer, was selected over runner-up Gregg Levy, the NFL's outside counsel.

Like Pash and Tagliabue, Levy had close ties to

the powerhouse Washington law firm Covington & Burling. Legal acumen has always been a supremely valued trait among top NFL executives, no surprise given that many of the "existential moments" in the league's history have involved megastakes litigation (losing the USFL's antitrust lawsuit in the 1980s could have been devastating, for instance—as opposed to the NFL's being forced to pay only $3 in damages). Even though Goodell won out in the end, he has empowered Pash as a kind of legal alter ego who, in the words of one owner, "plays on Roger's insecurities over not being a lawyer."

Along with Pash, there appear to be a number of ambitious operators at 345 Park—or "guys that think they're going to be the next commissioner," in the droll words of Joe Browne, the former spokesman and league lifer who started in 1965 under Pete Rozelle and was considered an institutional giant at Park Ave until his retirement in 2016 ("everybody's work father," one protégé described him).

Troy Vincent, the league's executive vice president of football operations, is a classic "guy that thinks he's going to be the next commissioner" at the league. Vincent, a defensive back for four teams, was president of the NFL Players Association from 2004 to 2008. He was gung-ho to succeed Gene Upshaw, the executive director of the union, after Upshaw's death in 2008. Or he started gunning for Upshaw's job before his death, according to certain people (Upshaw among them) who believed Vincent had spearheaded a failed coup attempt against his predecessor, a Hall of Fame offensive lineman who played sixteen seasons for the Oakland Raiders before retiring in 1981. Suspicion of Vincent ran deep inside the union, over both his loyalties and his questionable business dealings, which scuttled any hope of his ever replacing Upshaw. He then jumped to the league office, an unusual move for a union head, which made him an All-Pro traitor in the eyes of many fellow players and union colleagues.

Vincent played fifteen years in the league, made five consecutive Pro Bowl appearances with Philadelphia from 1999 to 2003, and had a distinguished career by any measure. When I met him in his office, Vincent was upbeat but cautious, prone to speaking in inspirational maxims. He drew freely from a devout Christian faith that he is quick to advertise. "I talked to my pastor this morning, and if you don't mind me sharing, I have to be one of the luckiest people in the world," Vincent confided. "I've gone from playing a game that I love for fifteen years, being a participant, and now having an opportunity to shape how the game is played and administer it going into the future." Vincent speaks about his job with a carefully enunciated awe.

On three occasions, Vincent emphasized whatever point he was making by pounding his desk. It drove home for me how serious Vincent was about his charge! That charge: to ensure "that everyone is playing under the same rules and under the same circumstance" (**pound**). He told me about a tropical storm a few years ago that threatened to postpone or delay a game between the Redskins and Eagles. "We will NEVER do anything to take resources away from the community," Vincent promised (**pound**). Also: "To whom much is given, much is required" (**pound**). "I am always conscious of how many people I affect," Vincent said, "and the world that I affect." It felt as though Vincent expected me to clap.

THE LEAGUE'S REPUTATION BUFFERS SEEMED to be punting entirely on the idea that Roger Goodell's image could be rehabbed. Their PR strategy amounted to holding their breath whenever the commissioner spoke, hoping for the best, and maybe cleaning up at the margins. The **Wall Street Journal**, for instance, would discover that Jane Goodell had set up an anonymous Twitter account to defend her husband from unflattering press reports—so there was that.

Otherwise, when it came to putting Goodell in front of the media, it was "What's the upside here?" That's what the league's gatekeepers would say, in so many words, when I asked if I could approach the overlord. The downsides were clear and present. Goodell could say the wrong thing (as he does), critics would pounce (as they do), and the Silly Circuit would spin it all into yet another self-made mash (as it does).

I spent a few weeks talking to NFL executives and a bunch of owners. They would, it was clear, report back to Goodell's protectors on the tenor of my questions and assess my threat level. I tried to pass myself off in these auditions as thoughtful and open-minded (as opposed to the spiteful and small-minded Boston fan that I was). And, go figure, it worked.

Here I was hanging with Rog on a football field, about an hour before the start of the NFC Championship Game: Arizona Cardinals and Carolina Panthers, Bank of America Stadium in Charlotte, January 24, 2016. We convened on the sideline as Goodell performed his ceremonial pregame rounds with the coaches and referees and countless auxiliaries.

On the surface, this should have been an exciting experience for me as an NFL junkie. I had never been on an NFL field before, much less on the occasion of such a Big Game. What better place and time to interview a Commissioner of Football than on the turf during Championship Sunday, the second-biggest national holiday on the NFL calendar? I try to remind myself of all the cool things I would never have gotten to do if, God help me, I had gone to law school.

But as a practical matter, this was a lousy environment to conduct an actual interview in. The stadium was pulsing with noise and the pregame sideline was rife with distraction—probably just how the NFL envisioned this. The interruption fodder would limit Goodell's exposure, curtail him from venturing into areas of hazardous depth, and minimize any chance of rapport between us, such as it was.

Beyond that, two to three feet of snow had fallen on much of the Northeast over the previous thirty-six hours, grounding most commercial flights. This forced me to drive eight hours from Washington, D.C., to Charlotte, the first leg through whiteout conditions. I barely made it to the stadium on time. Goodell, on the other hand, had his own plane and enjoyed a much more leisurely Sunday (which is not to suggest he relaxed for a second—or didn't work out like the **total animal** that he clearly is). Goodell volunteered that he had shoveled out the driveway of his home in Bronxville that morning, enabling him and the First Lady of the Shield to get in a Soul-Cycle class before he had to leave for the game. (What, you think these glorious abs happen by accident?) That morning's **New York Post** had greeted snowbound New Yorkers with a simple message that put Goodell in a bright mood. STAY HOME AND WATCH FOOTBALL was the front-page command. "I said, 'That's my headline!'" Goodell told me, about as close as he ever comes to boyish excitement.

Greg Aiello had summoned me to where he and the commissioner were standing at about the 40-yard line. Goodell got things rolling by telling me how much he loves **his** job. "I wake up"— around 5:30, works out, does his weights and cardio—"get jazzed up and then I'm ready to go." Goodell said his mind races during his workouts with all the things he's going to do that day. His schedule could change at a second's notice, which he appreciates. "I could go from talking to a senator, mayor, governor to some media CEO to meeting a bunch of Hall of Fame coaches and players and talking about the catch-versus-no-catch rule," he said. It could be one thing after another, or there could be a detour into something else. "You sometimes have to shift, and I love that," he said.

The commissioner keeps shifting, as people keep interrupting us. The general manager of the Panthers, the president of the Cardinals, someone named Isabella, some friend of the chief financial officer, a guy Goodell recognizes and who wanted a picture with him. One revelation to me was the sheer number of civilians who are allowed to be on an NFL field before a game. Hundreds, maybe thousands, of nonessential personnel are just hanging around—you'd think it would be more restrictive.

I tried to get in a few questions, including one—betraying my parochial interest—about whether Goodell had any regrets over how the league had handled Deflategate. "Fans want to know that we're going to make sure that the rules are enforced across all thirty-two teams," Goodell lectured me. He is, after all, the last line of integrity against all enemies of the Shield, foreign and domestic. "Thank you for looking after the game," people tell him. "I hear that a lot," Goodell said. "I hear that all around the country, all the time." This explains why Goodell is so beloved in fan surveys.

With politicians, sometimes I will ask them what it's like to be hated, from the get-go, by so many people. Not just unpopular, but hated, the way partisans and sports fans with social media accounts can hate—police protection, Hitler comparison, and death-threat-level hated. Invective becomes as basic as their daily oxygen. Did it give pause? Goodell went the football-as-life-lesson route. "You get knocked down, and you get up," he said. Nobody roots for the commissioner. "Most of these people don't know who you are," Goodell said. "They don't know you. But I know who I am."

Goodell toggles between the language of closed-off jock and the advanced glad-handing touches of a politician's son. He kept saying my name to punctuate his sentences—Mark this and Mark that. Like Leiweke and other executives at the league, Goodell will often default into management jargon. He tells me he is a big believer in "what I call the third solution." He explained to me what this meant. "You have one solution," Goodell said. "And you have another solution. But it's usually not either one, it's the **third** solution." (I totally get it!) That's what Goodell meant by "third solution." "If you work the process, you begin the process of working and listening, you get to a better place," he said.

"Come on, let's walk," Goodell told me. We were trying to get to a better place. "If we don't get away from the crowd, we'll never get this done." I asked Goodell to tell me about the "man cave" in Bronxville, from where he watches a lot of games. He apparently likes to talk about his man cave as it bolsters his "just-another-slob-on-the-couch" bona fides. His sanctorum, Goodell told me, is equipped with three TVs, which he watches simultaneously while checking multiple laptops. He watches as a fan, as a commissioner, and as a micromanager. He pesters his staff and fires off emails.

I asked Goodell if he had seen **Concussion**. The NFL's PR advisers, I later learned, had prepared him for this question, part of their larger "Ignore **Concussion**" strategy. If asked, Goodell was counseled to say that no, he had not seen the movie. He is so busy, he rarely has time to see movies; and when he does, his wife usually picks them out. Accordingly, Goodell told me that, in fact, he had not seen the movie. "I can't tell you the last time I've been to a movie," Goodell added. And then in the next breath he mentioned he had seen **The Intern**, starring Robert De Niro, just the night before, with his wife and teen daughters.

Broken football players were not a fun area for the commissioner—"player health and safety" would be the approved league term. Goodell had his standard "health and safety" ammunition ready (all the new rule changes, the first-class doctors and trainers in attendance for this game). But there was no shortage of "yes but on the other hand" for me to come back at him with. A few days earlier, former Steelers and Redskins wide receiver Antwaan Randle El had turned himself into that week's installment of what had become the NFL's own parallel reality show—a much darker one. Randle El was the latest ex-player to share his harrowing tale of postcareer physical and cognitive hardship. "I would play baseball," Randle El said in an interview with the **Pittsburgh Post-Gazette**. At only thirty-six, Randle El said he has bouts of memory loss and struggles to walk downstairs. When I asked Goodell about stories like this, he played the "we're generating awareness" card. "It is part of the conversation," he told me. Players and former players, he said, now feel freer to "come forward" to discuss their medical and mental issues. In fact, we should view the Antwaan Randle Els as signifiers of progress.

I mentioned to Goodell another recent example of our culture's enhanced "awareness": Pittsburgh and Cincinnati had met in a deranged spectacle two weeks earlier under the guise of a wild card playoff matchup. People had been talking about the game for days—another "national conversation" commenced, courtesy of our facilitators at the NFL. The contest featured a belligerent chaos of fights, cheap shots, rowdy fan behavior, ejections, and concussions. It was one of those would-the-center-hold cliff-hangers where you found yourself watching—past midnight—not just to see who won the game but also to see whether the end of civilization would be televised, live from Cincinnati. CBS announcer Phil Simms labeled the scene a "disgrace," echoing the opinion of many viewers, including at the league offices.

"I don't think that's what our fans want to see," Goodell told me when I asked about the debacle. "The fact that those hits stood out to so many people shows us how our culture has changed." Again, that game might have stuck out as a black eye for the NFL, but it was also proof of progress. Praise to the Shield, again. "Those hits were relatively common when I became commissioner," Goodell pointed out, for anyone keeping score.

Naturally Donald Trump, who was by then the front-runner for the 2016 GOP nomination, weighed in on the Steelers-Bengals bedlam. He, too, believed the game was a disgrace, but for different reasons. "I'm watching a game yesterday," he said at a campaign rally in Nevada. "What used to be considered a great tackle, a violent head-on tackle . . . you used to see these tackles, and it was incredible to watch, right?" That was back when America was still great, before everyone had gotten so politically correct and started throwing penalty flags over every little thing. "Football has become soft," Trump concluded. "Our country has become soft."

At minimum, these divergent responses to the Pittsburgh–Cincinnati game indicated that "awareness" cut in all directions. It also gave me an appreciation of how Goodell gets it from all sides, and how the Shield itself represents its own Rorschach test in the larger cultural skirmish.

Goodell and I had walked and talked about twenty yards down the field. I was grateful to have rated a Preferred Level customer on the commissioner's schedule during these crowded pregame moments. But it did not last long. Goodell had business to conduct. Arizona coach Bruce Arians had moved into schmoozing vicinity. Goodell walked over, wished him luck, and went in for the hug. There was an assistant coach and a referee to greet, someone's niece over there, panoramic respects to be paid.

While Goodell was otherwise occupied, I watched the closing minutes of the Patriots and Broncos in the AFC Championship Game up on the Bank of America scoreboard. Things looked bleak for the Pats, who were down 20–12 and had just given the ball back to Denver with a little over two minutes left.

As game time in Carolina approached, the scoreboard stopped playing the other game, leaving me to try to follow NE–DEN on my phone by way of ESPN.com. When Goodell turned back to me, he looked miffed. Why, he wanted to know, was I not following the AFC Championship Game on some app called "NFL Mobile"? I admitted I had no idea what "NFL Mobile" was. (Bad answer: apparently hell hath no fury like the commissioner confronting a barbarian not availed of some NFL consumer product gizmo.) Goodell held up his phone and tried to demonstrate for me the ease and pleasures of following a game via NFL Mobile. But his app was slow to load, as sometimes happens when you're in the middle of 75,000 people. "Watch, now it's going to screw up," Goodell said, frustrated. Panthers coach Ron Rivera walked over for a quick hug-hello. Goodell turned back to me again and his NFL Mobile was still not loading. He was becoming more and more agitated, which I admit I was a little pleased by given his earlier high horse.

"This pisses me off," he said.

As the scoreboard clock ticked down to kick-off, the Bank of America Stadium kept getting louder. The amped-up roar of a Panther kept crackling through the place. You hear these Sen-surround growls at the stadiums of teams whose mascots are predatory felines, like the Panthers, or the Nittany Lions of Penn State (whatever a Nit-tany Lion is, it sounds a lot like a panther in State College, Pennsylvania). Noise kept building in-side the coliseum until it suddenly became quiet.

"Where's the flag? I can't find the flag," Goodell said, scanning the field while preparing to observe "The Star-Spangled Banner." But in-stead of the anthem, this would be the prayer that would precede it.

And the commissioner closed his eyes and low-ered his head and struck a stern pose, the look of integrity.

ANTHEM DONE, WE WERE NOW GRACED BY THE presence of an actual member of The Elect. Pan-thers owner Jerry Richardson, one of the thirty-two precious subjects in Roger Goodell's royal pantheon, was seated nearby in a golf cart. Known around the Panthers as "the Big Cat" (or simply "Mister"), Richardson is, in terms of the commissioner's most valued customers, Elite Medallion Gold Level status. He has been the Panthers' only owner since the team entered the league in 1993 and very much fashions himself the singular towering figure of the franchise. He stands six-foot-three, or thirteen feet tall in the statue of Richardson that was being erected outside Bank of America Stadium.

Among the more respected and influential proprietors in the NFL, Richardson has been slowed by cardiac problems in recent years, including a heart transplant in 2009. Richardson was then the only owner who played in the NFL—two years as a receiver for the Johnny Unitas–era Colts—of which he can be quite fond of reminding people. Notwithstanding his history in pads, Richardson was known as the owner who most strongly encouraged the hardest line against the players' union during the lockout of 2011. He infamously patronized Peyton Manning during one negotiating session, reportedly asking him, "Do I need to help you read a revenue chart, son?" He also wondered to Manning, "What do you know about player health and safety?"

Richardson is like a lot of NFL owners in that he resembles a caricature drawing of what a certain type of old tycoon might look like—although at eighty, he is closer to "middle-aged" by Membership standards. If a cartoonist wanted to create Monopoly-like renderings of these aging show poodles, he would draw, say, Robert Kraft in his French cuff links seated on his owner's suite high chair, or Jerry Jones with his shiny white capped teeth (gleaming with dollar signs), or the Falcons' Arthur Blank with his impeccably groomed mustache.

Richardson, a small-town boy from Spring Hope, North Carolina, made his big-time fortune by buying up a bunch of Hardee's franchises. And he resembles precisely what you'd expect a Hardee's kingpin to look like. He has a comb-over helmet of white hair, a bulbous nose, chubby cheeks, and a face that looks like it should be jolly—like a fast-food mascot—but instead rests in a scowl. Think of the Baby Huey cartoon, but in a bad mood.

Richardson, who wore a tailored navy suit and nifty pocket squares for this occasion, had come out to perform his pregame custom of pounding four times on a massive blue-and-black drum that had been wheeled onto the field. KEEP POUNDING was imprinted twice on the drum. Ritual complete, Richardson returned his drumstick to a guy dressed up like a panther (one that eats five meals a day at Hardee's).

He then returned to the sidelines, where Goodell leaned over the Panther Patriarch's golf cart and engaged him in a hushed conversation. They locked eyes. This looked intense. I could not make out what the men were saying, but there were issues to work through.

The Panther Patriarch had been upset by how the Los Angeles treaty had gone down earlier in January. He had been a proponent of the Chargers-Raiders project in Carson, and did not take kindly to the late-game break in favor of the Rams in Inglewood. Richardson was seen as a loser in the L.A. clash, outmaneuvered by the big-eyed and blustering likes of Jerry Jones and the majestic ambitions (and bank account) of Stan Kroenke. Even though the Panthers were on the verge of playing in the franchise's second-ever Super Bowl, these backroom defeats pack their own special sting for a proud member like Richardson. He was now making noises like someone who was ready to take his ball and go home, at least as it related to league matters.

The Big Cat would check out for good in late 2017 when he put the Panthers up for sale, though it had nothing to do with Los Angeles. Richardson's self-styled reputation as a force for rectitude was incinerated in a hellfire of sexual harassment charges from team employees. A **Sports Illustrated** report detailed a twisted litany of accusations. They were notable for Richardson's keen interest in women's grooming. He was accused, among other things, of chiding female employees for not keeping their fingernails done to his liking, sponsoring their manicures, and, in multiple cases, asking if he could shave their legs for them(!). He would also, according to the **SI** report, arrive barefoot for private meetings with female underlings and ask for a foot massage. "Football" indeed.

AN ANNOUNCEMENT WAS MADE FOR EVERYONE to clear the field. I followed Goodell and Richardson into a tunnel where the Arizona players were waiting to be introduced. Goodell and Richardson continued their discussion while waiting for an elevator to take them up to their respective boxes. I tapped Goodell on the shoulder to thank him for his time, but he was locked into Richardson and did not move.

I joined a cluster of people who were watching the end of New England–Denver on a TV mounted to a wall. The Patriots were still down eight but now had the ball back and were driving into Bronco territory. And—whoa—Brady hit Rob Gronkowski on a fourth-and-10 bomb, followed by a 4-yard touchdown pass to Gronk to make it 20–18 with twelve seconds left. They needed just a two-point conversion to send the game to overtime.

Everyone in the tunnel was now fixated on the TV—random hangers-on, passing concessionaires, and even a few of the Cardinals players waiting to take the field. Football can be sublime. At its best, it can transcend everything—in my case driving eight hours, enduring a not-great interview with a tightly coiled commissioner with repeated interruptions; or in Brady's case (slightly more pertinent) being harassed by a zillion-dollar NFL investigation over nothing, being called a cheater in every corner of the country save the upper Northeast, and overcoming a ruthless Denver pass rush that had been brutalizing him all afternoon, sacking him four times and hitting him fourteen times.

As the teams lined up for the conversion try, I resolved that all of this would indeed be worth it if Brady could just get himself into another Super Bowl—Super Bowl 50, in his native San Francisco, home of his boyhood team (the 49ers) that drafted two forgotten quarterbacks instead of him. No one was thinking about concussions right then, or courtroom appeals, billionaires bickering, or a stone-cold commissioner. There is something about this sport that brings the story back to its most fascinating self. I would always tell people that whenever they would ask how I could keep watching football, despite everything I saw and everything we were learning. I say this every time: the best thing football has going for itself is football.

CBS cameras kept cutting to Denver's Peyton Manning, who was watching the last seconds from the sideline. Manning was a physical wreck and about to retire, so I guess I should admit that his ending up in the Super Bowl would be a good story, too. Brady's pass for Julian Edelman was tipped at the goal line and intercepted. Game over. And good for football, except when it kicks you in the head.

15.

THE BIG SPLAT

April 27, 2016

Eric Winston looked like your basic Big Ugly. That was what Keith Jackson, seminal football broadcaster of my youth, used to call offensive linemen. Winston was an unsung trench worker for four NFL teams over twelve years. He was six feet seven inches and three hundred pounds; not necessarily ugly, but Jackson meant the term as an affectionate catchall for the hulking grunts who blocked for the "scatbacks" who hogged all the facetime.

Winston was a third-round draft pick out of the University of Miami by the Houston Texans in 2006. He started at right tackle in his ninth pro game and remained a first-teamer for much of his career, earning close to $30 million during his time in the league. He also played for Arizona, Kansas City, and Cincinnati, for the most part in obscurity, except for one vivid close-up.

"It's sickening, it's one hundred percent sickening," Winston was saying on all the highlight shows one Sunday in 2012. "I've never been more embarrassed in my life to play football than at that moment right there." This was not your usual blitz of postgame platitudes. Winston's words came out loud and measured and his eyes were bugged. He was becoming uncomfortably philosophical about his profession. "We are not gladiators and this is not the Roman Coliseum," Winston said. "There are long-lasting ramifications to the game we play. I've already kind of come to the understanding that I won't live as long because I play this game, and that's okay." Was this man actually bringing up the taboo actuarial tables that players in the NFL rarely discuss, especially when surrounded by microphones?

It was the fifth week of that season when Winston, then twenty-eight and playing for the Chiefs, became briefly famous. Suddenly his scruffy visage was all over ESPN, CBS, Fox, NFL Network, YouTube, and every bit of coverage that accompanied the October 7 slate of games. The Chiefs had just lost 9–6 to the Ravens in a fully unmemorable slog, except for this big ugly rant in the locker room that followed.

Winston had been set off by a play that occurred in the final minutes of the game. The Chiefs' struggling quarterback, Matt Cassel, was knocked over by a Ravens lineman after a pass attempt. He struck his head on the Arrowhead Stadium turf, and then Winston, who was playing left tackle, stood over his quarterback and described seeing Cassel's eyes rolling back into his head. Trainers and doctors ran onto the field to tend to Cassel, Tom Brady's former backup. He was traded by the Pats after the 2008 season to Kansas City, where he became the starter. Cassel performed ably in KC at times but eventually wore out his welcome in Chiefs Nation. This fall from favor was most in evidence as Cassel was being wheeled off the field, woozy and concussed. Winston and his teammates heard the crowd cheering his departure.

"This is really fucked up," Winston told a fellow lineman, Ryan Lilja, on the field as Cassel's backup, Brady Quinn, took over the huddle. Winston remained upset through the end of the game and into the shower. His diatribe ensued.

"Hey, if he is not the best quarterback, he's not the best quarterback, and that's okay," Winston said as the crowd of cameras grew around him. "He's a person. And he got knocked out in a game and we've got seventy thousand people cheering that he got knocked out."

Eric Winston had my attention. He was crossing lines. Athletes are never supposed to criticize fans like this, especially home fans. According to the settled norms of pro sports, customers should enjoy full absolution for any form of verbal abuse they perpetrate, by the power vested in them by their status as "fans who spend their hard-earned money"—always **hard-earned**—"to buy their tickets and come to games." They pay the players' salaries, dammit.

So it was not surprising that Winston would catch heat within Chiefs Nation. Local fans and media became defensive, questioned whether in fact "seventy thousand people" were cheering Cassel's knockout and not just a scattered few. Or maybe some of the cheers were for Quinn entering the game. Winston stood by his outrage.

"This is a game that is going to cost us a lot down the road, that's okay, we picked it," Winston said, finishing his speech. "But we've got a lot of problems as a society if people think that's okay."

Winston's disillusionment had been building since he entered the league. Over time, he had come to realize that the majority of NFL fans cared about him only as a football player, not as a human being. He was merely a dancing elephant paid to perform. This should have been obvious all along but was placed into relief for him in 2011 when the owners instituted a 132-day lockout. The prevailing sentiment Winston heard from fans during that time was that players were paid well; they should just shut up and play. Then came the Cassel incident, and Winston's speech, which became a viral sensation. Winston was mostly praised in the national media. Fellow players, including some on opposing teams, sought him out on the field to thank him. Winston had struck a blow against the faceless noise machine of fantasy tough guys and message board heroes.

As soon as I saw Winston's harangue, he became someone I wanted to hear more from. Others did, too. He was inundated with interview requests and offered his own radio show. But he had to decline, at the urging of the Chiefs. They didn't need this "distraction" from an outspoken lineman. It violated the common football rule that no one, even when speaking in support of his brothers, should bring too much attention upon himself.

Winston's career would continue for another five seasons, mostly with the Bengals. In 2014, he was elected president of the NFL Players Association. I first met him in the spring of 2016 at the NFL Draft in Chicago. DeMaurice "De" Smith, the NFLPA's executive director, had invited me to a party the night before for incoming draft prospects at an Italian steakhouse (to be clear, I was not an incoming draft prospect, though I'm told I move well for a fifty-two-year-old with two reconstructed ACLs). Smith had been head of the union during the 2011 lockout, a bitter period in which the league was believed to have gotten the better of the eventual ten-year collective bargaining agreement. Of all the major sports unions, the NFLPA occupies the toughest bargaining position. Football players, who mostly play on non-guaranteed contracts, have the shortest careers and in most cases get paid only sixteen weeks out of the year to play in their injury-riddled league. Any time lost would cost them relatively large proportions of their career earning potential. It is difficult for that reason to keep unions together for a work stoppage.

In addition, football's view of the collective tends to follow the military model of top-down deference to coach and, especially, owner. NFL owners tend to have a greater need to flaunt their place atop the sports hierarchy than owners in other sports do. They feel the need, for whatever reason, to reinforce the Tex Schramm "You guys are cattle and we're the ranchers" sensibility. Such is the fragility of their egos and, perhaps, empires. Still, the violent foxholes that players endure together nurture bonds.

Banners and signs that said WELCOME TO THE FAMILY were draped all over Chicago. It was in keeping with the league's "Football Is Family" ad campaign then in full swing. But the question of whose family these wide-eyed bruisers were being welcomed into yielded different answers depending on whom you asked. At the very least, the draft extravaganza offered an early glimpse into the competing infantries that players serve.

The union recoiled at any notion that the Shield would be anything more than a short-term employer, much less a "family." Fans could be similarly jaded at the notion of a familial bond with the players they root for.

"Ownership" is another charged concept within the NFL, as is loyalty. I was at a party in D.C. several years ago and saw Daniel Snyder, the owner of the Redskins, parading around his newest quarterback-savior, Donovan McNabb. Snyder kept walking a few steps ahead of McNabb as if he were leading him on a leash, until McNabb got sidetracked to sign an autograph while Snyder continued into another room. "Hey, I've lost my owner," McNabb said. You often hear players referring to "my owner," innocently enough, but it's always jarring to hear. (Snyder might have been "my owner" at that moment, but McNabb's coach—Mike Shanahan—still disowned him at the end of his one season with the Redskins.)

Should a player's primary loyalty be to the organization he plays for, which will remain loyal in return—right up until the moment it decides to cut him? Should a player's loyalty be to his teammates, who might be competing for the same job or lined up on an opposing team a week later? Or should it be to his actual family, given that he has a very small window to make a living in a sport that, as Winston said, will likely inflict a long-term health cost? Prospects are pulled in a million different directions, nowhere more acutely than here.

George Atallah, the NFLPA's assistant executive director of external affairs, greeted me when I walked into the predraft party. He introduced me to Winston, as hulking as listed, who had a cluster of people around him trying to get a word in. It is a busy night for the president of the union, and Winston had a slightly harried and put-off vibe. "I loved that Matt Cassel thing you did," one man said upon meeting him, as if Winston had done nothing else in his career.

Atallah then led me up to a room where a group of draft prospects had assembled. They were, of course, supremely well conditioned and dressed in designer suits tailored for the occasion. I struck up a conversation with Shaq Lawson, a defensive end from Clemson who had just finished being photographed. Lawson told me he was intent on being one of the top fifteen players picked in the draft. He then showed off an impressive recall of the exact draft order of teams, one through fifteen. I asked Lawson whether he would rather be drafted to a team that he badly wanted to play for with the sixteenth pick (Tennessee) as opposed to a team he did not wish to play for, at fourteen (Oakland). Fourteen, Lawson said, no matter what team it was. It was a dream of his to go top-fifteen and that was that, end of discussion. I mentioned this later to Winston, who just shook his head. "These guys don't have a clue," he said. (Lawson wound up dropping to Buffalo at nineteenth, due to health concerns. He underwent shoulder surgery the next month and did not make his rookie debut until late October.)

Jermichael Finley, a former Packer, was sitting at a reserved table with his family. Atallah brought me over and asked if I knew who he was. Sure, I remembered Jermichael Finley: stud tight end, could motor for his size, tough to bring down. Whatever happened to him? Same thing that usually happens: "Most guys don't get to decide for themselves when they're done with the game," Finley said. "The game lets you know when it's done with you." The game—namely the Packers—let Finley know after six years in the league. He had suffered five concussions and a gruesome spinal injury to end his season in 2013. Finley received interest from a few teams but failed a physical with Seattle in 2014 and made his retirement official in October 2015, a few months before I met him in Chicago.

Finley was here with his wife and son, who was then seven. A $10 million insurance settlement had allowed him the financial security to support his family after leaving football at age twenty-eight. But Finley's transition had been difficult otherwise. So had the physical toll his career had taken on him, particularly his brain. He described the depression, memory loss, and irritability among the now-familiar laundry list of ailments you hear from former players. He missed the brotherhood of the locker room and felt increasingly isolated.

Finally, Finley had sought help from a holistic treatment and recovery center in Oxnard, California, where he underwent a thirty-day program of brain testing, meditation, therapy, and cognitive exercises. It helped, Finley said, to a point where if he didn't seek treatment, "ten years from now, I might have ended up one of those former players who put a bullet in his chest." But mostly Finley says his wife and four children have been his salvation. "I finally came to the realization that my relationship with the NFL was temporary," Finley said. "But my relationship with my wife and kids is permanent. It's forever." Everything else was "on the clock," to use the draft terminology.

Taking leave of Finley, Atallah wanted to make sure the former tight end knew who his real brothers were. The NFLPA was there for him. "We're your family, too," Atallah said. Finley just smiled and thanked the union for the party.

Chicago, this great urban melting pot and crossroads of America, had been transformed for a few late-April days into a Dungeons & Dragons convention for testosterone-addled sects. Fans of the Lions, Dolphins, and Bears (oh my), tribal denominations represented in face paint and by officially licensed jerseys: Chiefs reds, Cowboys blues, and Raiders silver and blacks; Cheeseheads, Viking horns, Steeler hardhats and Terrible Towels.

"The whole thing at the draft is a total blur, especially for these kids," Winston told me after the NFLPA bash. We had repaired to a tiki-themed Chinese restaurant with Atallah and Winston's friend and former teammate Dave Anderson, a wide receiver drafted the same year as Eric by the Texans. There were umbrella drinks, a pupu platter for four (dominated by Winston), and more umbrella drinks.

Winston compared the eve of the draft with "the last day of summer vacation," a line of demarcation between being the BMOC and the guy who carries the veterans' pads in training camp. Starting tomorrow, these coveted and sheltered amateurs become "owned." "It hits you fast," Winston said. "Few of these guys really know what's in store." You're sitting back in the greenroom, wearing the nicest clothes you've ever worn, and then boom, your name is called. "You're in the NFL."

I think of Pat Summerall, another seminal football narrator of my youth. He hosted an old NFL Films short: **They Call It Pro Football**, the production was called, making it all seem so grand and gritty. Here, as Winston said, was just total blur—and more umbrella drinks.

I was awakened in my hotel on draft day by a predawn call to worship. It came courtesy of a band of marauding Jets fans on the street below chanting, naturally, "J-E-T-S, JETS, JETS, JETS!" If I was being clear-eyed, I would acknowledge that this could have been any caste of drunken fans, not just Jets zealots. But it was four a.m. and I was not being clear-eyed, and admittedly I yelled things out the window that were not Football Is Family–friendly. Things escalated predictably ("Fuck you! Asshole," etc.). Eventually I stood down, shut the window, and returned to bed, secure in the judgment that I was the bigger man and, more important, rooted for a better football team.

THE MOOD WAS CONVIVIAL IN "DRAFT TOWN," the designated area around Grant Park, Congress Plaza, and the Auditorium Theatre where this affair would be held for the second year in a row (Philly would assume the "Draft Town" mantle in 2017, followed by Dallas in 2018). I talked to several fans who had traveled hundreds of miles and from several states away to attend the football Woodstock—200,000 of them in total would partake of the bazaar over three days

A few hours before things kicked off for real at seven p.m., Chicago time, I surveyed the clusters of fans lined up for blocks around the or-nate venue. Across from Grant Park, a parade of prospects walked "a red carpet" through portable bleachers packed with onlookers gathered to inspect these specimens one last time before they hugged Roger for keeps.

Ohio State running back Ezekiel Elliott showed up wearing a powder-blue tuxedo jacket over a dress shirt cropped a few inches above the navel to expose his helmet-hard abdomen. This was an early show-stealer on the red carpet until Elliott was eclipsed by Laremy Tunsil, a massive offensive tackle out of Ole Miss. He wore a bizarre pair of gold-studded shoes that resembled shiny pinecones engulfing his size-sixteen feet. Tunsil, who was accompanied by his mother, had been a hot topic of predraft discussion for reasons of actual football, not footwear. He was originally tapped as a potential first-overall pick by Tennessee, but the Titans wound up trading their pick to the Rams, who were desperate for a quarterback; same with the Eagles, who traded up for Cleveland's number two selection. Tunsil still remained a trendy choice to be the first nonquarterback taken in many mock drafts—at number three, by the Chargers.

"Who made those shoes, Laremy?" a TV "journalist" shouted at Tunsil. "How much did they cost? Did you have them made special for the draft?" Another Man in Makeup beside the red carpet tried to ask Tunsil whether he had heard anything from the Chargers and whether they might take him. An actual "football matter" is how the intrepid reporter prefaced his query, trying to rise above the fashion nonsense. (It's always amusing to watch sportswriters get indignant when others do not honor the sanctity of their "actual football questions.") Whatever Tunsil mumbled in response, I could not hear. He would learn his fate soon enough, as we all would.

Here's a partial spoiler: Tunsil's red carpet fuss would be nowhere close to the most memorable part of his draft day.

After the Prospect Runway ended, I walked a few blocks past a massive WELCOME TO THE FAM-ILY banner on the marquee of Roosevelt University to the historic draft venue. Opened in 1889, the Auditorium Theatre had once hosted the varied likes of John Philip Sousa, Booker T. Washington, and Teddy Roosevelt, the last of whom declared himself to be "as strong as a bull moose" during an appearance here in 1912. More than a century later, thousands of face-painted fanatics lined up for several blocks around the assembly hall to witness the NFL's annual job-placement extravaganza for strong-as-a-bull-moose "student-athletes."

As one would expect, it takes a certain hard-core fan to travel several hours, sometimes days, to attend such an ultimately action-free spectacle. These were NFL versions of what McDonald's called "heavy users," the restaurant's classification for customers who eat several meals a week at their feeding pens—sometimes more than twenty meals a month in the case of "super heavy users."

Superfans appear to travel a circuit. They cavort at Super Bowls and tailgate areas when their teams play each other. NFL drafts are "the Super Bowl of the off-season," league spokesman Brian McCarthy boasted to the **Chicago Tribune**. It was as if the NFL had thrown a big party and invited every family except for mine. This was the year Goodell had robbed New England of its first-round pick over Deflategate, which understandably kept many of my people away, not that anyone missed us.

I ENTERED THE VENUE, CLIMBED A FLIGHT OF stairs, and immediately confronted vomit. A shit-faced Bears fan in a #22 Matt Forte jersey was collapsed against the wall. It was not pretty. There is really no reason to mention this except that the sheer volume of the outburst was like nothing I'd seen—to a point where the man's issue flowed down the marble steps of the theater. Draft groupies tried to maneuver around the accident. Parents shielded their children's eyes. Football is family!

Goodell commenced the draft with a rare tweet: "here we go. #NFLDraft," the commissioner wrote, triggering the usual heave of responses from Twitter handles such as

@TB12BestEva, @FoxboroughFrank34, and @CountTheRingsBaby. These, too, were not pretty. First response: "@NFLCommish how can you even walk with a giant dildo in your ass?" The commissioner did not address the question.

But as the man said: "Here we go."

For as much alleged "expertise" goes into predicting it, the evening is usually good for a few surprises. There's something about the draft, if not mesmerizing for its action per se, then for the dressed-up crapshoot it all is. The draft makes for such a perfect set piece in the Shield's great reality show: thirty-two cliff-hangers packed into a few hours; big dreams and big money at stake, blue-chip belly buttons and gold-spiked shoes. Lions, Bears, and Browns fans can hope, root, and get excited over some new piece of strutting possibility. And when it's over they don't have to watch their teams lose for another few months.

About the only sure thing at a modern NFL Draft is that Roger Goodell will get booed. Repeatedly, and with gusto. Beyond that . . . wait, WHAT?

"Did you see this?" my colleague Ken Belson asked when I took the seat next to him in the designated press area. Here was our ticking time bomb, detonated before the Los Angeles Rams were even on the clock. Ken showed me a bizarre photo on his phone that was all over Twitter. It was a screenshot posted to Laremy Tunsil's account showing someone, apparently Tunsil, wearing a gas mask with a bong attached to it. This was not your grandpa's NFL Draft.

There are certain markers that show a society in decline. Was this one of those? Where have you gone, Roger Staubach? It seemed that every single person in Draft Town and beyond was now looking at this tweet and wondering what the hell it was. The extended family of NFL insiders and nugget-meisters were fully activated. So many questions: Is that actually Tunsil? Who posted this? Is it real? The tweet that will follow Laremy Tunsil for the rest of his days was quickly deleted. If only it was that easy. Screenshots popped up just as fast. Team Tunsil claimed his account was hacked.

"This whole social media scene makes me sick," Adam Schefter was saying as I walked past his ESPN perch in the middle of the room. Putting aside the obvious irony of this—the fact that Schefty himself **is** "a whole social media scene" unto himself—I took his point. This was a story out of control from the second it entered the hurricane of smear and guesswork that Twitter engenders (and the draft itself engenders). Well down on the list are facts, fairness, and yes, journalism, but mostly, we were all instantly in the vortex of **whatever the hell this was**.

To say that the Men in Makeup at the draft

were riled up over this tweet would be like saying that vultures had become riled up by the surprise arrival of a rhinoceros corpse. Schefter, of course, much prefers "actual football stories." Player signings, personnel moves, injury reports, contract values—that's his comfort food, not the off-field rococo like this that humanity will belch up (and God bless humanity!). Schefter owns these "actual football stories." No one comes close, and when someone dares trespass upon his "breaking news" dominion—the Bears are looking to trade into the first round!—he fashions a certain smirk, one that says: "You posers need to step aside while the real pros like me mine for golden nuggets—with a pickax, not a fucking pan!"

His colleagues humble themselves before Schefty. "Adam's the first pick in the draft," Sal Pal told me in awe. "He is the king. I just play right guard, wherever they need me." But Schefter was flustered by the Tunsil story. He was hesitant to "go on the air" with it. He had not yet received confirmation—**per sources**—that Tunsil was in fact the Lineman in the Gas Mask Attached to the Bong. Other outlets were reporting that it in fact was, and Schefter was getting pressure from his bosses to do the same. He called his fellow NFL insider Chris Mortensen, who was being treated for throat cancer in Houston at the time. Mort counseled caution. Schefter was torn. This was one red-hot story, awaiting his imprimatur.

He was still stinging from a major fail a few weeks earlier. Schefter had committed the unforgivable blunder of going to work out without his phone. It was only for twenty minutes, he said. But for the NFL insider-of-record, a phone-deprived twenty minutes can be lethal. "I never used to have my phone with me when I worked out," Schefter lamented. But then came that fateful spin class. "I get back to my phone to find eleven or twelve text messages," Schefter told me, slowly, as if spelling out the details of a trauma. "The number-one pick in the draft had been traded." Tennessee had shipped it to L.A. for the right to select quarterback Jared Goff out of Cal.

"And I had the story, too!" Schefter insisted. "But I was spinning." Lesson learned.

But this was no time to dwell. Schefter isn't much of a dweller anyway, but especially in the fire hose of draft night, fans are tuned in to their insider masters as they rarely are during the off-season. Goodell called out the first few picks: Goff to the Rams, quarterback Carson Wentz to the Eagles at number two, Zeke Elliott to the Cowboys at number four. But for all intents and purposes, there was one story right now: Laremy Tunsil.

First it was the gas mask photo, the hack and the postmodern social media absurdity of it all. It was not easy for anyone to get their heads around this situation, in the same way that it's not easy to fit a gas mask around an offensive lineman's massive head. Then came the next phase of the story, the one with a soundtrack: the big **splat** of a flesh-and-blood twenty-one-year-old's draft stock dropping off a cliff. No one was touching Tunsil; not teams that were projected to take him (the Chargers took Ohio State D-lineman Joey Bosa instead, at number three), not teams desperate for O-line help (the Ravens took Notre Dame tackle Ronnie Stanley instead, at number six).

What team would deliver Tunsil from this nightmare? Was the former "number one pick on the board" now too radioactive to be drafted at all? Pigskin pundits were calculating that Tunsil had lost close to $10 million in rookie earnings after he dropped out of the top ten. And counting. Like so many NFL stories today, this was riveting, sad, and uncomfortable at the same time.

Finally the Miami Dolphins halted this white-knuckle trip by picking Tunsil at thirteen. He strutted onto the draft stage as he had the red carpet earlier, except seemingly half the size. He posed with Goodell and his new aqua-blue jersey. He then subjected himself to his requisite first "interview" as a pro, from State Television. NFL Network "reporter" Deion Sanders asked about the "elephant in the room," or greenroom, where Tunsil said he first learned about the video, along with everybody else.

"Man, it was a mistake," he told Sanders. "You

Oakland (soon to be Vegas) Raiders owner Mark Davis in a red carpet pose.

New England Patriots owner Robert K. Kraft with his girlfriend, Ricki Noel Lander.

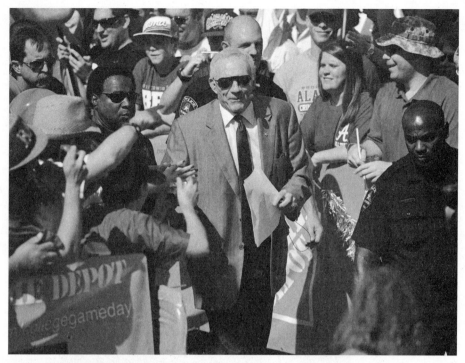

Dallas Cowboys owner Jerry Jones at ESPN College GameDay, Arlington, Texas.

Gold Jacket Jerry Jones with his beloved Hall of Fame self, in bust form.

Tom Brady in pre–Super Bowl shades, 2018.

Brady in pre–Super Bowl press conference ski hat, 2018.

Laremy Tunsil, Miami Dolphins O-lineman,
in the infamous gas mask bong that ruined
his draft night, 2016.

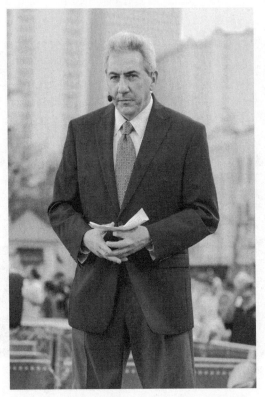

ESPN's Sal Paolantonio, reporting from somewhere (New Orleans, in this case).

ESPN's Adam Schefter—and his phone—on the set of *NFL Insiders*, pre–Super Bowl 2017.

NFL commissioner Roger Goodell at the draft, probably being booed.

Former Carolina Panthers owner Jerry Richardson, in better days, on his golf cart. (Richardson sold the Panthers in 2018 after receiving sexual harassment complaints from team employees.)

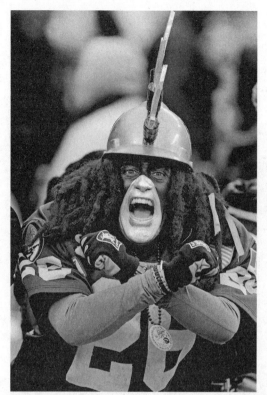

Oakland Raiders' Superfan Ray Perez (aka "Dr. Death"), in his element.

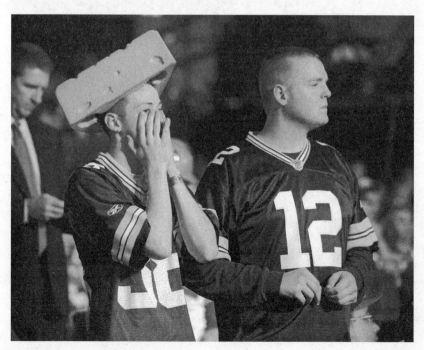

Green Bay Cheeseheads at the draft.

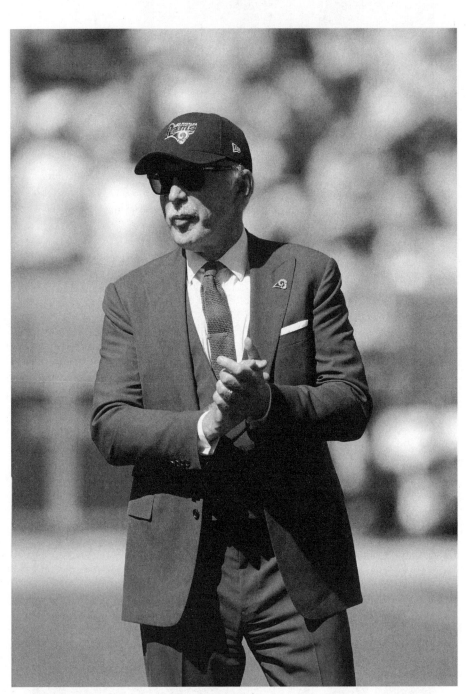

Los Angeles Rams owner Stan Kroenke on the sideline of his pre–Shangri-L.A. stadium (nowhere near St. Louis).

Gisele, being Gisele.

Underdog Nick Foles a few days before the Super Bowl that changed everything.

Giants co-owner Steve Tisch with then-fiancée, Katia Francesconi.

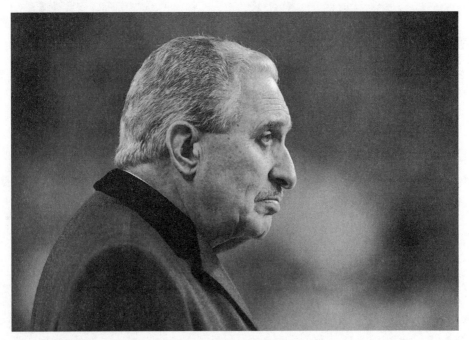

Falcons owner Arthur Blank, deep in thought, watching his team on a Monday night.

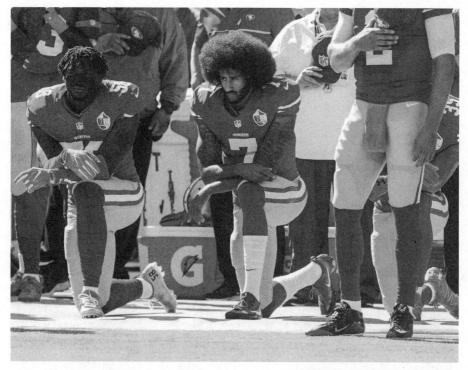

Former 49ers quarterback Colin Kaepernick (7), kneeling during the national anthem, before a game in 2016—which may be the last season Kaepernick would play a game in the NFL.

Postplaying-days Brett Favre, a few weeks before his Hall of Fame induction, 2016.

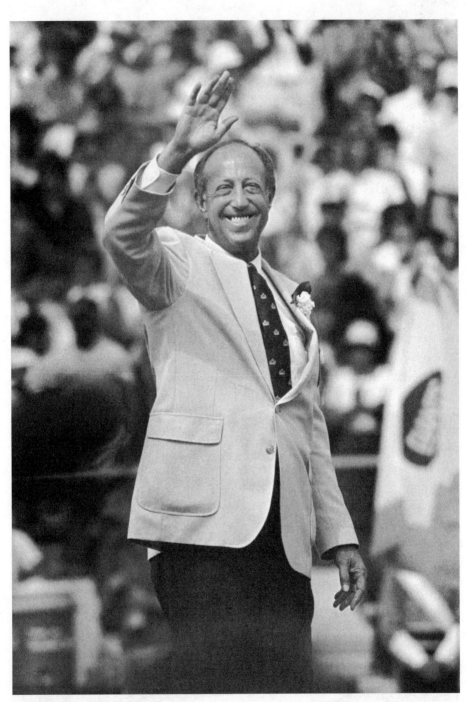

Pete Rozelle, NFL commissioner from 1960 to 1989, who steered the league on its modern trajectory of popularity and riches.

Vince Lombardi "treats us all the same," one player said of the legendary Packers coach. "Like dogs."

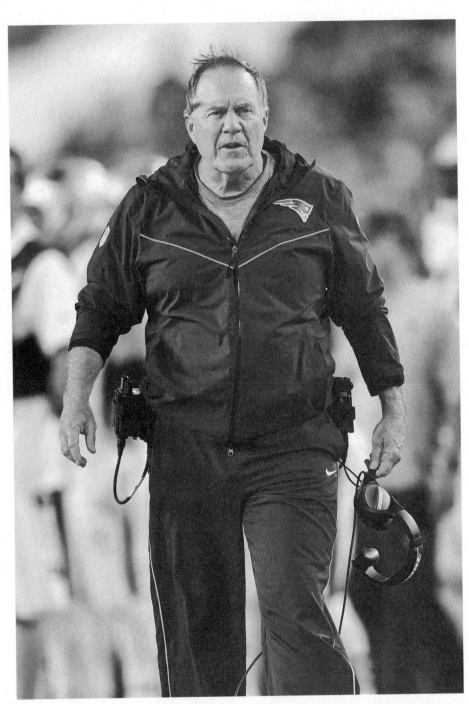

Bill Belichick, looking ecstatic on the sideline during a game against Tampa Bay in 2017.

know, it happened years ago. Like I said before, somebody hacked my Twitter account. That's how it got on there, man. It's just a crazy world— things happen for a reason." Tunsil appeared relatively composed, given everything. He relied on a few stock phrases (**"things happen for a reason," "I'm blessed to be a Miami Dolphin"**). Sanders ended his grilling with a "God bless you, man, I'm proud of you," and a hug.

After the Dolphins ended the suspense, and the tension in the room subsided for a bit, I wandered through the galleries of corporate appendages and sixty-something adolescents. In the lobby of the theater, I noted poster-size photos of select NFL greats shaking the commissioner's hand on-stage right after they were drafted. There was Pete Rozelle greeting the fresh-faced newcomers like Dan Marino and John Elway onstage in 1983. Next to them was a poster of the great . . . Troy Vincent? Hmm, wonder why he's in here, posing with Paul Tagliabue in 1992 after being drafted seventh by the Dolphins.

It was always clear when the next pick was coming because the hall would explode in boos as soon as Goodell walked out onstage. Abuse reduction efforts by the league were mostly futile. Walter Payton's widow accompanied Goodell onstage at one point, which might have dulled the edge for a few minutes. But the Human Shield technique has limited utility no matter how beloved or sympathetic the icon they pair with Goodell. Fans demonstrate impressive resolve when it comes to fulfilling their responsibility to beat up the commissioner. (The best example of this occurred at an unveiling of a Peyton Manning statue outside Lucas Oil Stadium in Indianapolis that fall. If ever there was a safe stage for Goodell, this would be it: congenial midwestern fans with no apparent ax to grind against the league, festive occasion for the Colts legend. And as an added buffer, the organizers sent Goodell out to introduce Hall of Famer Tony Dungy, the former Colts coach who—as Peter King pointed out—was probably the most venerated person there, except for Manning. Yet the hate still showered down, and hard.)

It is a mystery to me why Goodell allows this abuse to continue, pick after pick, round after round. Since the draft now shifts from city to city, the NFL could just as easily deputize a popular, nondemented home-team figure—say, retired Bears legend Brian Urlacher in Chicago—with the task of walking onstage a bunch of times, reading off names and posing for photos. How hard could that be? The bloodlusters might be deprived of their Goodell feedings, but it would at least spare the league the embarrassing look of having its commissioner booed savagely and repeatedly before the eyes of the world every single year. And don't think the Membership doesn't notice this, either. "Not good," Falcons owner

Arthur Blank told me, shaking his head when I asked him about this continuing tradition.

At one point in Chicago, I started canvassing fans on why exactly they were booing the commissioner. Some of them had parochial grievances—a few Chiefs fans, for instance, told me they were pissed that the league stripped their team of a third-round pick on a player-tampering rap that year. "If nothing else, I feel I have to boo him for the Ray Rice situation," a Bears fan, Larry Szwiec, told me. But mostly, the booing was an almost Pavlovian default reaction to the mere sight of Roger Goodell.

One impressive aspect of the commissioner's draft bloodbath is the stamina of his lion's den. The ardor in Chicago sustained itself well into the lower rounds. So committed were the hecklers that they would time the pauses in Goodell's announcement and then seize the brief silence for maximum impact. "With the seventeenth pick," Goodell would say, slight pause, and then the horde would scream into the void—**"Fuck You, Asshole," "Goodell sucks," "Shut up," "Go home," "Go Pats"**—before the commissioner could get his next set of words in to complete his fateful sentence ("the Atlanta Falcons select Keanu Neal . . .").

As round one neared completion, I headed to the press-filing center upstairs in search of the ultimate spoil for any self-respecting sportswriter—

free food. All I'd eaten that day were bags of Skittles and Cheetos from the NFL-issued gift bag at our press seats. (Who says we can't be bought?) But I managed to get lost as I navigated hallways and stairwells in the old building.

I turned a corner at one point, trying to right myself, only to wander into a small and dimly lit area that was inhabited by none other than the man of the hour, Laremy Tunsil. Holy damn, the Gas Mask Elvis himself!

Tunsil was in a hushed discussion with a young woman, presumably a handler assigned to him. She seemed completely overwhelmed. His eyes were red, as if he might have been crying. A security type looked sternly upon me and pointed to a doorway. **Get out**, I took this to mean. The doorway led into a converted classroom where the newly minted draft picks were holding their press conferences. Tunsil was up next, about to endure a thrown-to-the-wolves spectacle that somehow the league—and his own representatives— was allowing, as if the kid had not suffered enough already.

Apparently, Tunsil had just learned of yet another troubling development. This one involved an alleged hack of his Instagram account. Someone—again, Tunsil said he had no idea who— had now posted a series of old text messages between Tunsil and an Ole Miss assistant coach that strongly suggested an improper cash payment.

That was the backdrop against which Tunsil would be obligated to come out for his first press conference as a professional football player. He looked terrified.

The behemoth-in-the-headlights reiterated the same phrases he leaned on before. He was blessed to be here and happy to be part of the Dolphins and excited to get to work. Someone then asked him about the Instagram post. "I'm new to this," Tunsil said at one point, pleading for mercy. A reporter then asked if those text messages showed what they appeared to show—an exchange of cash between him and an assistant athletic director at Ole Miss.

"I would have to say yes," Tunsil said. He twice rubbed the gathering perspiration from his forehead with his sleeve. "I'm blessed," he said.

"Have you talked to the NCAA?" another reporter called out. Before Tunsil could answer, the young woman he was with before—the handler—swooped in for the overdue rescue. "He's got no more comment, thanks very much," the woman said, leading Tunsil off the podium like it was on fire.

Ken Belson, who was back in the hall writing the draft story for the next day's **Times**, called upstairs and asked me to please write him a feed from the Tunsil press conference (he wanted me to be an actual reporter on deadline, in other words, as opposed to a dilettante book writer—I hate when this happens). I tapped out a few paragraphs for Ken. My iPhone kept autocorrecting Tunsil as "tonsil."

In my forays behind the Shield, this might have been—and this is saying something—the single most mishandled fiasco I encountered. No one was making Tunsil play pro football, just like no one appeared to be forcing the gas-mask bong onto his then-teenage face. He made mistakes, like many college students do, and paid for it in over eight figures in lost earnings. And then there was the added humiliation Tunsil was forced to endure, the whole perverse scene: Welcome to the family, Laremy Tunsil. He was completely on his own.

Eric Winston, who had left Chicago before the draft, became more disgusted as he watched the affair unfold. "Last night everyone saw a young man's dream turn into a nightmare," Winston would tweet the next day. "What did the NFL do? Nothing." What really enraged Winston was something Goodell said when he was asked about the Tunsil saga during a morning-after interview on ESPN's **Mike & Mike**.

"I think it's all part of what makes the draft so exciting," Goodell said.

And with that Winston was moved to launch into the second most memorable rant of his career, this time via Twitter (everything via Twitter). Never mind a young man's nightmare, Winston tweeted of Tunsil's televised ordeal. "If Roger is to be believed, they loved it because it made the draft 'so exciting,'" he said. I took "they" to mean the NFL and "it" to mean the prime reality show meat that we had all feasted on.

"The NFL invested big on this marketing campaign of 'family,'" Winston persisted. "Let me dish out some free advice to the young men coming into the league this weekend: they are not your family. This is a business." It hits you fast.

They call it pro football.

16.

IMMORTALITY GETS OLD

August 4, 2016

After a few false starts, I made my first proper journey that summer to Canton, Ohio, battered Rust Belt birthplace of the machine that batters bodies, prints money, and kills our Sundays. Originally called the American Professional Football Association, the NFL got its start here in 1920 with the Canton Bulldogs running back Jim Thorpe designated as the league's first president. The founding confab took place at a Hupmobile car dealership; and it felt fitting that this seminal American creation—the NFL—would be born in a showroom of hustlers.

As Elvis fans make pilgrimages to Graceland, football zealots come to Canton. Where to begin with Canton? I came for the indoctrination ceremonies for the Pro Football Hall of Fame's class of 2016. "Enshrinement Weekend," as this early August festival is known, marks a reunion of returning Hall of Famers who are "welcomed home" to Canton in a grand three-day cotillion. Let's maybe begin with that notion: "Home."

A little over three hundred Hall of Famers have a "home" in Canton. They reside permanently here in brass bust form. While many can't make it in the flesh, their legends loom: Canton is laden with myth, glory, and ghost. "Here's the deal," the coach and broadcaster John Madden explained during his 2006 induction speech. After the Hall of Fame closes for the day, and all the fans and visitors and maintenance people depart, something happens with the immortals left in the building. "I believe that the busts talk to each other," Madden said. Vince Lombardi, Walter Payton, and now John Madden himself would be "forever and ever talking about whatever," Madden said.

"That's what I believe."

"Canton" rates as one of those iconic American place-names, like "Cooperstown" or "Gettysburg." Football is of course the franchise here. But the city also conjures impressions particular to the sport's heavier impacts. By contrast, when baseball's Hall of Famers show up in Cooperstown for their sport's induction rite, the gathering marks a celebration of a game that's allowed its stars to age softly. Whitey Ford, Hank Aaron, and Sandy Koufax all look stellar as old men, sitting on the back porch of the Otesaga Resort Hotel. Here, Canton's homecoming is both a celebration of the game they excelled in and a showcase of its hazards. Immortality loses some luster if you can't remember why you're here.

You can identify the royalty of Canton by their signature "gold jackets." They're actually more canary yellow, better suited to an announcer for a regional sports network. A significant number of dead Hall of Famers request burial in their hallowed attire. But here among the still-walking, these garments demarcate primacy, as cardinals in Rome are set apart by their scarlet robes (blood-colored, reflecting willingness to die for their faith).

Canton is the football Vatican. The shrine is rich with pomp, freighted with demons, and roamed, gingerly, by elect beings who have come "home." The rest of us may only visit.

I flew to Cleveland and drove about sixty miles south to Canton, seat of Stark County, Ohio, and final resting place of President William McKinley. Canton is like many Rust Belt cities that have bled manufacturing jobs and been forced to adapt to service-economy realities. Its recoveries have been uneven and its blemishes present themselves over dreary blocks of abandoned homes and buildings. As with the game that made it famous, Canton has expended its share of worry over what's coming next.

Whatever the city's future holds, past and present are polished clean for the enshrinement ceremonies. Streets downtown are decked out with American flags on lampposts and WELCOME HOME banners on the sides of buildings. Every bit of signage bears the Hall of Fame logo, a miniaturized version of the circular temple that is effectively the Flag of Canton.

"Are you here for induction?" I was asked a few times, as if I were pregnant. The construction threw me at first (it's simply "induction," not "**the** induction"—like "prom," as opposed to "**the** prom"). But it was meant to be welcoming, and Cantonians could not have been more so.

Festivities began Thursday night with the enshrinee's Gold Jacket Dinner at the Canton Memorial Civic Center. This was a can't-miss affair, according to all who'd been here before. I arrived early, made my way through the waiting crowd that included a lineup of pageant contestants, the Enshrinement Queen, Miss Canton, a bunch of city and Hall dignitaries, a brass band, and a mosh pit of Gold Jackets.

Tony Dorsett was the first football cardinal I recognized, and not just by the jacket. He was a foot or two in front of me waiting to enter the Civic Center. His face was as fresh and boyish as I remember him, if not his brain or body. "I will never forget that ninety-nine-yard run you had," I told Dorsett without hesitation. Something about Canton melts your instinct for respectful distance and restores you (or me) to the unabashed fan boy who used to hang out in the lobby of the Newton Marriott and hounded visiting players for autographs when they came to town to play the Pats.

That epic Dorsett dash from 1983 remained vivid to me. It was the longest run from scrimmage in NFL history (a record that can only be tied). "I was in high school and watching that game with my brother," I took this opportunity to inform Touchdown Tony, as if he gave a damn. It was against Minnesota on a Monday night, I recalled helpfully. Dorsett was kind to humor me.

"Ten men on the field," he said. Yes, the Cowboys happened to be a man short on that play. Fullback Ron Springs had gotten mixed up and remained on the sideline. I'm guessing Dorsett could have recited every last detail of that thirty-five-year-old event—the blocking scheme, the name of the formation, the exact play call, everything. But I've read enough about Dorsett's post-playing days to also know the price of these memories.

Dorsett's short-term recall is shot. "He just can't tell you who dropped him off at his house no more than 10 minutes ago," Gary Myers of the **Daily News** wrote of Dorsett in what has become the evergreen genre of stories about demolished former NFL players living out their days in pain and fog. Several Gold Jackets have been the subjects of these agonized hero-in-winter yarns. They include similar refrains ("I have good days and I have bad days," Dorsett told Myers), similar retroactive fatalism ("If you play as long as I did, you are going to have something wrong with you"), and similar lines of frustration ("I looked in the mirror and I say 'Who are you,'" Dorsett told CNN in 2013). In most cases, the accounts will conclude with some declaration from the broken player that he has no regrets. "Hell yeah," Dorsett said, "I would do it again."

NFL Network carried the Gold Jacket Dinner live over three full hours. A few dozen banquet tables were set up across the McKinley Room, each circular setting anchored by a blue bucket of Bud Light bottles. I found a seat in the back of the hall, in the middle of a bunch of Packer fans with Cheesehead hats who had come to witness the induction of their Gunslinger God, #4, Brett Favre. We watched the eminences file in. Forrest Gregg was in a wheelchair, Willie Roaf had become obese, and Lynn Swann (a trained ballet dancer, whom Curt Gowdy once called "the Baryshnikov of football") looked like he could still play. ESPN's Chris Berman was a most approachable destination for the selfie-swarms.

Rich Eisen, the perky über-host of the NFL Network, began a serviceable lounge act as the evening's master of ceremonies. He welcomed all "football-loving people" to Canton. He said "welcome home" to the 141 Gold Jackets who had returned and teased the induction of the 8 newest Hall of Famers. For the first time, he said, these newcomers would "don their gold jackets, unveil the busts, and become permanent residents of Canton, Ohio." Eisen also extended a special thank-you to Haggar, the menswear company that had been making the Gold Jackets since 1978. That—1978—might have been the last time I thought of Haggar, which I guess used to advertise a lot during sporting events. Canton reeked of throwback garments, like the mothballed yellow slacks I found in my father's closet after he died.

Maybe it was because I came to football in the seventies, but that's what Canton conjured for me: the NFL in the time of those Miller Lite ads of the "Hey, you're Boog Powell" era. When men were men and concussions were "dings" and only Broadway Joe was allowed gender ambiguity. "My wife still wears panty hose because of Joe Namath," Canton mayor Thomas Bernabei informed the banquet-goers, by way of welcoming us.

Paul Anka was in the banquet room, too, because of course Paul Anka was in the banquet room—an actual throwback lounge act (like Haggar, who knew he was still in business?). He performed a version of "My Way" with verses fashioned into rhyming ditties for each new inductee. I saw a few of the Gold Jackets stifling chuckles. Anka wore a three-piece vested suit and really should have been smoking Merits.

Goodell spoke briefly and was treated mildly by the crowd, except for a few scattered jeers (allaying some concern from Park Ave that Goodell might actually hear boos from the "football-loving people" of Canton, as close as a commissioner ever comes to a home-field advantage). Speakers who acknowledged Goodell spoke of him with a hint of pity, as if they were talking about a wounded horse. "The majority of executives and players appreciate you," retiring PR czar Joe Browne reassured Goodell, turning to him on the dais.

Hall of Fame president David Baker welcomed the returning Gold Jackets back to "this city of excellence." "The most inspiring place on earth," he called Canton. Baker, who towers six feet nine inches and weighs four hundred pounds, has a taste for bright white suits that make him resemble a cartoon polar bear. He is an affable behemoth of bullshit—which I don't mean to be disparaging, necessarily, because you'd want a true believer presiding at the temple, right? Baker fits this bill, if not his suit.

"There is a special bond between football and America," proselytized Baker, the former commissioner of the Arena Football League. Baker referred to the Hall as "the ecumenical church of football" and himself as "the Knights Templar of the holy game of football." Like Baker, the Hall of Fame lays it on thick with the "excellence, excellence, excellence" message. Its mission statement— displayed conspicuously—is relentless: Honor the Heroes of the Game, it says on banners and signs. "Preserve its history. Promote its values. Celebrate excellence EVERYWHERE." ALL CAPS is the official style.

Implied, also, is an unspoken mission of the Pro Football Hall of Fame: to keep certain subjects off-limits.

Unlike baseball, football's Legion of Honor does not discriminate for bad behavior. Shoeless Joe Jackson and Barry Bonds can be banned from Cooperstown, but they would be welcomed in Canton if they played football. Gold Jackets can be stained but still worn.

The punishing Charger linebacker Junior Seau was enshrined in the Hall of Fame the previous summer, three years after he committed suicide at forty-three with a CTE-addled brain. His surviving daughter, Sydney, planned to deliver a speech about her father at his induction ceremony, in keeping with his dying wishes. But the Hall did not allow it, citing a recent policy forbidding speeches on behalf of dead members. Instead, the Hall planned to show a video highlighting the copious excellence of Seau's career, but leaving out the grief that came after. There would be no mention of Seau's head trauma, suicide, or (certainly not) the wrongful death lawsuit that his family had filed against the NFL. "Our mission is to honor the heroes of the game, and Junior is a hero of the game," Baker explained to the **New York Times**. "We're going to celebrate his life, not the death and other issues."

The finessing of "other issues" during En-shrinement Weekend makes for many elephants in many rooms. Denial is practiced aggressively. Checkered histories hide in plain view.

Still, there was part of me that appreciated this, the idea that on-field excellence would be the only measure of judgment here, consistent with the spirit of respite. Would the busts of Unitas and Lombardi shun the bust of, say, O. J. Simpson after hours? It would seem wrong if they did.

As the Gold Jacket Dinner dishes were cleared, the Class of 2016 was called to the Pigskin Torah to receive their sacred garments. Brett Favre was the exalted name of the group. Proper testament to his excellence was paid in an inspiring video tribute. But there was not, to be sure, anything about his painkiller addiction, his concussions, or the unwelcome penis selfies he was caught sending to a female reporter, among "other issues" that pocked his career. No mention, either, of the shooting in Philadelphia that inductee Marvin Harrison, Peyton Manning's favorite receiver in Indianapolis, was caught up in in 2008 (Harrison was not charged); or the gambling fraud scandal that earned five-time Super Bowl winner Eddie DeBartolo a one-year ban from the league and eventually cost him control of the 49ers, which he had owned for twenty-three years.

The new class received their proper Gold Jacket due and welcome "home" hugs from their new brothers in immortality. Well, not **all**, because Kenny ("the Snake") Stabler—dazzling Raiders quarterback of my youth—had passed away from a world of suffering the previous summer. This was a few months before Stabler was diagnosed, posthumously, with CTE and voted (also posthumously) into Canton. Immortality loses even more luster when you die too young.

Stabler was the Brett Favre of his era, a southpaw model of the scrambling free spirited good ol' boy who was thrilling to watch. The Snake was synonymous with the outlaw Raider teams of the 1970s. "A perfect marriage between quarterback and team" is how his special video described Stabler and the Raiders. (There was apparently some strain on the marriage, however, evidenced by the bizarre absence of any Raider gear in Stabler's Hall of Fame display; instead there was an AFC Pro Bowl uniform, a game ball, and Stabler's helmet from the New Orleans Saints, for whom he played a forgettable nineteen games at the tail end of his career.)

By 10:30 p.m., the Gold Jacket Dinner was officially dragging. It was time to bid good night to

Miss Canton and the Enshrinement Queen and flee the Civic Center. One can only celebrate so much excellence in a single evening, even with all the commercial breaks to run up the score (or ad revenue) for the NFL Network. I was also famished, having received neither Gold Jacket nor dinner at the Gold Jacket Dinner, and ready to brave the fine dining void of Canton, Ohio, late on a Thursday night.

I wound up at the bar at the McKinley Grand Hotel, called Thorpe's. Rich Eisen himself walked in and took a seat across the bar. He ordered vodka on the rocks and started bitching to the person he was sitting with about the length of the dinner he had just presided over. His companion, as it turned out, was his NFL Network colleague Marshall Faulk, the Hall of Fame running back. Like seemingly half of all living and sentient Gold Jackets, Faulk is on the payroll of either NFL Network, ESPN, or some other of the Shield's **valued broadcast partners**.

I introduced myself to Eisen, the only NFL Network employee who has his own PR guy (I know this because I'd tried to reach him previously through official channels). As with Adam Schefter, Eisen was another University of Michigan alumnus. We bonded over Ann Arbor and Michigan football for a few minutes until another Hall of Famer, Warren Sapp, entered the bar and made a beeline for Faulk, Eisen, and, by proximity, me.

Sapp, a handful of a defensive tackle for the Buccaneers and Raiders, had a career checkered with "other issues" as well. He had also been part of the NFL Network's full-employment program for Gold Jackets until he was dismissed the previous year following his arrest on suspicion of soliciting a prostitute and two counts of assault. (Unlike the Hall of Fame, the NFL Network does enforce standards of conduct. Charges against Sapp were eventually dismissed. Faulk was eventually dumped by the network, too, in his case over sexual harassment complaints.) As Sapp joined our scrum, wearing a University of Miami polo shirt, he and Eisen engaged in the following dialogue:

SAPP (pointing at Eisen): "Dude!"

EISEN (pointing at Sapp): "Dude!"

SAPP (shaking head and pointing back): "Dude?"

EISEN (nodding affirmatively): "Dude!"

Faulk and I tried to follow this battle of ideas back-and-forth, which probably looked like a pair of dogs watching a Ping-Pong match. It all seemed to be leading nowhere, except a logical place to call it a night.

17.

"START BLOW-DRYING
TEDDY KOPPEL'S HAIR
'CAUSE THIS ONE'S DONE"

August 5, 2016

Friday dawned, and I made my first visit to the Hall of Fame proper, at least as a fan or nominal "sportswriter." Technically I'd been here once before, but as a political reporter. Future vice president and lifelong Steeler fan Joe Biden had stopped in for a photo op a few weeks before the 2008 election. Our press pooler on that day was Perry Bacon, a burly African American reporter who was working for the **Washington Post**. "You look like you played some, man," Biden said. Bacon told him that he in fact had never played football. Biden then jabbed Bacon in the chest, which he apparently judged too soft. "You need to work on your pecs," the running mate said. Canton makes for such freakish associations, or maybe it's just Biden who does.

The main Hall of Fame museum is a round stone structure with a cone-headed top. From the outside, it resembles a giant orange-juice squeezer. Inside, it is a smaller and more intimate affair, a short walk between the various exhibits, theaters, galleries of busts, and a large gift shop, which was my first stop. A TV near the checkout counter played ESPN, which at that moment featured Tom Brady speaking for the first time that summer after observing a media lockdown through training camp. These were his first public words since a panel of appeals judges reversed a lower-court decision and sided with the NFL in ruling that Brady must serve his four-game Deflategate suspension after all. Brady, who a few weeks earlier announced on his Facebook page that he would not appeal the decision any further, was his usual insipid self before the microphones. Actually, he might have been even worse than before, although it hardly stopped the Court of Foxborough from hanging on the quarterback's every word like he was Socrates in Athens.

"I tried to come out here and just focus on what I need to do to get better and help our team," Brady said. "I'll be excited to be back when I'm back, and I'll be cheering our team on, hoping they can go out and win every game." Commenting from the ESPN studio, former Patriot teammate Damien Woody described Brady's remarks as "emotional." The only emotion it stirred in me was boredom.

Back to live action in the gift shop, I turned around and found myself face-to-belly with a mountainous former player. His face I could not recognize, only his Gold Jacket. "Who's that?" I whispered to the guy next to the hulk—perhaps the most commonly uttered question of the weekend, especially around anonymous old linemen. It turned out to be Walter Jones, the mainstay offensive tackle of the Seahawks and Hall of Fame Class of 2014. He was shopping for a white shirt to wear to the Hall of Fame parade through Canton the next morning. I asked Jones if Gold Jackets had to pay for stuff in the gift shop (I always try to get smarter, no matter where I am). He replied that a Hall of Famer is given gift cards in exchange for signing autographs.

There was something affecting about being at the Hall of Fame when so many Gold Jackets were "home." I watched a film about the previous Super Bowl, in all of the game's high-definition action. It was one of those full-sensory theaters where you could experience the crunch and acrobatics of the field and hear the coaches' amped-up pep talks and, for a few seconds, feel like you could run through a wall yourself. No one creates reality distortion like the NFL, and I admit to being a total sucker for this stuff.

And then I walked out of the darkened theater and was confronted—without breaking stride—with a couple of Hall of Famers walking slowly down a hallway. Steve Young, the once fleet and nimble 49ers quarterback, nearly veered into me. He wore a Gold Jacket and a blank expression. I don't want to read too much into one split-second visage but my mind jumped to some of the more harrowing concussion sequences I'd ever witnessed on TV, both involving late-career Steve Young.

One came in 1997, courtesy of a sack from the aforementioned Warren Sapp (with follow-up knee-to-the-head by Sapp's Buccaneers teammate Hardy Nickerson). Another came two years later, with Young getting pulverized on an unblocked safety blitz by future Hall of Famer Aeneas Williams, of Arizona, leaving Young motionless on his side, as if he were suddenly asleep. That sack—resulting in his second concussion in three weeks—would be the last play of Young's career.

Young was one of the handful of Gold Jackets that the Hall of Fame offered up to speak to the media that afternoon. We were summoned to a room at McKinley High School, a short walk from the main museum, past an overhanging sign touting the Hall's mission statement (again), another declaration of OUR VALUES (INTEGRITY listed twice), and a massive photo collage of the Class of 2016 (captioned with another CELEBRATE EXCELLENCE EVERYWHERE).

Unfortunately, Young was a no-show at the media meat market, the stated reason being that he was "not feeling well." A dozen other Hall of Famers held court at stations across the room, including most of the new class. Demand upon them varied: Orlando Pace, the stud offensive tackle for the Rams, was pretty much left alone, consistent with the unsung position he played and the now-abandoned NFL city—St. Louis—he played in.

Brett Favre, not surprisingly, was swarmed. I could barely get within fifteen feet of him, but close enough to hear the Gunslinger parry a series of admiring queries from the Pigskin Pravda. "What made you Brett Favre?" was one of the first questions, which turned out to be representative of the pointed grilling he would not be receiving from the Fourth Estate. "I was watching some old highlights of myself, and I was actually pretty good," Favre said.

"What made you Brett Favre?" the reporter tried again.

"Arm strength?" Favre said, shrugging, as if he were taking a wild guess.

I always found Favre, whose playing career ended in 2010 after a few stutter-step retirements, to be a wildly compelling figure. He was a self-fashioned bumpkin prone to big rolls of the dice, big plays, and big mistakes at the worst possible late-game moments. You never knew what you were going to get with the audacious Favre, except for a high-wire act, for better or worse. He was the banged-up opposite of the hypersmooth control freak of a Brady.

Seeing Favre at close range, it occurred to me that I'd always had a bit of a fan-crush on the guy. He inhabited his dumb-jock charisma with a mischievous exuberance. If I stepped back I'd probably have to concede that Favre cut a far more winning and accessible personality than my master of mistake-free football and optimized living, Mr. TB12 himself. Favre was a mess, who put his teams—and their fans—through emotional hell rides. If I was being objective, I'd probably prefer Favre's flawed humanity on most days to Brady's cool strut on the edge of hubris. But I'm not being objective.

Favre, who wore a blue polo shirt and long khaki shorts, was asked how he would spend his first day as a Hall of Famer back home in his native Mississippi. "Probably cut grass on my front lawn with my gold jacket on, I don't know," he said. Favre added that he had heard Mississippi had more football Hall of Famers than any other state. They do, a reporter confirmed, "per capita."

"I don't know what that means, but it sounds good to me," said Favre.

After a few minutes of Favre, I made my way around the Gold Jacket spin room. At this point in the weekend, I was officially burned out on the feel-good parade and determined to at least drizzle on it. I made a point of asking the Gold Jackets about the state of their health. I figured it would make for a less comfortable line of questioning.

But most of the answers were thoughtful and even carried a whiff of relief, as if the Hall of Famers welcomed the chance to pierce the propaganda veil. "I have aches and pains all over the old body," Dermontti Dawson, the longtime center for the Steelers, told me. He was standing off in a corner, and I had him pretty much to myself, which made it easier to converse on these more delicate issues. "As players, we all know we're going to have residual effects," Dawson said. He listed a few of his recent ones: he had his rotator cuff repaired the previous September, he was about to have his other shoulder replaced, he had bad carpal tunnel in both hands. "But it is normal," Dawson said. "We played a high-impact game. You know there will be fallout. It may not be immediate, but there will be fallout." Another reporter walked over, listened for a bit and chimed in: "Dermontti, tell me about your induction, your memories of that special day?"

Dawson dutifully shared his memories. But then he turned back to me, and I asked if he had he seen **Concussion**.

"Oh yeah, I cried through it," said Dawson, who played with some of the players featured in the film, including its most tragic protagonist,

Mike Webster, whom he would succeed as the Steelers' center. "I just had tears coming out of my eyes. And I started worrying about myself, what's going to happen to me down the road." Another reporter tried to ask Dawson about "what it meant" for him to "come home" to Canton. But Dawson talked over him, something I appreciated. He kept looking at me. I asked Dawson if he had felt any neurological effects from his career.

"Yeah, I've had some short-term memory problems," Dawson said. "And sometimes I think too much. I can't shut my mind off. I can't sleep too well, just general stuff like that." He said he has tried to combat damage to his brain by "keeping my mind active," doing puzzles and playing brain games that he has on his iPad. "I try to do that, read all the time," Dawson said. "But you never know what's going to happen to you down the road."

An official-looking guy in a suit walked over, maybe sensing danger as if a trip wire had been activated (keyword: "Concussion").

I moved on to another scrum, this one anchored by Dawson's former teammate the defensive end Kevin Greene. Greene, a holy terror of a pass rusher, played fifteen years in the NFL and was part of the 2016 Hall of Fame class. Greene's lawless blond mane that once flew out the back of his helmet was now cropped and neat. But with bulging forearms and a white goatee, he retained

an aura of menace about him, like an aging professional wrestler. Even at fifty-four, Greene's still-
crazed eyes were not what you'd want staring at
you across a neutral zone.

Another Gold Jacket walked by us and set up
shop across the room. Jim Kelly! I loved Jim Kelly,
the hard-bitten quarterback who led the Buffalo
Bills to four Super Bowls in the early 1990s, all
losses. Buffalo's glory years coincided with some
awful Patriots teams, so it was never enough of a
fair fight to even bother resenting the Bills. I had
only positive associations with Kelly, the brash or-
chestrator of the Bills' unrelenting no-huddle offense. Their Super Bowl futility also lent them a
lovable loser's cachet.

Kelly has suffered through a brutal run of
hardship after his retirement in 1997. His son
Hunter was born with Krabbe disease, a rare neurological disorder that resulted in his death at the
age of eight. "It's been said that the trademark of
my career was toughness," Kelly said in his Hall
of Fame induction speech in 2002, when Hunter
was five. "The toughest person I ever met in my
life was my hero, my soldier, my son, Hunter. I
love you buddy." Kelly, who has dedicated much
of his post-playing life to a Krabbe disease advo-
cacy group he and his wife established in Hunter's
honor, was diagnosed with cancer of the upper
jaw in 2013. Kelly endured surgeries, chemo, radiation, and all manner of indignity, only to have

the cancer return in 2014. Two months after Kelly was declared cancer-free for a second time, he was additionally diagnosed with MRSA (staph infection). (In March 2018, Kelly announced his cancer had returned, and he was being treated once again.)

It felt almost silly to ask Kelly about something as relatively pedestrian to an ex–football player as brain health. He spoke of "getting dinged" with a kind of neutral remove. The new rule changes and concussion protocols were "just kind of how the game has evolved," he said, not taking a position on them either way. Kelly was part of a generation of mobile quarterbacks, along with Favre, Young, Warren Moon, and Troy Aikman, who enjoyed peak seasons during the 1990s. They were all bold and mobile enough to have each suffered and played through multiple concussions. To varying degrees, each had spoken with concern if not regret about the impact the game had had on their cognitive health. Aikman and Favre have both said they would hesitate to let their hypothetical sons play football. Not Kelly. "If my son was still alive today, I would not hold him back from playing," he said. He spoke of his own dings with an element of comic nostalgia, like he was reliving a wild old time.

"I remember playing the New Orleans Saints one time, and I'm laying on the turf, and the whole dome is spinning." Kelly laughs and a few of the reporters giggled along with him. He says that he could not get his eyes to focus and had to come out of the game for a while but eventually came back in.

"And I remember the Super Bowl against the Washington Redskins," Kelly kept going. "I think I played the whole last quarter with a concussion." He even threw a couple of postconcussive touchdown passes. "So maybe they should have hit me a little earlier, I'd have done better," Kelly said to more laughter.

One of the reporters asked Kelly to give his definition of a ding. "Is what happened in New Orleans a 'ding'?" he said.

"Yeah, that was minor," Kelly said, smiling. He seemed to notice that the group of media around him had grown, and that not everyone was smiling back at him. "Well, of course I played back when that was considered minor," he said. "These days, I might have not gone back in that football game." He said he agreed "as a parent" with the new vigilance about head safety. Another reporter asked when Kelly learned he had suffered a concussion in the Super Bowl against Washington. "After the game, when I had no clue where I was at," Kelly said, laughing again.

I heard Kelly's tone as more happy-go-lucky than cavalier. He had been through worse and should be free to enjoy his memories of less burdened times—a retroactive respite. By now, though, the only laughter coming back at Kelly was of the nervous variety, especially after he recalled being disoriented after the Redskins Super Bowl, not knowing where his family was or why he had gone back to the team hotel. "To make a long story short, it's no fun," Kelly said, "but you know what?"

Before he could conclude his summation, a reporter asked whether Kelly had any memory today of that fourth quarter of the Super Bowl. "No," he said. "I mean I know we lost." At this point, a referee inserted himself, a league or Hall of Fame official. "Last question," the man announced. This was the PR equivalent of placing a too-talkative former player into the concussion protocol.

The media fair broke up and the Gold Jackets scattered. I followed Brett Favre out a back exit and through a darkened auditorium. Favre moved with something between a swagger and a limp. He had an induction speech to prepare and needed to rest up. "I'm tired," he said.

Appendix: The Hall of Fame Game

The Hall of Fame Game is an appendage tacked on to an already-gratuitous body of preseason games. Think of a benign growth upon the appendix—something extraneous upon the extraneous. This year's cysts were the Packers and Colts.

The only Hall of Fame Game that I have any memory of involved the Patriots, in 2000, against the 49ers. It was the first game that Belichick coached for New England, and the first pro game ever played by the rookie quarterback from Michigan, Tom Brady.

Also debuting that night in the ABC booth was Dennis Miller, the verbose comedian whose brief stint as a **Monday Night Football** commentator was, in my lonely view, a guilty pleasure. Miller approached the Hall of Fame contest with perfectly appropriate sarcasm. "If there's anybody in this stadium more pumped up than me they wouldn't pass the league's standardized drug test," Miller told his highly amused broadcast partner, Al Michaels.

As that first Brady-Belichick game wound down, with the Pats beating the 49ers 20–0, Miller tried to adopt his own version of Dandy Don Meredith's "Turn out the lights, the party's over" tagline to signal that the result was sealed. "Start blow-drying Teddy Koppel's hair," Miller said to conclude his maiden broadcast, "'cause this one's done."

I admit, I giggled at this, which partly explains why I'm not in the business of making decisions about TV careers. Miller was let go after two seasons on **MNF**. But it's something, at least, that I still remember these lines—and who even remembers **anything** about a Hall of Fame Game, much less seventeen years later?

Actually, people might remember this year's Hall of Fame Game for the same reason that you only think about your appendix when something goes wrong, i.e., appendicitis. This was appendicitis:

CANTON, Ohio
August 7, 2016

Sunday night's Hall of Fame Game between the Green Bay Packers and Indianapolis Colts was cancelled because of poor field conditions.

Yes, this happened. "I thought it was a joke at first, honestly," Colts quarterback Andrew Luck said. It was not. Apparently the paint used to make the big Hall of Fame logo in the middle of the field and in the end zones had hardened, making the surfaces at once slippery and cement-like. The field was "kind of congealing and rubberized," David Baker said, and efforts to fix the problem were not satisfactory.

Fans would receive refunds, Baker reassured all the football-loving people who had made the hike to Canton and went home hungry.

18.

AMERICAN CARNAGE

September 2016

I've heard players say that after the first few days
of training camp, about 90 percent of them want
to retire. Few do, obviously, but it's easy to appreciate why these would be prime days for players
to question whether their football furnaces still
burned. They are being put through sadistic conditioning drills, subjected to endless meetings, and
standing around for hours in peak heat. They become reacquainted with football's everyday pain.

If baseball's spring training is mythologized
as a ritual of rebirth (hope springing eternal and
such), NFL training camp is a death slog. It,
too, is mythologized, but as a misery saga. Reality shows such as HBO's **Hard Knocks** and
Amazon's **All or Nothing** have a perverse appeal,

like those late-night prison documentaries on the high-numbered cable channels.

Fan readiness can't be measured with scales and stopwatches, or I might have failed my physical at the start of the 2016 season. I was not contemplating retirement or making any protest statements over concussions or greed or, for that matter, Tom Brady being sidelined for four games over nothing. But I had grown weary of the legal, procedural, and moral agonizing that surrounded the game as I journeyed deeper in. I could have used a longer off-season.

It was also a busy fall in my day job. I had a presidential campaign to cover—a respite from the respite, which in fact was not at all a respite since the 2016 general election was every bit as scary and dispiriting as the NFL was on its worst day. My plan was to skip most of the NFL regular season and tune back in after Thanksgiving. This was not a rigid vow. There would be exceptions, and obviously the NFL (like the presidential campaign) could be impossible to avoid. I watched the Kickoff Game on TV, a Super Bowl rematch between the Broncos and the Panthers. It featured the reigning MVP, Cam Newton, getting pounded silly throughout the game by Bronco defenders— at least four helmet-to-helmet shots as tallied by reporters, but it seemed like more from my view on the couch. The Broncos were not assessed a single penalty for any of them. Newton was not checked for any concussion symptoms. The NFL's supposedly enhanced concussion policy appeared, shall we say, lacking. Denver won the game 21–20 on a missed last-second field goal. Newton was asked afterward about his battering. "It's not fun to get hit in the head," he concluded. That needs to be the title of somebody's memoir.

This seemed to be a good time for me to "step away from the game" for a while. Or "take a knee," as 49ers quarterback Colin Kaepernick had started doing while "The Star-Spangled Banner" played before preseason games. This was something new and incendiary, especially for the patriotic domain of football. The NFL is the most conservative, Republican, and nationalistic of the major sports leagues, despite the socialist profit-sharing agreement that the billionaire owners enter into. Kaepernick, who is of mixed race, said he was kneeling to protest injustice against African Americans and other minorities, namely by police. More than 83 percent of NFL fans are white, according to a Reuters report citing a 2007 study, and fans are 20 percent more likely to be Republicans than Democrats. Nearly 70 percent of the players, meanwhile, are black, according to data from the Institute for Diversity and Ethics in Sport. NFL owners, with a few exceptions, lean Republican; several of them donated to Trump's campaign, and some donated $1 million apiece to his inauguration committee.

Kaepernick, who led the 49ers to the Super Bowl in 2013, had seen his play decline since. He lost his starting position to the submediocre Blaine Gabbert and then went on to become the most conspicuous backup quarterback in NFL history. Kaepernick was joined in his protests by about a dozen other players around the league, who would either take knees or raise their fists during the anthem. He was photographed kneeling for the cover of **Time** magazine ("The Perilous Fight"), drew a slew of death threats, and was called all sorts of bad things in the press by anonymous owners and league executives. ("I don't want him anywhere near my team," one front office executive told **Bleacher Report**'s Mike Freeman. "He's a traitor.") Kaepernick was also blamed for a hiccup in the NFL's TV ratings—about an 11 percent drop over the first half of the season—though the saturation coverage of the election was cited as a bigger factor. Neither saga was mutually exclusive; Kaepernick and football, Donald Trump and Hillary Clinton all occupied distinct corners in the seething cultural combat zone of 2016.

FOOTBALL HAD BECOME ITS OWN SPRAWLING mess of a cause célèbre, another battleground in the culture wars that seemed to be breaking out everywhere. The game is "the last bastion of hope for toughness in America in men," said University of Michigan coach Jim Harbaugh (John's brother), defending football to HBO's Andrea Kremer, and it was only a matter of seconds before someone looked askance. Studio host Bryant Gumbel called the quote "not exactly a quote for the Age of Enlightenment," which set off Rush Limbaugh in the predictable direction ("Gumbel epitomizes the modern day cultural left"). Whether or not they represent a silent majority, a vocal and substantial population today will dismiss any criticism of football as an elitist affront to their selfhood. "People that say, 'I won't let my son play [football]' are fools," former Arizona coach Bruce Arians told Peter King. "We have this fear of concussion that is real, but not all of those statistics, I think, can prove anything."

The coach's words carry a whiff of persecution. Not just of the sport, but of the ethic and culture that has grown around it—something conservative and essential to American traditions. "This makes football akin to the Confederate Flag, or Christmas decorations in public spaces or taxpayer supported art depicting Jesus in a tank of urine," wrote Chuck Klosterman in his essay "Sudden Death (Over Time)." Football, he continued, "becomes intractable precisely because so many people want to see it eliminated."

Trump's campaign was predicated on many of the cultural, generational, and demographic tensions that football had incubated for years.

Football had become overregulated and sissified, Trump's criticism boiled down to.

Football's biggest critics, they said, were the same bubble-world liberals in the media, ivory-tower scientists (who overplay the dangers of concussions), and soft coastal suits who never played the game—and never met a Trump voter.

IT WAS ONLY A MATTER OF TIME BEFORE TRUMP served up Kaepernick, the vegan quarterback, as red meat to his base. Kaepernick was a Trumpian villain straight out of Central Casting—big 'fro, swarthy skin, and a San Francisco jersey. If Kaepernick did not exist, some ingenious Russian troll-bot would invent him. "The NFL is way down in their ratings," Trump taunted the league at a campaign rally in Greeley, Colorado, a week before the election. He said that politics was "a much rougher game than football" and also more exciting. "We've taken a lot of people away from the NFL," Trump boasted. "And the other reason"— he paused—"is Kaepernick! Kaepernick!"

Cries of displeasure, cued: **"Booooo!" "Traitor!" "U.S.A., U.S.A.!"**

Trump had mentioned Kaepernick before, after he first started kneeling. "Maybe he should find a country that works better for him," Trump said of Kaepernick to a conservative radio host in Seattle. "Let him try. It won't happen." It was only a matter of time before Trump-style politics crashed into the NFL coliseum.

Allegiance to sports team and political tribe had become two of our culture's strongest identity markers. You hear the word "fan" used interchangeably with "diehard"—as in "faith dies hard."

Trump's business model was predicated on drawing faith from willing fans at the expense of easy foils. Winning itself was the highest imperative he could offer. There was no call to the broader American community, its diversity or better angels; just the notion that he himself is a winner. America no longer won, so Trump—he alone—was what the country needed. His pitch was akin to a team hiring a new coach because he had "won everywhere he's ever been."

As with any good salesman, Trump could tell a simple, or simplistic, story. His story was that our government was occupied by a corrupt political "establishment"; we had neglected our borders, indulged political correctness, and made our country less than great. To Trump, the NFL represented its own kind of establishment. It was an issue that was personal to him as someone who had tried and failed for decades to join its ranks. It, too, was stagnant, increasingly delicate, and overtolerant of political correctness, as Kaepernick embodied.

The NFL was reality TV, like Trump; it operated on a star system, as Trump's campaign did (himself). Insomuch as politics had referees—the mainstream media, rules of decorum, ethical norms—they were ripe for flouting and abuse. Trump tipped politics onto a level of unregulated personal fouls. Who knew where the story would lead and who would win? That's the reality TV part, and the Master Don of the genre dominated the campaign.

Winning **is** everything, isn't it? And the crowd went nuts in both directions as another loser—the scrawny Kaepernick in this case, playing for the 2–14 49ers—was carted off, never (as of this writing) to play a down in the NFL again.

AS IT HAPPENED, A FEW MONTHS AFTER I WROTE about Brady I embarked on a profile of Trump. His political ascendance had mirrored my time with the NFL, and there were obvious parallels between the circuses. Both offered showcases for American carnage, hubris, and mythmaking. It made sense that America's chief crossover between reality TV and politics, Trump, would be obsessed with pro football.

Trump had wanted into the NFL Membership for years, even though his earlier foray into football with the USFL's New Jersey Generals in the 1980s met with a disastrous end. The USFL folded in 1986 and Trump received heavy blame for, among other things, paying exorbitant salaries to lure name players such as Herschel Walker and Doug Flutie to the Generals, even though his counterparts would bankrupt themselves if they tried to keep pace. Trump was also the driving force behind the league's moving its games from spring to fall to compete directly with the NFL. From the start, Trump's motive with the USFL was to get himself into the NFL, either through a merger or by making the Generals so enticing that the big boys could not refuse him. Trump in 1984 finagled a meeting with NFL commissioner Pete Rozelle at the Pierre Hotel in New York in which he told Rozelle he would do whatever it took to get into the league. Rozelle was not impressed, according to an account of the meeting by Jeff Pearlman, author of an upcoming book on the USFL. "They just saw him as this scumbag huckster," Pearlman said of Trump. "He was this New York, fast-talking, kind of con man."

The NFL had long factored in Trump's well-documented Wannabe Complex: his craving for acceptance from the real billionaires and real tough guys whose ranks he desperately wanted to join. His most recent play for entry came in 2014, when he attempted to buy the Buffalo Bills, a franchise that was most definitely not tired of winning. No one thought Trump was serious. They figured it was just another one of his publicity stunts, like running for president, something that would never (ahem) amount to anything. Trump did not come close to passing muster with the Membership. He was, for starters, not considered sufficiently solvent or transparent to proffer a serious bid. Football owners, as it turns out, get a much closer look at a candidate's finances than electorates do.

The Bills wound up selling to the Pennsylvania shale fracking magnates Terry and Kim Pegula, for $1.4 billion. This was disappointing to Trump, who was in fact very serious about wanting the Bills, and was reportedly one of the three serious candidates for the team (the third was a Toronto-based investor group that included Jon Bon Jovi). Trump became upset with Kraft, his longtime friend, wishing that Kraft had done more to grease his entry with the Membership board. It created a rift between the two that lasted until the summer of 2016, when Kraft approached Ivanka Trump in Aspen and told her how much he missed Donald, who had recently become the newly minted Republican presidential nominee.

As for the Bills, Trump took the loss with his customary grace and magnanimity. He assured fans via Twitter that he had dodged calamity. "Wow, @nfl ratings are down big league," he wrote shortly after the Pegulas bought the team. "Glad I didn't get the Bills." This feeling was quite mutual and considerably more sincere coming back from the league. But Trump, as he does, would not let the matter go. "Even though I refused to pay a ridiculous price for the Buffalo Bills, I would have produced a winner," he tweeted a few days later. (These were more innocent times, before DJT's tweets were poking at nuclear-armed madmen.)

In the end, a seat at the NFL Membership table is so exclusive that even the White House itself has become a consolation prize. By no means, though, was Trump done with the NFL.

Trump knew I had profiled Brady earlier, and he would not shut up about how he and the handsome quarterback were special friends. They initially met in 2002 after Brady led the Patriots to their first Super Bowl win and Trump enlisted him to judge the Miss Universe Pageant in Gary, Indiana. "If one thing stands out about Tom Brady," Trump told **Sports Illustrated** at the time, it "is that he loves those women. And guess what? They love him, too." Trump even tried to offer up Ivanka to Brady at the pageant. "I think he and Ivanka would make a great combination," Trump told Howard Stern. The mind recoils: in a parallel universe, Brady could now be filling the powerful son-in-law role in the West Wing, quarterbacking Middle East peace talks.

Donny and Tommy golfed together a bunch of times over the years. Trump would call Brady after his games, and sometimes, if the call came in when Brady was driving home from the stadium, he would put Trump on the speaker phone for the other passengers to hear—because it's such a kick to have the actual voice of Donald Trump coming over the phone; and it was for Trump, too, to have Brady's on the line (also on the speaker). This is one of these mutually fetishistic dances that the Very Famous engage in. What's the use of having shiny friends if you can't show them off?

Trump showed me the Patriots helmet and autographed Brady football next to his desk at Trump Tower. He kept bringing up Deflategate, which he also called a "witch hunt" and seemed more interested in discussing than many of the policy issues that were coming up in the campaign. "It's so ridiculous what they're doing to him," Trump said of Brady, mentioning again that he had just spoken to Tom.

"He said: 'Mr. Trump'—he calls me Mr. Trump, which he shouldn't, because we play golf all the time. Anyway, he says: 'Mr. Trump—Donald,' he doesn't even know what the fuck to call me. It's the craziest thing. He's a friend of mine. **A really good friend of mine**."

Standing across the room was the not-yet-famous Hope Hicks, Trump's ever-present campaign press aide and the future White House communications director. Her father, Paul Hicks, was then the top flack (sorry, **executive vice president for communications and public affairs**) at the NFL. But Hope happened to mention that he had just resigned that morning. "You're kidding, what happened?" Trump asked her. "It was just too much, right?" Trump replied (to his own question). "He probably thought, 'You people are crazy.'" Hope shrugged, nodded. A few weeks later, the future president was showing me around Trump National Golf Club in Rancho Palos Verdes, California. We were accompanied by Damon Winter, a **Times** photographer who had, a few months earlier, photographed Brady for the earlier profile. At one point, as Trump showed me around his 7,242-yard golf paradise on the Pacific, he looked over at Winter. "Who's got a better body, me or Tom Brady?" he asked. No answer from Winter that I recall.

Trump kept urging me to call Brady and ask him about his "great friendship with Trump." Brady would say great things, no doubt. "Ask him, 'How is Trump as a golfer?'"

After Trump kept insisting, I finally reached out to Brady, fully expecting a polite stiff-arm from the quarterback. "I really have no interest in political talk right now," Brady confirmed promptly. "I have learned way too much about politics the last seven months."

19.

PATRIOTISM

November 2016

I tried to be judicious in reaching out to Brady. It would be wrong to abuse the privilege. And I would be loath to ever impose on the Almighty, especially for frivolous reasons (only life-altering ones, as when Brady won another Super Bowl and I just **needed** to congratulate him).

Every few months, though, I would send Brady an email to tell him how this project was progressing. Inevitably my emails to TB would come with an appeal: could we talk again? I had many more questions, I would say, and was curious to get his perspective on all that had transpired since we'd last spoken. I was eager to hear more about the TB12 method that he was continuing to ride to "peak performance" on the field and a fledgling lifestyle empire off it. I really didn't mean the third part: caring about TB12—"the method," "the lifestyle," "pliability," and all that whatnot. To the extent I did, I figured the results spoke for themselves. TB12 plainly worked for Tom Brady and, by extension, for all of us who rooted for his success on the field: Robert Kraft and all of his heirs, Timmy from Danvers on the car phone, all of Brady's "owners" on DraftKings, bettors in Vegas, and abettors in Foxborough.

If I was an aging NFL quarterback intent on "sustained peak performance," maybe I would care more about "the method" and "the lifestyle." However: I am not. I am a middle-aged print hack and retired high school athlete bent on "decent performance." I felt little need to delve deeper into the Tao of TB12 beyond the tutorial Brady (and Guerrero) provided me a few years back.

If "Gods do not answer letters," as John Updike once wrote about Ted Williams, they do reply to emails—or at least Brady does. He was always responsive and would typically write back within a day. He was thoughtful, polite, and, as far as agreeing to meet again, graciously noncommittal. He was always busy, he would say, believably. He was tied up with commitments in addition to his work and his family. He never closed the door all the way. It might have just been his way of being nice, but at least Brady's stiff-arms were more of

the "not now" variety rather than a simple definitive "no."

I was in touch with enough people in Brady's
circle to get updates on his nonfootball life.
His mother, Galynn, had been diagnosed with
two forms of cancer in the space of a year, first
smoldering myeloma and then breast cancer. She
underwent a regimen of surgeries, radiation, and
chemotherapy treatments, and her prognosis was
uncertain for much of 2015 and 2016. Before she
was diagnosed, when she first began feeling sick,
Galynn had anguished hard over Deflategate, following every development. "She was as whacked
out as a towel would be when it was wrung dry
by Tommy's situation," Tom Senior told me. Her
illness would make it impossible for the Bradys to
travel to any Patriots games in 2016.

In the midst of Brady's suspension, I sent Tom
an email. "Hope all's well with you and family," I
wrote, "and that you're keeping the Moneymaker
pliable." I asked if TB had any interest in letting
me visit with him during his suspension. Because
I'm such a good friend, and I figured he might
require my support.

Brady replied promptly, thanked and affirmed me. "As you know by now, Pliability is the
way!!!" Brady said (the GOAT likes his exclama-
tion points!!!). "There is no other way," he emphasized. Brady, as I expected, then let me down
gently. "I'm gonna lay low the rest of the year out-

side of my existing obligations as there are A LOT of those," he wrote. "Look forward to seeing you around. Best of luck to you always!"

And "btw" Brady added, he had seen me on TV the previous morning while he was warming up on the treadmill. I was doing some talking head routine on CBS during the presidential campaign—and apparently I had achieved peak pundit performance in the eyes of the Prince of Pliability. "Nice job," Brady said. (**Shit**, I felt like writing back, **I see YOU on TV, too, Tommy**, but that felt too giddy.)

Like so many people, Brady, who had previously expressed great uninterest in politics, could not avoid the Trump-Clinton brawl of 2016. Maybe more to the point, the campaign could not avoid Brady. It began in September 2015 when Trump friend Bob Kraft stuck a Make America Great Again hat in Brady's locker between a canister of Listerine and a tube of deodorant. A reporter spotted the hat and questions ensued. Brady deemed it "amazing" what Trump had accomplished on the campaign to that point. "He obviously appeals to a lot of people," Brady said in an interview on WEEI. "And he's a hell of a lot of fun to play golf with."

Brady's "total focus" on football has always bought him license to be oblivious to the outside world, at least in the "stick to football" contexts where he was called upon to speak (locker-room interviews, his weekly sports radio interviews). But Brady's ability to aw-shucks his way through Trump had limits in light of the intensely divisive feelings Trump was stirring up. Brady seemed to realize this soon enough as the Trump questions kept coming and took on an edgier urgency— to a point where Brady would reflexively take a knee every time someone mentioned Trump's name to him. "Can I just stay out of this debate?" an exasperated Brady said later in the fall after a WEEI host asked him another Trump-related question.

But Trump kept right on dropping Brady's name at every opportunity. He would always tout their "great friendship" and the "great love" he had received in New England due to Brady's "great support." He attributed his victory in the Massachusetts Republican primary to a "Tom Brady effect" (this "effect" did not extend to the general election as Clinton won all six New England states except for a single electoral vote in northern Maine). Bizarrely, Trump's Brady bro boasts were not just restricted to Patriots Country, either. "We love Tom Brady, right?" Trump yelled out at a rally on the Eastern Shore of Maryland, in a room full of Ravens fans who booed loudly.

I couldn't help myself, and emailed news of that episode to Brady. "How to read a room there, Donald," I wrote.

"Funny," Brady replied. "That made my day!"

In addition to Brady, Trump was also not

shy about advertising his "great friendship" with Kraft, or for that matter Belichick. When I wrote about Trump in October 2015, he kept insisting to me that he was a huge fan—meaning that Belichick was a huge fan of **his**, that the coach "really loves me." Everyone just assumes that Belichick is "a really rough guy," Trump said. And maybe he is a really rough guy, he allowed, but there's just something about the Donald that melts the hoodie's heart.

"So I go to the Patriots game last year," Trump told me. "I'm on the sidelines with Kraft. He's got Les Moonves right here. He's got a lot of different people. And Belichick comes over in his Patriots sweatshirt and the hoodie and the whole thing. He hugs me, and he kisses me, and he said: 'I love you. You're the greatest.'"

Yes, that sounds **exactly** like Belichick.

I worried for a second that I might not have hidden my skepticism when Trump told me this. But he did not appear to notice. He sat at his desk in Trump Tower and seemed almost dreamy at this memory, as if the reception he received from Belichick that day had moved him a great deal. "He just feels warmly toward me, Belichick does," Trump said. "Isn't that the craziest thing?"

Well, yes. And I remained dubious. Besides the fact that Belichick strikes no one as a "hugs me, kisses me" type, on or off the sidelines, he had been reputed over the years to be a progressive, at least culturally. He supposedly loved the Grateful Dead, did attend Wesleyan University in Connecticut, and has worked quietly on liberal causes, such as visiting prisons with Hall of Fame running back (and ex-felon) Jim Brown. Brown has praised Belichick's contributions to an organization he established that supports inmates, gang members, and underprivileged children. "He has been face to face with my gangsters in L.A. and in Cleveland," Brown said of Belichick, adding that Belichick's commitment to humanitarian causes placed him on a par with Boston Celtic great Bill Russell as a social activist. Brown described the Patriots coach as "a free-thinker."

As it turned out, Belichick's freethinking did indeed lead him to great affection for Donald Trump. The day before the election, Trump was campaigning in New Hampshire, at a rally in Manchester. When he came to the requisite "I love the New England Patriots and they love me back" part of his speech, Trump added a special enhancement. He had received a "beautiful letter" of support for his campaign—from Coach Belichick.

Again, I was dubious. Did Belichick write "beautiful letters" to celebrity politicians? My suspicion was that either Trump made this up, or, if Belichick did write the letter, the last thing he would have expected—or wanted—was to have Trump read it out loud. It would have dropped

Belichick right into the middle of the most bit-
terly contested presidential campaign in decades,
and right in the middle of the season.

I was wrong, twice. Not only did Belichick
write Trump the letter, Trump apparently called
to ask Belichick if he had his permission to share
its contents at a rally; and Belichick apparently
told Trump that if he planned to do that, he
would go back and write Trump a second letter,
an even more effusive one, that he could then read
at the rally—which he did.

This became an immediate issue in Foxborough.
Belichick was asked about the letter repeatedly in
his weekly press conference. "My comments are
not politically motivated," Belichick said. "I have
a friendship and loyalty to Donald." At the very
least, this confirmed that Belichick had in fact
written these words to Trump: "Congratulations
on a tremendous campaign," he wrote, according to Trump, reading from the letter. Belichick
praised Trump for "coming out beautifully" despite having had to deal with "an unbelievable
slanted and negative media." Trump had proven
himself to be "the ultimate competitive fighter,"
Belichick wrote. "Your leadership is amazing."
The love note went on for a while longer, con-
cluding with the coach expressing his hope that
the next day's election results would "give the opportunity to make America great again."

Amazing, Belichick even spoke in the Trumpian

message lexicon. After a few too many follow-up queries for Belichick's liking (i.e., one), he returned to his own message: increasingly gruff variations on "We're focused on Seattle."

Passions around the 2016 election were stratospherically high, in New England as everywhere. Say what you will about Donald Trump, but there is no question he has been a transformative figure. His campaign, presidency, and shattering of norms have been an unsettling force in America, for better or worse. I know many people who count themselves in the "worse" camp. I am related to many of them, live in a city (D.C.) full of them, and work in a profession that Trump has essentially declared war on (the "unbelievable slanted and negative media," in Belichick's grandiloquence). Also, a whole lot of these people live in New England and root for the Pats and were thrown into a conniption of cognitive dissonance over Trump's full-on (and mutual) embrace of their team.

Trump was always wrapping himself in the Pats flag in some fashion. No football team was more closely associated with a future president, or perhaps any president, at least since Richard Nixon adopted the Washington Redskins as his own and even called occasional plays for coach George Allen. Similar to Trump, the Patriots were a divisive juggernaut that inspired strong feelings. The team represented a sporting ideal of Trump's promise to make "America win so much, you'll be bored of winning." New England had indeed won so much that a lot of America had become, yes, bored of its winning. And no small number of them also believed that the Patriots, like Trump, had achieved their victories through questionable means.

If the Patriots weren't polarizing enough, they now represented a culture war grenade. It worked both ways. People outside of New England who had no reason to hate the team, but who hated Trump, now had a fully formed Evil Empire to root against whose helmets might as well have been emblazoned with MAKE AMERICA GREAT AGAIN. And people who had no reason to support the Patriots, but who loved Trump, could now identify with Brady, Belichick, and Kraft as Patriotic soldiers for their cause.

The dynamic reminded me of the 1980s, during the epic NBA rivalry days of Magic Johnson's Lakers and Larry Bird's Celtics. I was, naturally, a Bird-Boston guy, and in college at the time in Ann Arbor. Being a Celtics fan not only won me the ire of the many fans on campus who rooted for the emerging Detroit Pistons, the Celtics' chief rival in the Eastern Conference; it also made me have to answer for Boston's bitter history of racism, the perception that nothing had changed about the city since the worst days of the busing crisis of the 1970s, and the notion that the Celtics, with their white stars and predominately white roster (ten players on their 1986 championship team), were the unofficial team of White America.

No matter what I said—talking points included the Celts' being the first team with a black player and a black coach—it wouldn't register. My African American friends, especially, hated the Celtics. This even extended to many blacks who lived in Boston. Of the relatively few blacks in my suburban schools in the late seventies and early eighties, a large number rooted for the Dr. J–era Philadelphia 76ers. In ESPN's **30 for 30** documentary about the Celtics–Lakers rivalry, "Best of Enemies," Magic Johnson told of African Americans sidling up to him whenever he played in Boston and declaring themselves to be Laker fans, despite where they'd lived their entire lives.

Similarly, I knew many white people in college, from rural areas of Michigan not close to Detroit, who took Bird's greatness as a validator of white achievement. I remember visiting a friend's cottage on Lake Michigan and watching Game 7 of the 1987 Eastern Conference Finals between the Celtics and Pistons. We were at a small-town bar, about three or four hours from Detroit, no blacks in sight for miles. Everyone in the bar who was paying attention was rooting for the Celtics. When I asked one guy why he wasn't rooting for the home-state Pistons, he discharged a stunning flurry of invective against the city of Detroit and African Americans in general. The Celtics, he believed, had the best chance to defeat the "Tinseltown Niggers" in the finals.

Three decades later, rooting for the Patriots had also become a racially and socially fraught identity. Trump's willingness to inflame so many minority groups and women, his ability to inspire his "silent majority" (the Nixonian term he adopted for his mostly white supporters), and his insistence on shouting out to the Patriots whenever possible made him an unshakable piece of baggage for the team. White nationalists embraced the Patriots as their own. Neo-Klansman Richard Spencer dubbed Brady an "Aryan Avatar" and said the Patriots' winning the Super Bowl would be "a victory for the #AltRight." Spencer also tweeted his approval that the team employed "three white wide receivers" and was "consistently NFL's whitest team."

The latter was not true—the Patriots' makeup of white and African American players has been in line with the league average. Whatever, this was not fun. And as someone who has been an eager apologist for the Patriots over many years— through cheating scandals, a murder trial, and all manner of arrogant behavior—the Trump connection was a bigger drag on the team's image than anything that came before, at least in the (admittedly politicized) circles I traveled in. It was a much hotter button of an issue than Deflategate ever was, back in those days of innocence.

My common response to any anti-Trump fervor that accrued against the Patriots was that fame trumps politics in many cases. "Friendship" becomes different when you're living at a certain sea level of public life. You become part of a select club made up of people who play golf together and attend one another's weddings and funerals. They call to congratulate one another on presidential elections and Super Bowl wins and those types of everyday things. The rest of us could never begin to understand. We should keep our heroes in their lanes and never expect crossover perfection.

But damn if the 2016 campaign did not exhaust and deflate. No one was safe. Football was not safe. The election came and went but never seemed to end.

I spent Election Night in New York performing my talking head duty at CBS and being stunned with all the rest of the media geniuses. I left CBS Studios on Fifty-seventh Street at around 2:30 a.m. and headed back to my hotel on Seventh Avenue. Whom should I spot walking in the other direction but Jets owner Woody Johnson. He was wearing a MAKE AMERICA GREAT AGAIN hat and heading home from Trump's Election Night party. Last time I saw Johnson, we were in Boca

Raton, at a party at the league meetings in March 2016. He had been a big Jeb Bush supporter and was then working up the stomach to embrace Trump, which he soon did. He told me in Boca that he had made a great deal of money in the 1990s, when Bill Clinton was president—which I took as Johnson's way of indicating he would be just fine if Hillary was elected, too. I was relieved to hear that.

"Woody!" I called out to the Johnson & Johnson heir on the sidewalk. I was somewhat fog-headed from the late hour and did not, thus, address "Mr. Johnson" in the proper fashion. The Wood Man did not seem to mind. He said he was thrilled with Trump's victory and predicted it would bring "hope" to all the "blue-collar guys" he knew in Staten Island. Feeling free to be a wiseass, I asked Woody whether Trump "could even bring hope to the New York Jets?"

Johnson peered over his glasses and played along. "Do you really think he could help the Jets?" he said. It turned out maybe Trump could: by sending Woody out of the country. He wound up appointing him ambassador to the United Kingdom.

Five days later, I watched the Patriots host the Seahawks on **Sunday Night Football**. This had all the makings of a great game—two elite teams, Super Bowl rematch from two years earlier, Seahawks coach Pete Carroll (he of the fateful decision to pass at the goal line in 2015) returning to Foxborough to play the team that fired him in 1999, paving the way for the Belichick Century. It really did turn out to be a great game, eight lead changes, terrific performances by Rob Gronkowski and Seattle quarterback Russell Wilson. The Pats had four chances to tie the game from inside the 3-yard line in the final minute; a last-ditch pass to Gronk on fourth down was broken up in the end zone.

But what was remarkable about this game was how numb everything seemed in the stadium. Sometimes it's hard to judge a crowd from TV; this was not one of those times. Everything felt sleepy and muted. I could have been projecting my own exhaustion with football and the fractured days we were all living through. But I was not alone in noticing the pall.

"Man, have you ever heard seventy thousand people quieter than this?" Al Michaels mused at one point in the NBC broadcast. Foxborough has for years been a reliably nonraucous environment compared with other NFL venues. Yet something was different about this. It felt as if everyone watching were still nursing a hangover from our nasty bender of an election, as if the country were playing hurt.

"There was a time when they kicked their last field goal to go ahead and it was like a round of applause for a nice effort," Carroll observed after the game, speaking about the mood at Gillette Stadium. "Not a great place" is how he summed up the environment. Carroll attributed the crowd's impassivity to being spoiled by the Patriots' success. Perhaps they were, or to use the Trumpian construct, the crowd was just "tired of winning," or maybe tired of something else.

There was a time, not even a year before, when I could watch a down-to-the-wire Pats game like this and get worked into a palpitating dander. Win or lose, it would be useless for me to even try to sleep for at least two hours after it ended. My shirt would be drenched, my brain would be racing, and I'd have to absorb every word of "rapid reaction" on the Internet.

It goes with our commitment to leaving it all out on the vicarious field we inhabit as fans. But not tonight, my heart was not in this. The stakes felt really low for a Big Game. The Pats were headed for the postseason either way. I would try to be ready for the playoffs.

20.

CHEESEHEAD ELEGY

**Mental toughness is many things
and rather difficult to explain.**

—VINCE LOMBARDI

Dress as if you're going ice fishing.

—MAN IN HA HA CLINTON-DIX
#21 JERSEY IN LOBBY OF THE
HAMPTON INN, GREEN BAY,
WISCONSIN

January 8, 2017

As a general rule, Jews don't go ice fishing. But
the message was not complicated. Packer fans set
winning examples before approaching God's tun-
dra. They were spread out all over the lobby with

shock-and-awe piles of wool, fleece, and Canada goose. They stood before their offerings like they represented some essential totems of manhood. They were exhibiting **superior preparation.**
My pile is bigger! I packed more layers!

Falling back in love can require forethought. You need to "put yourself in a position to win," as Coach Belichick would say. For consumers of football, politics, and life in America, this had been a brutal season. Efforts at reconciliation were in order.

Bill Parcells used to call this part of the year "the Tournament," as in playoffs. The Pats would be there, as usual, their fourteenth time since 2001 and the seventh season in a row they had earned a first-round bye. I am indeed spoiled. But I needed a karmic infusion and knew where to find it. It was not Foxborough, and certainly not Washington, D.C.

Since Trump's election, my adult hometown felt like a fortressed village bracing for a guerrilla invasion. There was none of the postelection cooling of tensions we would normally enjoy with a new president. Instead, a shell-shocked aura hung over large sectors of the city. The Redskins had once again underachieved and missed the playoffs—which did please me, but didn't help the prevailing mood. I vowed to get away as often as possible before the inauguration.

I had never been to Lambeau Field, this most

hallowed of ground in this the Middlest of Football Americas. The Packers were hosting the Giants in the NFC Wild Card Game. It was 10 degrees at game time and I stood on the hearty shoulders of giants who froze before me. Their Rules for Living have been conveyed through Lambeau's generations, reaching down to tourists like me.

The first rule was, no complaining about the cold. Visitors learn this immediately. "The weather is like **Fight Club**," Giants coach Ben McAdoo said. "We don't talk about **Fight Club**."

Everything climate related in Green Bay is relative—to the Ice Bowl. On the day of the Championship Game in 1967 wind chills were supposedly pushing below minus-50. Today's bright sun and temps in the double digits (okay, so it was 10) were a Green Bay data point for global warming. And if you don't possess the mental toughness (**"rather difficult to explain"**), someone else does. Lambeau has sold out every game since 1960 and there's a deep bench of fans on a decades-long waiting list for tickets.

More wisdom: I was instructed by multiple parties to eat and drink at Hinterland Brewery or Titletown Brewing Co. My pal Belson kept pushing me toward a bar called the Sardine Can, whose owner, Chris Hansen (he once went on Letterman and drank a beer through his nose), plugged his place as "a dump." On game day, it is also important to check for last-minute logistical information—road closures, injury reports—in the **Green Bay Press Gazette**, the local daily whose sports editor a century ago, George W. Calhoun, cofounded the Packers along with a former Notre Dame football star, Curly Lambeau.

Saturday's **Press Gazette** featured a lineup of gluttony options around town—a seven-pound burrito (at Sangria's Mexican Grille), a forty-ounce steak (at Prime Quarter Steak Club), and (at the stadium proper) a special "Lam Bowl," created for the playoffs, filled with three pounds of sausage, cheese curds, bacon, and tater tots, topped with Bavarian Dunkel Beer Cheese and Red Cherry Peppers (sold in a souvenir Lam-Bowl). Let the healing begin.

My flight was late getting into Milwaukee Friday night, which along with the two-hour drive north to Green Bay made for slim pickings food-wise—as in, Brett Favre's Steakhouse. Brett's was the only place that was still serving dinner. If only someone had intercepted me, in the best Favre tradition. Brett, I hate to say it, your steakhouse was suboptimal: I ate an overcooked leather of a filet and mashed potatoes that tasted like chunky sour cream.

But my waitress, Carol, wore a Packers bow tie and was tremendous. Her husband and son were off ice-fishing for the weekend, and she was moonlighting from her job as a prison administrator at the Columbia Correctional Institution, once the home of Jeffrey Dahmer. Carol told me the same basic rule applied at both of her jobs: just treat everyone the same. She asked where I was from. Washington, D.C., I said. Did I know Trump? Not really, I said.

Talk of politics was minimal otherwise. People here are unfailingly nice—"Wisconsin Nice"—but the election had gotten intense. Green Bay, with a population of about 100,000 (Lambeau's capacity is 81,441), is the seat of Brown County, which Trump won by just a sliver over Hillary Clinton, 48 percent to 47 percent. November felt forever ago and yesterday. But now we were on to something else in this, the smallest city in America to have a major sports team. Green Bay is not a red or blue state, but green and yellow America.

Just treat everyone the same. Mind your layers. Go Packers.

Green Bay and the Packers have been held up as the embodiment of something the league had gotten right. It is a crown jewel of small-town pride, a community invested literally in a team that is the only one in sports owned entirely by shareholders. Every one of these 360,000 owners is Membership. I much prefer them to the billionaires.

"I think a lot of people around the league look at us and they wonder, 'How does it work there?'" said Mark Murphy, a former defensive back for the

Redskins who now serves as the Packers' CEO, representing the team's shareholders. On league matters, including official votes, Murphy effectively serves as the Packers' owner. "My wife calls me a **faux**-ner," Murphy told me. "That means I'm an owner but without the money."

Candidates for national office have tried over the years to reap reflective glory from this Pigskin Paradise, at times clumsily (John Kerry's fumbled reference to "Lambert Field" during a 2004 campaign stop in Wisconsin is something he should never live down). Green Bay's go-to God is of course Coach Lombardi, the philosopher-bully whose legend as a paragon of American leadership made him a rare consensus icon during an even more divided era. Both Richard Nixon and Hubert Humphrey considered Lombardi as their running mates during the 1968 election, according to David Maraniss, author of the definitive Lombardi biography from 1999, **When Pride Still Mattered**. Lombardi, a Kennedy Democrat, had no interest in the job.

"If Brett Favre was the team's Christ-like redeemer," wrote Austin Smith in the January 2017 **Harper's** ("The Lords of Lambeau"), "Lombardi was its Old Testament God." His scripture is invoked all over Green Bay and around football, including by even the worst of actors. Greg Hardy, the former All-Pro defensive end for the Panthers and Cowboys, and repeated batterer of women, applied Lombardi to his own comeback attempt in the league. "It's not whether you get knocked out, it's whether you get back up," Hardy said, quoting Lombardi, rather unfortunately.

I took a ride around Green Bay late on the night before the game, enjoying the idea that these were the same streets Lombardi used to drive while obsessing over his game plans. Many of the roads had different names then, including one now named for the sideline sage himself (Lombardi Avenue). Subsequent coaches earned street designations after they won Super Bowls with the Packers—although Mike Holmgren and Mike McCarthy only rated "ways."

Peter King, the longtime pro football writer for **Sports Illustrated** and connoisseur of NFL road food, shared the best Lambeau advice I received. Show up about five hours before kickoff. Wander through the parking lot and strike up conversations with tailgaters. Be there and be friendly and the beer, brats, and brotherhood will flow. He was correct. A few people even offered me their stray tickets but I had already dropped $250 on StubHub for a single on the 30-yard line, Section 328. I wore seven layers. It was not enough.

Again, though, it's relative: The sun was out. Lots of tailgaters went topless except for their chest paint. I had always assumed that the bare-chested bozos on TV in frigid stadiums are just showing off for cameras, or too drunk to feel anything. But

I spotted maybe two dozen of them in the tailgate lot, and no cameras were anywhere. Maybe some were in the too-drunk-to-feel-anything camp, but there was honor in these men. It was less a fashion statement than a declaration of pride and place.

Also impressive was that two tailgaters I spoke to possessed the situational awareness to apply sunscreen to their goose-pimpled torsos. "You can get a nasty burn on a day like this if you're not careful," a tailgater named Nick warned me. He had driven six hours from Minnesota. Cold air can lull you into thinking the sun can't burn, he said; and it can indeed, which Nick learned the hard way coming to Packer games for thirty years. Veteran move. He offered me sunscreen and a bratwurst. I took the bratwurst.

Other new friends included four bare-chested teammates from the Miami University of Ohio football team, who drove in from Cincinnati, each of their shivering pecs and bellies painted in yellow-green letters, spelling out:

P (O-lineman Tommy Doyle), **A** (wide receiver Jack Sorenson), **C** (tight end Andrew Homer), and **K** (D-lineman Ben Kimpler).

A post-Christmas Santa Claus with green-and-yellow beard hugged me. I took a selfie with a guy in yellow-striped Packer overalls unstrapped to expose a Packer tattoo over his bare nipple—which I then tweeted, a tourist move, but I needed to share.

At the suggestion of one of the tailgaters, I stopped by the All Things Jerky truck and perused a menu that included reindeer jerky, boar BBQ jerky, kangaroo jerky, and alligator jerky—the latter two presumably imported from somewhere Not Wisconsin. According to my tailgate friend, jerky "keeps your blood warm in the cold," so it's good to stock up. This struck me as bullshit jerky, but what did I know? (I wasn't even wearing sunscreen.)

To warm up before entering the stadium, I stepped into the heated tent area called the "tailgate zone." The AFC Wild Card Game between Miami at Pittsburgh was on a big TV. I watched Dolphins quarterback Matt Moore rolling out to his right and getting blasted by Steeler linebacker Bud Dupree as he released his pass. Moore was left writhing on the ground and bleeding from the mouth. A Packer fan watching next to me grunted in something between thrill and horror. He stood under a poster-size photo hanging from the ceiling of Packer mauler Ray Nitschke standing over an opponent—#66 in a classic kill shot.

"You gotta see this," the fan said, calling his friend over to watch the replays. And there were replays, five in the two minutes it took for Moore to get off the turf and the referees to assess the offsetting personal foul penalties (one for roughing the passer, the other for the retaliating Dolphins who attacked Dupree). "He gets hit right in the jaw!" CBS's Phil Simms marveled during the final replay.

"And made a terrific throw, too."

Football!

Moore came out for only one play and then returned to the game. I headed into the stadium.

My seat was near the top of the bowl. Next to me was a guy named Jake, a bar manager from Oshkosh, who spent much of the first quarter trying to start chants about Giants quarterback Eli Manning ("Eli eats boogers, Eli eats boogers"). None caught on. Other than that, Jake was definitely Wisconsin Nice, or Wisconsin Drunk. He kept trying to initiate high fives on every Packer offensive play that gained more than ten yards. This became tiresome after a while, at least to me (Masshole Nice isn't really a thing). He also took delight in Giants receiver Odell Beckham Jr. dropping two passes in the first quarter. Beckham and some Giants teammates had faced a tabloid/talk radio/Twitter shit-storm during the week when they were photographed on a boat in Miami after jetting south on their off day. They should have been gearing up for frigid Green Bay instead, per hot take sources. This was not a good look for a team preparing for its first playoff game since 2011—a **distraction** at the very least. Beckham, as if playing exclusively to the peanut gallery, missed two more catchable balls early in the second quarter that Twitter immediately blamed on the Miami boat ride.

But the Giants' defense started warm in Green Bay and dominated much of the first half. They led 6–0 until just before the two-minute warning, when Aaron Rodgers defrosted and that was that. On second and goal from the Giants' 5, the quarterback stutter-stepped around the pocket, avoided three rushers, ran to his left and, at the last second, threw a bullet to Davante Adams in the end zone to give the Packers a 7–6 lead. Adams then ran to a corner and observed the Green Bay tradition of the scoring Packer launching himself over the padded wall and into the first rows of exulting supplicants—the Lambeau Leap. Fans converge like frozen love piranhas, enveloping the Packer in a frenzy of hugs and head-slaps. This is most definitely a Top-10 best tradition in American sports, if not American life in general, or maybe even the entire history of human achievement.

The Giants regained the ball for just forty-two seconds before punting it back to Rodgers. He drove the Packers 80 yards in 1:38, more than half of which came on a 42-yard Hail Mary to Randall Cobb on the last play of the half. Rodgers in his career had now hit on three desperation heaves of more than 40 yards at the end of halves or regulation time. I had seen them all on video but it was something to witness live. On TV, you can't appreciate the full loft Rodgers had to put on the ball to allow his receivers to get downfield— four or five seconds, it seemed, longer than many punts. The crowd reupped their delirium, Cobb sprang up off the frozen ground and Lambeau Leaped into the hands of joy.

I shared a high five with Jake and also a bag of my jerky at halftime—the kangaroo, I think it was (I warned him it might be a little tough this time of year). Green Bay went into the locker room up 14–6 but the game felt effectively over. The Giants looked beat on their slow walks to the locker room. It was as if Rodgers had lulled them into false hope before breaking New York with a flurry of gut-punches to end the round. The game was not close after that, with the Packers winning, 38–13. If the game had gone another half, Green Bay might have won 100–13 and I could have lost four toes.

House of Pain's "Jump Around" broke out in the stadium at the end of the third quarter. The early-nineties hip-hop anthem had become a Lambeau tradition following one that had begun twenty years ago at the University of Wisconsin's Camp Randall Stadium. This was not your Lombardi's Lambeau, but it still worked. I adopted Green Bay as my NFC team this postseason while I jumped around on numb feet.

21.

"WE DON'T WANT YOU
IN LOS ANGELES"

**God will never forsake you—
unlike the Chargers.**

—SIGN OUTSIDE THE COMMUNITY BAPTIST CHURCH,

FALLBROOK, CALIFORNIA,

NEAR SAN DIEGO

January 18, 2017

Football's grand future sprawls over a big field of dirt just east of LAX. It covers 298 acres on the site of the Hollywood Park racetrack in Inglewood. Here is the dusty canvas where "Stan's vision" would be realized, someday, at least that's the plan (says Stan). "Stan" is Stan Kroenke, the serial entrepreneur, Walmart heir by marriage, and owner of the new L.A. Rams, among other pro sports teams.

Whatever plutocrat's wet dream gets constructed here will become the new home of the Rams and Chargers beginning in about 2020 (the projected finish was originally 2019 but building started slowly due to heavy rains). I heard from a lot of people at the league that I needed to check out this Manhattan Project of stadia in L.A. So I headed west after Green Bay, to warm up, watch the four divisional round playoff games on TV, and get a peek at Stan's Vision. It wasn't much to see yet, this vision, unless you get off on inspecting big, early-stage construction grounds, which I do barely at all—maybe a fifteen-minute capacity, tops. The meter was running.

I met up first in a construction trailer with Kevin Demoff, the Rams' chief operating officer, and the chief cheerleader for Stan's Vision. "You have a good reputation," I told Demoff, upon meeting him—which he does, at least around the league. "You haven't been to St. Louis lately," cautioned Demoff, who is forty-one years old and almost entirely gray (largely because of St. Louis). To wit: KTVI Channel 2 in St. Louis had recently identified Demoff in a graphic as "Rams Chief Operating Officer/Professional Liar."

Anyway, the agenda for the visit was for Demoff to sell me on all the wondrous things about the in-progress stadium. But really I was more interested in talking about the elephant in the room, that being the Chargers' deciding to come here, too, even though nobody wanted them. I wasn't subtle about this, either. "You want the Chargers to fail, right?" I asked Demoff. He smiled, but couldn't play along. "I want us to succeed," he said. At which point I was sent out to view the big pile of dirt.

My tour guides were a pair of hard-hatted project managers from Legends, the stadium construction and hospitality firm co-owned by the Cowboys and New York Yankees. The project managers—Dale Koger and Scott Owens—kept tossing out fun facts about Shangri LA, mostly related to dirt: more than four million cubic yards, for instance, had been excavated thus far and they would eventually reach eight million cubic yards. Their construction vehicles picked up sixty yards of dirt per minute and seventy thousand yards in a day.

We were standing on a twenty-foot-high platform and surveying the grand gravel view, orange hued like Cleveland Browns helmets. Big machines zigzagged across the soil in jagged formations. "Look at that man standing out there in the middle," Dale said, pointing out a single hard hat in the middle of the megapit. "He looks like an ant, doesn't he?" Indeed he did, and with that my meter expired.

There was a better show down the road at the famed Forum, onetime seat of L.A. glamour, home of the Showtime Lakers, and now site of a debacle-in-the-making scheduled for eleven a.m.: a "Welcome to L.A." pep rally for the team that had until a few days earlier been known as the San Diego Chargers.

The Rams' coming "home" to Los Angeles party seemed to be going so well, too. But then the embattled Chargers owner Dean Spanos, peeved that San Diego's government and taxpayers would not subsidize him a new stadium, decided to bolt for L.A., where he and the Bolts would effectively be crashing on Stan's couch once his Football Vanity Village was complete.

There are many aspects to this particular pile of NFL turmoil, but start with this: No one wanted the "Los Angeles Chargers" to happen. Not the people of San Diego, who had supported their team for fifty-six years. Not the league or the other owners, who did not want to abandon a loyal fan base in one of the fastest-growing markets in the league. Los Angeles itself, at least the subset that cared about football, had made its position on the Chargers clear in a number of ways. The new L.A. Chargers logo was viciously booed upon its unveiling at a Clippers-Lakers game at the Staples Center. The team scrapped the logo and vowed to come up with a new one, but that wasn't quite the point. MESSAGE TO CHARGERS: WE

DON'T WANT YOU IN LOS ANGELES was the headline over a column by Bill Plaschke in the **Los Angeles Times**. There was no need to read further to understand where he was coming from.

The Rams, to quote Coach Obvious, were also not happy. When all is said and done—factoring in relocation fees and moving costs—Stan Kroenke would be spending close to $4 billion to realize his "vision" in Inglewood. Kroenke would have invested a decade of groundwork in the project and made himself a pariah in his home state of Missouri (where he was named for the St. Louis Cardinal idol Stan Musial), and also among a few of his business partners who came away bitter after he'd prevailed in the intra-owner bloodbath over L.A.

Spanos would have been one of the leading pissed-offees. He remained hurt that his partners had overwhelmingly opted for Brother Stan and the Rams project over the Chargers-Raiders combo platter in Carson. To placate Spanos, Goodell engineered this consolation arrangement in which the Chargers would own a one-year option to become the Rams' tenant in Inglewood. No one thought Spanos would actually do this. "Dean just seemed so wounded after we voted for Stan, Roger needed to give him something," an AFC team executive told me after the vote was taken in Houston. "We should have given him a puppy."

Instead Spanos got rights to sloppy seconds in L.A. Goodell and the Membership figured Spanos would work out some deal in San Diego, because that's what everyone wanted him to do and it made the most sense and the alternative made none. Yet here was Spanos calling Stan Kroenke to say, "Hey, I'm coming, dude, what can I bring?" (definitely paraphrasing here).

Kroenke, who had learned the news with everyone else—via ESPN's Adam Schefter—was not happy. Spanos's phone call went to voice mail. When I visited Inglewood about a week later Silent Stan had yet to return the call. They definitely had some repair work to do, Kroenke and Spanos did, perhaps a support group for socially awkward rich guys who have screwed over entire fan bases. Kroenke also managed to be out of town on the day of the Chargers' "Welcome to L.A." rally. I, however, was thrilled to be in Inglewood, as any connoisseur of NFL clown shows would be.

How do you stage a housewarming rally for someone nobody wants in the neighborhood—let alone your landlord? This even included the "someone" who was being "welcomed." Philip Rivers, the Chargers quarterback for the previous thirteen seasons, was plainly unhappy. He choked up and stammered his way through a radio interview on the subject of having to uproot from (or commute from) his longtime home in San Diego to L.A. When the team held a news conference to announce its new head coach, Anthony Lynn, Lynn declared himself "so pumped" and "so proud to be the head coach of the San Diego— uhh, L.A. Chargers." Lynn quickly acknowledged his mistake with a simple "Oops," which, according to the **Los Angeles Times**, could also work nicely as the Chargers' new slogan.

Dean Spanos, whose father Alex became majority owner of the Chargers in 1984, had said repeatedly that he did not want to leave San Diego. He loved the place, it was his home. He pleaded with the voters and public officials of San Diego to build him a new domicile. When that failed, he begged his fellow owners to help pay for one. He was now the most hated man in his hometown and an unwanted tenant in his adopted one. "Now I know how Art Modell feels," he told one NFC owner, referring to the longtime Cleveland Browns owner who moved the team to Baltimore, became the most reviled figure in northeast Ohio, and then never set foot in Cleveland again. Dino got little sympathy from his fellow owners. They were miffed at him for turning what had appeared to be a somewhat elegant solution to the L.A. problem into a towering embarrassment.

This was something the NFL under Goodell had become quite adept at. If "Stan's Vision" to build a transformational manor in the City of Dreams represented the pinnacle of NFL boldness and wherewithal, the deal that allowed

the Chargers to storm the palace represented
NFL politics, pettiness, and greed at its worst. If
the Rams' going to L.A. was akin to winning the
Super Bowl, the Chargers' following behind was
Deflategate.

I drove about a mile to the Forum and pulled
in behind two buses. The buses carried batches
of "Charger fans" adorned in powder-blue jerseys,
L.A. CHARGERS hats, and green-blue face paint.
Where did they find these people? Were they
bused in from San Diego? Did the Chargers
offer $50 and a bunch of L.A. CHARGERS gear
to the track workers at Hollywood Park if they
were willing to run over to the Forum after their
shift? I was dubious about this, as were others. "I
have still never met a single Chargers fan," Bill
Plaschke wrote.

The "fans" filed off the bus and looked too
perfect—the face-paint jobs, the newly printed
uniforms. There was a bunch of reports, mostly
on Twitter, that a casting call had gone out for
people to play "Charger fans" and make a bunch
of noise at the rally. None of these reports were
confirmed, although I tried to interview at least
three of these "fans" and they were strangely coy
about where they lived and what they did for a living and what brought them here. When I asked,
only one of the three could name the Chargers'
new coach.

San Diego Union-Tribune columnist Kevin

Acee deemed the whole "self-welcome rally" to be a "wondrous metaphor" for the Chargers' new history. "A fabricated event so perfectly Los Angeles," he wrote. One of the rally speakers said it was "so fitting" that this party to celebrate the future of the NFL in L.A. would be held at the Fabulous Forum, one of the landmark venues of the city's entertainment scene.

One could also say (as I will say here) that the Forum, opened in 1967, was also a fitting spot for this spectacle because who knew if it would even still be here in ten years?

Everything about this rally was bizarre, beginning with the metal detectors. Maybe this is standard procedure for any production that features high-profile scoundrels—in this case Dean Spanos and Roger Goodell—but it seemed like an odd precaution for a "welcome rally" that would draw 150 people tops, a bunch of local dignitaries, and Chargers cheerleaders. A fair number of current and former Chargers also shuffled in. One was Rivers, who sat onstage as he waited to speak, not looking happy at all. He slumped in his chair and (poorly) hid a smirk. Goodell sat a few seats over, looking about as happy.

The commissioner was called up to say a few words. And the crowd did not even boo him properly (no way these were real NFL fans). It was more like courteous applause. Goodell did his fatherly pep talk routine with the sad-looking

Spanos. "Dean, welcome, we're proud of you, and welcome to your new home," Goodell said. This was after Goodell twice mentioned "Stan's Vision" that would "set a new standard for entertainment complexes in the whole world." You had to figure Roger's pilot was firing up the private jet at that point.

Spanos has slicked-back hair and a jowly face, resembling a short man's version of ESPN's Chris Berman or a rich-guy's version of a brunette Barney Rubble. He appeared nervous and uncomfortable. That tends to be his public default mode, but his unease was conspicuous here. "Let me dispel the myth," Spanos felt the need to insist, as he pointed behind him to Rivers. "Yes, he is happy to be here." Rivers managed a cursory wave. Spanos aptly described this occasion as "surreal."

To that point, the self-welcome had been a relatively polite gathering, if hardly raucous. There were a few "L.A. Chargers" chants and half-assed dancing along to blasted songs like "Uptown Funk." Glitter showered onto the stage. But then, as Spanos spoke, a heckler went to work. "Way to screw over San Diego," screamed a Chargers diehard, Joseph MacRae. He was in from San Diego, middle fingers raised. He said his profane piece while part of the crowd tried to drown him out with an "L.A. Chargers" chant. MacRae eventually headed for the exit but was shoved from behind by a burly Chargers "fan" in a vintage

Lance Alworth jersey. MacRae spun around, as if we might see an actual fight—or the actors might be staging one for us.

But then MacRae thought better of it and San Diego stayed classy-ish. MacRae would be heard from again, raising money to pay for a billboard on I-405 near the Chargers' temporary home in Carson. The sign featured, among other things, a cartoon likeness of Goodell in a clown nose next to the NFL's "Football Is Family" slogan covered in dollar signs.

Spanos looked shaken by the interruption. His speech became halting and he rushed through the rest of it. Coach Lynn followed, managing to say "Los Angeles Chargers" this time. Rivers stepped up in the pocket and reassured the "home" fans, though backhandedly. "All I heard the last few days is that nobody wanted us up here," Rivers said. He paused, and for a second I thought— hoped!—Rivers might actually finish the sentence with something like "Well, I don't want to be here either." That would have been **so good**. But it was not to be. Rivers spat out an "I guess we're gonna be okay" and returned to his chair. L.A. already had enough actors.

22.

"I'M DRUNK, I'M STUPID,
I'M A PATS FAN,"
THE MAN TOLD POLICE

January 23, 2017

Before I left L.A., I stopped by the NFL Network studios, located in a warehouse park in Culver City, which also doubles as a human warehouse to dozens of former NFL greats who are now employed as on-air "personalities." Introduced in 2003, NFL Network views itself as a quasi-journalistic enterprise. But many team officials and executives at the NFL—half of the league's workforce is employed by NFL Network—would prefer a more **quasi** approach and less journalistic. Such is the dilemma built in to being a network that devotes 24–7 to covering its own workforce. Not only would it become understandably awkward when, say, a New England Patriots employee (Aaron Hernandez) murders someone or a Baltimore Ravens employee (Ray Rice) cold-cocks his fiancée or an actual owner (the Colts' Jim Irsay) gets a DUI. It can rankle Park Ave and the individual teams when the network strays too far from its house organ mission.

The Culver City studio has a towel-snappy ambience. It is muscled with youngish-looking men who enjoy showing off their impressive recall of 40-yard dash times from the Scouting Combine. Rare here is the sight of gray hair, or many females. Being an NFL fan is obviously encouraged, so long as there's no veering too far into fan-boy behavior. "On my first day at NFL Media I signed paperwork promising that I wouldn't harass players for autographs," wrote Diana Moskovitz in a **Deadspin** essay about what it's like to be a woman employee at NFL Network. "That struck me as odd, given that I was a professional reporter being hired to work in a newsroom."

As it is, the network does neither journalism nor propaganda that well. But I do spend a lot of time watching it, as I imagine any serious football fan with access to the channel would. If nothing else, the Pigskin Pravda offers plenty of highlights and the full library of NFL Films, a jewel of the league's media empire. The network produces some solid original programs, like the **A Football Life** documentary series; and it also favors us (or used to) with such fine artwork as **Behind the Pom-Poms**, a show that asks actual NFL cheerleaders what **they** like about football—and just so we know they're legit professionals, the cheerleaders are made to wear their skin-hugging uniforms on the show. (**Behind the Pom-Poms** appeared to be discontinued in 2014, a few years before several of NFL Network's former player-employees would be suspended in a hail of sexual harassment allegations.)

NFL Network also reaps great material from the off-field reality shows that the teams and players generate. A few days before I visited Culver City, the network had managed to piss off the New York Giants PR department by tweeting out something about the Giants' party boat scandal in Miami. On the afternoon I was there, the network was doing saturation coverage of another perfect installment in **Real World—NFL**. In the Steelers' locker room following their playoff win over Kansas City, Pittsburgh's star receiver Antonio Brown made a Facebook Live video of himself. In the background, Steelers coach Mike Tomlin can be heard delivering a postgame speech, with many of his words audible—including the part where he referred to Pittsburgh's next opponent, my Patriots, as "those assholes."

Few would be surprised that an NFL coach talked that way in a locker room speech, especially, in this case, about a team that much of the league would characterize the same way. The Patriots, who had defeated the Texans 34–16 in the divisional round, had been a particular bane to the Steelers on big stages, going back to the AFC Championship Game in 2002. So of course Tomlin has every right to call the Pats assholes, I probably would, too—**and I root for the motherfuckers**.

Antonio Brown was criticized for placing himself above the team, or placing other considerations above the team (i.e., Facebook, which, according to the **Wall Street Journal**, had paid him $244,000 to serve as a "social media influencer" on its site). But Brown's more egregious sin was that he violated the **sanctity of the locker room**. He not only provided bulletin board fodder to the opposition but also created a **distraction**. Tomlin even extended the matter a couple days by refusing to let the distraction die, reiterating again and again how stupid and immature Brown was. Distraction is the bane of NFL coaches and locker rooms—or, if you're the NFL Network, essential to your business model.

Social media swarmed over Brown with memes and ridicule. He was the fresh meat of distraction. Tomlin called Brown's act "foolish," "inconsiderate," and "selfish," among other things; he apologized not just in his capacity as head coach of the Steelers, but also "as a parent" and "as a member of the community." Tomlin directed his apology to pretty much everybody in America, except the Patriots.

IN OTHER NEWS, THE OAKLAND RAIDERS AN-
nounced that they had applied to the league to
relocate their franchise to Las Vegas. This meant
that the two teams who had lost out to the Rams
in the L.A. sweepstakes, the Chargers and Raiders, would be fleeing passionate NFL markets
where they had enjoyed rich histories and loyal
fans. As the gambling capital of America, Vegas
had always been avoided by the NFL like a Super-
fund site. Steering clear was essential to the NFL's
preserving its charade of rectitude, or "the Integrity of the Game" as Goodell would say. (Two
years earlier the league put the kibosh on a fantasy
football convention in Vegas organized by then-
Cowboy quarterback Tony Romo because it was
held at a place whose naming rights were sold to
a casino.) But then Sin City happened to flash a
near-billion-dollar stadium deal in front of Mark
Davis like a high roller dangling a C-note at a
strip club. So never mind the city's crumbling
roads and swelling class sizes. "Las Vegas Raiders" had a certain ring to it all of a sudden.

Would Roger finally show up in Foxborough?
This was another storyline that presented itself
before the league championship games. Goodell
had avoided the Patriots' home since he attended
a January 2015 playoff game two weeks before
Deflategate got rolling. He could have just shown

up, maybe unannounced, at some innocuous regular-season game and that could have ended this quietly (Goodell's home in Bronxville is just 186 miles down Interstate 95 from Gillette). But by staying away for the next two seasons while visiting every other league venue at least once, Goodell constructed a slow-building embarrassment for himself—one of his better skills.

The NFL's PR geniuses compounded things by concocting cover stories for the commissioner's absence. They claimed, for instance, that Goodell wanted to be in Atlanta for the first-round game between the Seahawks and Falcons because it might turn out to be the last game the Falcons ever played in the Georgia Dome. Yeah, this would be the absolutely hallowed Georgia Dome, certifiable Lambeau-of-the-South. The Falcons were vacating this never-beloved bubble after the season. Opened in 1992, the Georgia Dome's most memorable event might have been its own implosion just twenty-five years later. Roger just needed to be there for Seahawks-Falcons in case this was indeed (choking back tears) good-bye to the fucking Georgia Dome. He is apparently sentimental about certain things.

Sure enough, the Falcons beat the Seahawks and would host the Packers in the NFC Championship the following Sunday—granting another last gasp for the Grand Ol' Dome. The question then became, would Goodell finally do the honorable thing and show up in Foxborough for the AFC Championship Game? Surely, since he had just bid his farewell to the Georgia Dome the week before, he could not compound his cowardice further. I sent a sarcastic email to an NFL flack asking if Goodell would be returning for one last look at the Dome. Yes, the flack said, seemingly without return sarcasm, Goodell in fact would be returning to Atlanta. And the flack even tried to justify it by explaining that Goodell had not seen the Packers play in person yet that year, and had already seen the Steelers play twice, so fair's fair.

Like Goodell, I, too, had been avoiding Foxborough, although in my case no one noticed or cared. Mostly I stayed away because getting there was a chore and I'd just as soon avoid the traffic and urine-soaked hell of postgame Route 1. If Lambeau was the NFL's Louvre, Gillette two weeks later would be like going to Hooters for a nightcap.

But a friend came through with two excellent tickets on the 20-yard line, so I flew up Sunday to see if Tommy could complete the last step of his vindication tour en route to the Super Bowl. Naturally "Where's Rahjah?" had provided hours of sports-radio mirth in New England. By the time I was heading south from Logan airport in my rental car, however, a new preoccupation had come up. In the predawn hours of that morning, some yahoo Masshole pulled the fire alarm in

Pittsburgh's hotel in Boston (as yahoo Massholes do), sending the groggy Steelers out into the cold. Nice. Someone on WEEI was comparing this with the old rat-fucking shenanigans that Red Auerbach used to pull to "gain an edge" on the competition. The late Boston Celtics patriarch was notorious for supposedly orchestrating stunts like these—turning off the hot water in the visitors' shower room, for instance. There were similar tales of fire alarms going off in the wee hours at the Lakers' hotel during the NBA finals. A certain mystique had grown up around these capers, in the vein of "doing what it takes" to mess with an opponent and "getting in their heads." That's the point the caller on the radio was trying to make. Personally I had a hard time thinking of these things as anything other than classic dick moves, but I figured the listeners of WEEI could do without my opinion on this.

Not surprisingly, the fire alarm mastermind was busted, arrested, and identified—as Dennis Harrison, twenty-five, of Boston. "I'm drunk, I'm stupid, I'm a Pats fan," he told police. Harrison might have coined the perfect mantra for us.

I went to the Pats-Steelers game with my old pal Nem, an artist who now lives in nearby Watertown. Nem adopted the Pats later in life. Like me he was excited to be going to such a fateful game but also pining slightly for his warm living room, eating chili, drinking for free, and peeing without a long hike or line. Nem and I were both fifty-two years old and increasingly biased against hassle and unnecessary discomfort. Hunter S. Thompson put it well, if not succinctly, in a gonzo treatment he did in **Rolling Stone** about Super Bowl 8 in 1974. "I hope to Christ I never again succumb to whatever kind of weakness or madness it is that causes a person to endure the incoherent hell that comes with going out to a cold and rainy stadium for three hours on a Sunday afternoon and trying to get involved with whatever seems to be happening down there on that far-below field."

But Nem and I were also closer to death than we used to be and figured that as we age, events like this become ways to measure your life, like weddings and funerals. We got to Foxborough early, watched the Falcons cruise to NFC primacy on a tailgater's TV (so much for my Packers). We chatted with a few groups of Steelers fans in the parking lot, a few of them interspersed with Pats counterparts in Sons of Belichick jerseys and happy to share their food and booze. Good-lucks were exchanged. We respect you guys, I said to my new Pittsburgh friends. Really, there was no reason to be assholes before we kicked Black and Gold ass.

It was a wet chill of a night, 35 degrees and drizzly. The cold was raw and clingy, more insidious than the straight-up freeze of Green Bay. As is true of many Pats fans, I had become complacent and took my comfort for granted. Shame on me for skimping on layers—**not** superior preparation!

This was Nem's first time at Gillette. He took note of the directives from the scoreboard for us to "make noise, make noise." "It's so easy to be a fan," Nem remarked, "they tell you what to do at every second." After sufficient noise was made, the scoreboard declared "Fan Power" and we all felt, sure enough, **empowered.** Nem ran off to the concession stand before kickoff and came back with a big plastic cup of red wine. He came to Foxborough for the Pats and stayed for the Merlot.

The game was never close. Pittsburgh seemed to be playing half asleep, especially after their brilliant running back Le'Veon Bell went out with a groin injury. Brady threw for 384 yards and three touchdowns; receiver Chris Hogan caught nine balls for 180 yards and two touchdowns. It was 34–9 after three, leaving only the "Where's Rahjah" chants to build and the final score to be registered (36–17). Nem and I stuck around for the trophy presentation. Nothing about this result was surprising, but I tried to make myself feel grateful, if not exhilarated by the once-hapless Pats' earning their seventh trip to the Super Bowl in sixteen years. I saw a woman in a Steelers #7 jersey sobbing in the concourse. "You'll be back next year," I said, trying to be reassuring, but a big part of me felt nothing. Maybe it was a self-protection. Last time Pats fans tried to enjoy a blowout win in the AFC Championship Game, after all, we got promptly deflated. But this felt like something else, maybe how rich people become overindulged when they lose the ability to savor and great fortune becomes mundane.

Bob Kraft did another one of his self-satisfied trophy hoistings on national TV. "For a number of reasons, all of you in this stadium understand how big this win was," Kraft cried, sounding a bit befuddled (or "drunk" to use the word teasing some of the YouTube clips). "But we have to go to Houston and win one . . ." And with that, Kraft stopped abruptly, raised the trophy again, and ended his remarks in mid-sentence—which was strange, but really fine.

As Nem and I made our way out of the stadium, a shot of elation appeared on the sideline in front of us. Martellus Bennett, the Patriots tight end, had grabbed a pair of red, white, and blue pom-poms from a cheerleader and began dancing and singing along to Whitney Houston's "I Wanna Dance with Somebody." Somebody book this man on **Behind the Pom-Poms**!

Bennett, a journeyman eccentric who wore out his welcome with three NFL teams and never won with any of them, had served as a blocking and pass-catching mainstay for the Pats after Gronk went down in November. Known as "Marty"— **Mahty** in New England—Bennett had become a fan favorite and bracing alternative to the drab personalities that Belichick preferred in his locker room. Bennett wrote a children's book (**Hey A.J., It's Saturday**), produced an animated film (**Zoovie: A Warm and Fuzzy Tale**), and released a mixtape on his Twitter account (**Year of the Orange Dinosaur**). He visited Boston Children's Hospital dressed as Pikachu. He was also a quote machine, who once compared the Patriots' dread-locked bowling ball of a running back, LeGarrette Blount, with Bambi. On another occasion he claimed that his previous team, the Bears, never won because "we just had a bunch of bitches on the roster."

Now here was Bennett galloping off to his first Super Bowl. New England's assholes had made easy work of Tomlin's bitches. And here was my blast of joy, the visceral thing you remember. I would think of this scene whenever I heard the candied "I Wanna Dance with Somebody" play-ing somewhere. It always awakens the souvenir image: Mahty jumping around with cheerleaders, dancing in the rain on Route 1.

23.

THE TV REPORTER IN THE
BELICHICK UNDERWEAR

January 30, 2017

Donald Trump was not elected for subtlety. "This American carnage stops right here and stops right now," he announced in what would become the billboard line of his inaugural address. "American carnage" needn't be unpleasant. It could even be riveting, like pro wrestling and pro football (both Trump obsessions). It could draw huge crowds, as Trump America's grand opening drew "the largest audience to witness an inauguration, period," in the words of incoming White House mouthpiece Sean Spicer. The claim was as plausible as pro wrestling, but Spicer was just using "alternative facts," as the White House counselor Kellyanne Conway defended her beleaguered-from-day-1 colleague. They worked in the service of the new president's mission: to be the biggest spectacle in the world at all times, and to create a Maximum America in his own image.

This pitted Trump from the get-go against the incumbent megaspectacle on the American carnage calendar: the Super Bowl. It was scheduled for two weeks later in Houston (an event also not invented for subtlety). A collision course between Trump and the NFL was probably inevitable: there was only so much room in the American headspace.

Lamar Hunt, founder of the AFL and Kansas City Chiefs, originally coined the term "Super Bowl." It was a play on the bouncy "Super Ball" toy, originally intended as a placeholder until the game's grand masters could come up with a better, more dignified name. But "Super Bowl" stuck as the permanent solution as this grand pageant of excess as we know it today took hold. The AFL-NFL Championship Game (or "World Championship Game," as the first two contests were called) grew into a culture-stopping extravaganza.

A few days after Trump's inauguration, I headed for the alternative chaos of Houston. It was good to escape Washington, if not the politics of it, which remained hard to escape after Trump took his hand off the Bible. His swearing-in begot nationwide protests. His first actions included a ban on refugees and restrictions on immigrants from Muslim-majority countries. It set off bed-

lam at airports, court challenges, and more protests. Super Bowl 51 would not be your average
stick-to-sports extravaganza.

"I'm not talking politics at all," Tom Brady
said in response to the first of several questions
that concerned just that—specifically, his golfing buddy, now in the White House. Brady was
getting a lot of Trump questions, beginning
with Super Bowl week's Opening Night at Minute Maid Park in Houston. Brady tried to shut
them down, always easier when operating in his
managed bubble. But this was not Foxborough.
Brady's podium was being overrun with **distraction** questions. "I'm just a positive person" became
his go-to blow-off. "I'm focused on positive things
in my life," Brady said. This presumably did not
include refugees.

Shortly before Opening Night began, Trump
fired Acting Attorney General Sally Yates after she
advised the Justice Department that Trump's executive order keeping out citizens from Muslim-
majority countries was not constitutional. Several
Falcons and Patriots players were invited to
weigh in but mostly demurred. The Falcons receiver Mohamed Sanu, a practicing Muslim,
was asked to discuss Trump's executive order. "A
very tough situation," he called it, and "hard for
me to talk about right now." I asked two of the
more thoughtful Patriots, defensive linemen Alan
Branch and Chris Long, if they had thoughts on

Trump. Both said they did, and would speak at some point, but did not wish to "distract" during Super Bowl week. League and team officials did their best to fumigate the event of any political contamination. They went as far as scrubbing the official transcripts of the interviews of nearly every mention of "Trump" or "president," despite the words' coming up through the evening.

Typically, Super Bowl Opening Night ("fueled by Gatorade," because everything must now be **fueled** or **powered** by some big-paying sponsor) makes up its own goofy mob scene. Players and coaches are required to make themselves available in a mosh pit of quasi-media. They are eager to learn, the quasi-media are, things like whether Falcons running back Devonta Freeman had a favorite type of fish to eat (yes, tilapia) or if Patriots center David Andrews had a favorite breakfast cereal (yes, Cap'n Crunch with Crunch Berries, the Crunch Berries providing "an important source of fruit," he confided to me).

A female TV reporter from Alaska told Belichick that she always wears "Bill Belichick underwear on game days." Coach, who had just announced that his "focus was on football," managed a pained look of amusement (or was it an amused look of pain?). "Did you even know there was Bill Belichick underwear?" she pressed. "I guess I missed that one," he muttered back.

Belichick also mentioned that he'd never been to Alaska.

Super Bowl week is like a national political convention in that little of consequence actually happens until the final night, and even that is often an anticlimax. Still, every majordomo in politics—or in this case football—tends to show up so the rubber-necking factor is high. Entourages pass through the lobbies of the hotels inside the secured Super Bowl "village": sights of Dan Fouts signing a football, Mean Joe Greene at a reception desk at the Hilton, Odell Beckham's entourage nearly trampling a slow-moving pack of Gold Jackets emerging from a luncheon. "They make us wear 'em here," Hall of Fame defensive back Mel Renfro told me, referring to the Gold Jackets on parade this week.

So much football eminence operating in close quarters enhances potential for something noteworthy occurring, if not "news" per se (e.g., Johnny Manziel signing autographs for $99, or $50 for selfies). Earl Campbell, the bulldozer running back of the Houston Oilers in the late 1970s and early 1980s, made headlines early in the week when he complained that the modern NFL had grown soft compared with when he played. Campbell suggested that players were now too quick to succumb to injuries, including head injuries. "I can't play because I didn't get a pedicure this week," Campbell told **USA Today**, mocking the current generation. "I don't play because my head hurt. That wouldn't have got the job done back in my day."

Campbell, the son of rose growers in Tyler, Texas, played with a demolishing abandon that made plenty of his contemporaries soft, too. "Every time you hit him you lower your own IQ," Redskins linebacker Pete Wysocki said of Campbell. In Campbell's prime, health was the only thing some people thought could stop him. Never much for evading tacklers, the Tyler Rose preferred a more punitive approach. No one who saw Earl Campbell play forgot him—and it was satisfying in that football at its most basic is a straight-ahead contest of attempted domination. How sustainable was another matter. Campbell played only eight years in the league, retired in 1985, and was enshrined in Canton as perhaps the most merciless running back ever to play in the NFL. "Punishment" was the operative theme when discussing Earl Campbell. "The hardest-hitting running back I ever played against," Cowboys safety Cliff Harris said after Campbell retired. "When you finished a game against Earl, you had to sit in a tub with Epsom salts."

As Houston football royalty, Campbell was a ubiquitous artifact at this Super Bowl week. Now sixty-one, he was also another example of how punishment in football can be a two-way game, and that his "back in my day" nostalgia comes with a price. Campbell has had both knees replaced, endured five back surgeries, severe arthritis, foot drop caused by nerve damage, spinal stenosis, and a rehab program for addiction to OxyContin, among other things that Epsom salts couldn't help. He had an unruly white beard and moved with the aid of a walker.

I watched Campbell inch through the room at the annual Super Bowl party put on by Leigh Steinberg, his former agent. Like Campbell, Steinberg had seen better days since his peak as the game's premier superagent representing top players of the eighties and nineties. Several wound up firing or suing him, and Steinberg wound up filing for bankruptcy and being treated for addiction, among other fall-from-grace standbys. I'd spoken to him a few times, and read a memoir he wrote about his life as an agent in the NFL. He is a tireless name-dropper and self-promoter but not without insights.

In his heyday, Steinberg hosted the week's essential Super Bowl party. He had made a bit of a comeback in recent years, recruiting first-round-drafted quarterbacks Paxton Lynch and Patrick Mahomes as clients. He was also trying to keep alive his Super Bowl party, which he described to me as "legendary." This would be the thirtieth he would host. Not knowing better, I figured this would be a primo destination, baby. But like

Steinberg (and me), the party was solidly B-list. Long lines of fans filed into the Hughes Manor, a multitented event space a few miles from Super Bowl "village." There were plates of sweaty cheese, silent auctions, and junior hustlers getting all excited about their networking opportunities.

Campbell was one of the few stars I recognized. Others also recognized Campbell, and mobbed him. His hobbled condition made it difficult for him to evade the pursuit, though Campbell did not mind. He smiled through a procession of photo requests, many of them younger fans who seemed not to know who Campbell was. But his older groupies did. They were less interested in photos and autographs, more interested in regaling Campbell with their memories of his memories. "You were an absolute beast," one supplicant told Campbell. He wore a new cowboy hat and spoke with a New England accent (what's more pathetic than a Masshole in a cowboy hat?). The man said he wore #34 in Pop Warner in honor of Campbell. "There was no one like you, Earl," he said, shaking Campbell's arthritic hand. He spoke to his hero in the past tense, like he was a ghost.

Commissioner Goodell managed to tear himself away from the Georgia Dome and get himself to Houston. Goodell was scheduled to host his annual State-of-the-NFL press conference on Wednesday. This is a Super Bowl week tradition in which we watch Roger Dodger stand on his

Shielded soapbox next to the Lombardi Trophy and ride out a rush of media questions—and perhaps this year, skip the part about how people take risks by "sitting on the couch."

I happened to walk into the George R. Brown Convention Center behind El Generalísimo. His security detail and about ten league executives were in tow. They moved briskly and all wore dark suits (in lieu of military fatigues). They also looked nervous, perhaps owing to "couch" flashbacks, but the Strong Man was all game face. Several of the questions were at least semiconfrontational. Goodell's preclenched body would grow visibly more so when selected keywords were mentioned—words like "San Diego," "St. Louis," "Oakland," "concussions," and of course "Brady." A San Diego reporter threatened early with a question about "what message the league sends to its fans" when the Chargers can leave San Diego after fifty-six years after the owners can't secure public money for a new stadium. "These are painful processes," Goodell said (drink!), and we were off.

New England reporters came eager to relitigate the evergreen topic of football air pressure. The **Globe**'s Dan Shaughnessy referred to comments Goodell made a few days earlier in which he said it would be an "honor" to hand the Lombardi Trophy to Tom Brady. Brady's dad, bless the man, took exception. "Somebody that has Roger

Goodell's ethics doesn't belong on any stage that Tom Brady is on," Tom Senior said. Tom Junior promptly imposed a media ban on his father.

Shaughnessy also wondered about the commissioner's two-year absence from Foxborough. This triggered what might have been the commissioner's most hilarious response of the day, intended or (more likely) not. "If I'm invited back to Foxborough, I'll come," Goodell said. Wait, so he was just waiting for the proper invite? That's what this was all about? I saw Robert and Jonathan Kraft just look at each other.

LATER THAT DAY, I WOULD TAKE A HIATUS FROM Houston to fly to Boston and visit my father in the hospital. He was eighty-three, had a worn-down heart, and was a few days away from entering hospice care. His name was Miguel Leibovich, an immigrant from Argentina who came to Massachusetts via Tennessee in 1958. He met my mother, they married and moved to the suburbs and eventually divorced. They raised three kids and, tragically, lost one in a car crash—my little brother, Phil, a great sports fan and my best friend; our last conversation was about the Pats beating the Seahawks in a November game in 1985, sealed by a late interception by Fred Marion. My father was not without his demons and, certainly, not without his heartaches, but they were far outpaced by his deep love of family and friends and appreciation for life's boundless amusements.

He never bothered much with American sports. It made me jealous of my friends who got to play catch with their fathers. It frustrated me that we could never connect over sports, which was something I clearly followed closely and performed well in (as opposed to, say, school). But I sought out some surrogate "American dads" who could fill the gaps for my foreign model—my grandfather in Brooklyn taught me baseball and took me to Mets games, my friend Josh's dad, Dr. King, took us to Fenway and Foxborough. And Miguel and I developed a lively affinity as we both grew older. We became great laughing friends, would talk for a few minutes on the phone a few times a week, mostly about our respective comings and goings and whatever was going on in the world. I never stopped trying to get him interested in sports.

At the very least, Miguel liked the idea of celebrating victories. Argentina used to shut down for rejoicing after a win in the World Cup, people cheering through the streets, beeping their horns. He loved a party. He loved being part of a community, especially a happy one. He once drove my friends and me to Logan airport at five a.m. to welcome the Larry Bird Celtics as they arrived back from Philly after they beat the 76ers in a big Game 6. In 2004, when the Red Sox were about to win their first World Series in eighty-six years,

I was watching the deciding game by myself in an Iowa hotel room. The person I called before the final out was Miguel, though I had little expectation he was watching. He would, at the very least, appreciate that I was calling at a meaningful moment, and that his adopted hometown would soon be breaking out in euphoria—unless heartache intervened, as it does. He told me that if the Red Sox held on, he would race around downtown Boston in his car beeping his horn.

Miguel lived life as if it were a timed sprint through the aisles of a market, trying to fill his cart with as many worthwhile experiences as he could before time expired. He always appreciated the metaphor of a race against time. He once told me, when I was probably too young to hear it, that he never expected to live a long life. He was lucky enough to defy his own prediction, with a big assist from modern medicine. He was never religious and could in fact be quite defiant of any rules that could restrict his pleasures and hostile to any God that could allow, among other things, his son to be taken at such a young age. That might sound self-centered and indulgent, but that was also Miguel. He hated confinement in any form, especially at the end of his life.

My plan was to fly in to Boston from Houston, spend Thursday with Miguel, and then fly back Friday. But I would return only if his condition seemed stable enough to leave him. Or, if not, I would just stay in Boston with Miguel and miss the game. But he had no patience for the second option. No way was I missing the Super Bowl on account of his bad heart, he said. He knew the Pats were playing. He knew the Super Bowl was the ultimate American party—and did I mention that he loved a party? "You only have so many chances for memories," Miguel would say. "Listen to your father."

This might be a slight reach of a parallel, but Tom Brady also talked about racing time. In his case, he was racing the standard assumptions of how long a person can play football at his insane level. Brady's coconspirator in this race was his doctrinal commitment to his "lifestyle"—and to Guru Guerrero himself.

Beyond his TB12 salesmanship proposition, Brady is at his core a killer control freak. My dad was, too. Both were determined, and again lucky, to be able to live their lives in a way that allowed them optimal control over their time and freedom to pursue their zeal to the fullest. That's about where their similarities ended (and needless to say, Miguel couldn't throw a spiral to save his life). But there are few privileges greater than having ample time at the helm of a shopping cart.

Mortality takes many forms, and death is only the most literal expression of it. There are obvious parallels between our human fears of death and our desperation to maximize and extend something we cherish—a career, a season, or a passion for something. In a livelihood sense, we're all athletes. If lucky, maybe we get twenty years to perform at a high level doing something that we love, before something or someone comes along to take it away. Ideally, that love does not come with any long-term health risks, but even when it does, in the case of football players, most will say they have no regrets. No one said the end was supposed to be easy for them, or for anyone, or that it had to come without a fight.

One thing that stood out from my time with Brady was how certain of his philosophies he could seem. This might have been the salesman Brady talking, or just the messianic tone of someone who dabbled in motivational speaking (Brady would headline a Tony Robbins event in 2017, which, to be honest, bummed me out a little when I heard about it). You can't help being skeptical of anyone hawking **answers**. But beyond that, Brady could become vulnerable at certain points. Once was when he started talking to me about his own father and his voice cracked. He said he wished Tom Senior took better care of himself. "He says, 'I'd rather die than not eat ice cream,'" Brady said of his father. "But my dad is the most optimistic guy I've ever met. He will meet someone and three weeks later, he'll think they're best friends. I take on a little of that. Kraft would always tell me there's a naïveté to me, you know, like, he'll say it in a good way, I think."

Brady went on about how difficult it is to persuade his father to change his lifestyle. "You can't control what people do, even people you love so much," Brady said. There was this exchange at the beginning of Super Bowl week as Brady was completing his Opening Night media duties. When he wasn't warding off questions about Trump and Deflategate, Brady took a question from a kid reporter named Joseph who was seated on the shoulders of ESPN's Trent Dilfer. "Many people say you're their hero," Joseph asked. "Who is your hero?"

Brady smiled, said it was a great question, and then nearly lost it. "I think my dad is my hero, because he's someone I look up to every day," Brady said, and then he stopped and nodded his head as his eyes welled up. "And, uh . . . " he tried to continue, "just my dad."

Tom Junior had alluded to his mother's "health issues" without getting into details. "Yeah, this year my mom hasn't been to a game this season and my dad hasn't been to one," he said. "It is very atypical." But I was struck that what triggered Brady's emotion was the mention of his father, the caretaker, and not the parent who was actually sick. The Toms had an unusually close father-son friendship, maybe slightly fraught. I thought of Tom Senior's recollection of how devastated he was when his pal opted for faraway Ann Arbor over nearby Berkeley, and how Tom Junior was wise enough at that age to realize that this might have been a necessary separation. But clearly their bond had evolved, endured, and has taken some sad turns down fragile roads of old age, cross-country distance, an unforgiving league, and the prospect of the Unbeaten Opponent, mortality.

The expectation was that Galynn Brady would be well enough to travel to Houston for the game. But I had spoken to Tom Senior, who told me that his wife of forty-six years had been suffering from pneumonia and shingles, so it was looking like a game-time decision. Death might be the ultimate game clock that's beyond our control, but there are worse goals to shoot for than getting to a Super Bowl—or a seventh.

24.

CLOCKS AND SITCOMS

February 5, 2017

By the time I arrived back in Houston on Friday, the city had gone from being a zoo to a party penitentiary. The weekend's arrival brought a swarm of football merrymakers trying to navigate closed roads and clampdown security checkpoints. I scored a few sweet party invites. I saw some things, such as: Mark Davis at the "Commissioner's Party" being taunted by the daughter of Broncos owner Pat Bowlen. "I really like the Raiders," she told him. "Especially when we're kicking your ass." Her tone captivated Davis. "I like the sound of that," he said, and I left the Membership kids to their devices.

Her Majesty of the Shield, Jane Goodell, sarcastically thanked me for "really starting the week out on the right note for us." She was referring to a story I had published in the **Times** a few days earlier in which I'd recycled a bunch of unused but newly relevant quotes that Trump had given me for a story a year and a half earlier—a practice known in journalism circles as "composting" (making use of discarded material—very green). "The commissioner is a weak guy," I had quoted Trump saying. He had also referred to Goodell as "a dope."

Also composted in the story: Trump criticized Kraft for not suing the league over Deflategate. Kraft did not perform well under pressure, Trump said. He should never have trusted Goodell. "He choked, just like Romney choked," Trump said of Kraft. Kraft pulled me aside at a pregame tailgate party the league had hosted next to NRG Stadium.

"Did Trump really say that I choked?" Kraft wanted to know. Yes, I told him, though it was a throwaway line from about eighteen months earlier. But Kraft did seem wounded. "Did he really compare me to Romney?" Yes, I said again, but it was in the context of Deflategate—and besides, sir, your team is about to play in another Super Bowl, why are you worried about this? Kraft, who wore an aqua blue suit with pocket squares, shook his head. Even at pinnacle moments, it is always essential to be loved and respected at the most powerful levels. "It was a shock to read that," Kraft said.

By now I'd been to enough of these quasi-exclusive NFL parties to gain a déjà vu sense of Usual Suspects assembled (and reassembled) in a swamp. I had arrived at a similar impression about D.C. parties years earlier. For a while, you're a bit dazzled to be in the presence of—and even cultivated by—high-level politicians. But over time, they acquire the sameness of familiar characters going through high-level motions. They are afflicted with the same boredoms, insecurities, hang-ups, and discomforts as the rest of us. Billionaires, commissioners, and Gold Jackets can just as easily become Usual Suspects. It's all the same sitcom.

Woody Johnson was commiserating about all the disclosure forms he had to fill out after Trump had designated him ambassador to the United Kingdom. His audience was Sam Skinner, a former cabinet official and White House chief of staff under President George H. W. Bush, as well as Roger Goodell's father-in-law. Johnson wore a bright white Jets cap and had his young sons from his second marriage with him. They kept running up to show off their newest autographs. "Jerry Jones!" one of the boys told him. "Shaquille O'Neal," the other one one-upped. "That's great," the proud father told his boys, and Woody stood humanized before my eyes.

L.A. bridesmaids Mark Davis and Dean Spanos stood together a few feet away from the

Wood Man, both wearing white (think of Davis as the bowl-headed Jim Carrey in **Dumb and Dumber**, with Spanos played by Jeff Daniels). I heard "Dino" getting some "best wishes" for finally getting his Chargers to L.A. He received them with a pained smile, like he was being congratulated for a hernia.

Davis, meanwhile, was fielding queries about the Raiders' fleeing Oakland. "Is Vegas real?" Shaquille O'Neal wanted to know. It might be, Davis said. "You need a tight end?" O'Neal wondered.

Before getting his answer, Shaq lumbered away to pose for more pictures, leaving me alone with Davis and in need of an icebreaker. As always, I was prepared with an obscure detail. I had just been reading an old book about the NFL (**The League**, by David Harris) in which Al Davis went off on a riff about how incredible his son's bar mitzvah was. "I was just reading about how proud your father was of your bar mitzvah," I said to Mark Davis, who melted when I said this.

"It was a great bar mitzvah," he agreed, grinning. "It was near Lake Merritt in Oakland. A lot of the Raiders were there."

"LOOKING GOOD, SAL," SOMEONE CALLED OUT to ESPN's Sal Paolantonio, posing for photos with a bunch of Pats fans waiting to get into NRG Stadium. This seemed a good way to begin a live

Super Bowl experience, the visage of Sal Pal ministering to his communicants. I snapped a picture for the Sal Pal photo essay that Belson and I were curating from our various safaris. This will include several shots of Sal Pal's big face filling TVs over hotel bars.

Super Bowl crowds are made up heavily of fat cats, league types, and others with minimal rooting interest—thus subdued. It heightens the studio feel inside the coliseum, the sense that we're all extras at America's ultimate TV production. But something else felt different about this Super Bowl. It had to do with the political moment we were living through, as if the game had become a proxy for our national divisions. Super Bowls are promoted by the league as unifying spectacles. They celebrate competition, brute strength, and branding prowess. But the struggle must always be leavened with fun commercials, booze, and feel-good performances (Up with People used to play at halftime until Pete Rozelle killed the tradition—another mark of his good judgment). This Super Bowl, though, felt less like a civic rivalry—my town versus your town—and more like a theater for a cultural bar fight. Coalitions of the "Us" and the "Them" are inexact, but there was a decided bent in this game of Make America Great Again versus The Resistance; the dynasty rooted on by Richard Spencer and Donald Trump versus the team whose season ticket base is 40 percent black and whose slogan was #RiseUp. In a pregame interview with Fox, Trump again asserted that he has great friends on the Patriots and predicted a New England win by eight points. It all felt like an opening Hunger Game in the broader Trump-era divide. Things were only getting started.

When Atlanta scored first, the reaction on Twitter reinforced the idea of a political grudge match on turf. "America 7—Trump voters 0" distilled this pretty well (courtesy of @NotBillWalton); so did "The Falcons respect an independent judiciary." I spent more time on Twitter than usual during a game I cared about. Being the Super Bowl, there were ceremonies and longer breaks, thus more time to fill. Plus, as a Pats fan—and everyone knows how this game went—the first half was dreadful, though much of America seemed ecstatic. Twitter also reflected the fact that many Super Bowl commercials were playing to the political environment, particularly as they related to Trump's immigration orders and plans for a border wall. Once a melting pot of cheesy dips and wagering, this Super Bowl Sunday felt more like a family Thanksgiving during divorce proceedings. Did everyone see that Budweiser ad that followed the journey of company founder Adolphus Busch as he immigrated to America from Germany? Discuss. Apparently it was a pretty woke message from Bud;

or, if you prefer, an attempt at liberal pandering. A #BoycottBudweiser hashtag was born by halftime.

"These commercials have been a bonanza of leftist activism," a **Breitbart** editor complained. "Two immigration commercials, a feminist commercial, now an eco wacko commercial? Am I missing anything?"

Personally, I was missing something—my football team.

THE FALCONS LED 21–3 AT THE HALF. BRADY threw a pick-six, his receivers kept getting crushed and dropping passes, and Atlanta's skill players—orders of magnitude faster than New England's defenders—were running free.

I hate Super Bowl halftimes. They are endless. Give me more football, ASAP. But this one felt like a nice break from the carnage. Lady Gaga was scheduled to perform. Would she get political? This was a bit of a cliff-hanger—and the game's result was looking less like one, so we'll take the drama where we can. It was not out of the question that Ms. Gaga would make some political statement, given her liberal and provocateur proclivities. But she kept it clean, making her entrance into the stadium via suspension wires from the stadium roof.

Atlanta scored first in the second half, another

touchdown: 28–3. It was more of the same. Until it wasn't; and then things got blurry.

Patriot running back James White caught a short touchdown pass from Brady with 2:06 left in the third quarter. Stephen Gostkowski missed the extra point. It was that kind of day. The Pats got the ball back, moved down the field; but the drive stalled, they settled for a field goal (that kind of day): 28–12.

Brady and his receivers were starting to click, finally. But time was the issue, as it often is. There was no one better at racing it than Brady, but MVP Matt Ryan now controlled the clock and ball. Until he didn't! Sack, fumble, and Brady back on the field. No more Twitter and politics, hello football game.

The Falcons controlled the ball for less than a minute—they burned almost no time on the clock. Brady didn't either. He hit a six-yard touchdown pass to Danny Amendola, two-point conversion run by White, 28–20 with 5:56 left.

There was now actual noise in the stadium. Pats fans travel much louder than their Foxborough versions. But the full comeback was still a long shot—again, because of time. If Ryan and the most potent offense in the NFL could get two or three first downs and a field goal, it would be over. Julio Jones caught an insane 27-yard pass along the right sideline to give the Falcons a second first down of the drive and put them at the

Patriots' 22, well inside field-goal range. Now they would surely run the ball three times, kill some clock, kick a field goal, and that would be the end. Unless it wasn't.

A sack and holding penalty took Atlanta out of range; an incomplete pass on third down froze the clock. The punting team came out and Brady started at his own 9.

Belson kept reading me things off Twitter but I wasn't listening. Brady was suddenly in one of those mechanical zones of his: passes to Chris Hogan, Malcolm Mitchell, Amendola, two to White, and a fingertip-on-turf revelation by Julian Edelman. I envisioned Brady humming to himself as he worked.

The Falcons' defense looked like they were running in sand. Another touchdown by White, conversion by Amendola, and we were headed to overtime. The ending felt determined at this point, even before the Pats won the coin toss and Atlanta's body language resembled Sunday morning at a frat house. The comeback materialized so fast yet also felt suspended in clouds. But it was only a matter of time.

(Spoiler alert:) 34–28, Pats in OT. James White again, TD from two yards out, ruling on the field confirmed.

On an escalator to the postgame avails, I was a few steps down from an older African American gentleman wearing a Patriots #31 jersey. "Jonathan Jones," the man told me when I asked who 31 was. "He's my son." Really! "He made some plays," I said. Jones was an undrafted rookie free agent out of Auburn, an undersized cornerback who made the roster as a special teams demon. His dad looked like he could have been crying but might have been just spent. I congratulated him. "My son won the Super Bowl," Mr. Jones said in response, saying it like a question, as if he wasn't sure it was real.

I struggled through the bedlam. Martellus Bennett had his three-year-old daughter, Jett, on his lap. She hijacked his press conference (talking about her dog peeing on a rug) until he took it back. "It's like waking up and eating cake for breakfast," Bennett said of this experience. "It's super cool."

Patriots started filing out of their locker room. It sounded raucous in there. Offensive linemen were smoking cigars. A bunch of players were holding boxes of pizza as they walked out. They were headed to some victory party and fully prepared (with pizza!). Brady had his game jersey swiped in the postgame commotion, it was later learned. Kraft would compare the heist of Tommy's shirt to "taking a great Chagall or Picasso." The FBI became involved, among other international law enforcement entities—more off-season reality-show fodder. Eventually the jersey would be recovered from the media figure who swiped it. The guy was from Mexico! Really, how on-message can Trump's team be? Or maybe this was a moment to put our national divorce on hold and submit to the powers of pliability.

I caught Brady and Guerrero walking out together. Brady's face was stuck in a far-off smile. They walked down the hallway and crowds parted for him. The whole tableau was a groggy trance. No one—not even participants—had processed what just occurred. This would require film review. I rewatched the Fox broadcast five times, though it never took that long because I always started at 28–3. When you can control the clock, you do it.

Miguel would die a few days later. He would rewind some things if he could—and who wouldn't? But I made it back in time to be with him at the end, and that was a hell of a party.

25.

TURN-ONS

February 2017

Literally no one is happy for you, Patriots fans. Everything good about sports is wasted on you. Any enjoyment to be had as a neutral observer of last night's game—objectively, it really was one of the greatest Super Bowls ever, if not THE greatest—is soured by the fact that you bloated bags of shit are, through sheer cosmic luck, the beneficiaries of the Patriots' greatness.

—DREW MAGARY, DEADSPIN,
FEBRUARY 6, 2017

I was really beginning to think that people don't like us. Where do we apologize? Oh, fuck it.

> **Congrats, Patriots fans! You are the official team of the alt-right! They're all yours. More important, your team is now emblematic of an America that is distorted beyond recognition: a place where people are less revered than the bold and brave companies that maximize delivery and efficiency by phasing out every last trace of humanity and treating people like coal to be shoveled into a furnace.**
>
> —MAGARY, DEADSPIN, SEPTEMBER 7, 2017

Tough but fair. But where were we?

At the posh league tailgate before the Super Bowl, I had parked myself next to a five-star table where Bob Kraft was seated along with his son Jonathan, Jerry Jones with his son Stephen (the Cowboys' CEO), and a few others. As owners of one of the participating Super Bowl teams, the Krafts were enjoying Prom Queen status at the party. People kept coming over, hugging them, and saying things into their ears, paying respects.

Jerry Jones was riding high on the Cowboy

saddle himself, even more than usual. He had learned the night before he would be part of the Hall of Fame class of 2017. David Baker had informed the finalists of their fates. "If you don't make it in, you get a phone call," Jones explained to me. "If you're in, Dave Baker himself comes to your room."

Jones had been in a suite with his family, hoping for the phone not to ring. And then, wouldn't you know it, God knocked on the door just after dinner with word of Jerry's immortality. He would be introduced on the field, along with the rest of his Hall of Fame class, at the end of the first quarter—Jerry would be introduced I mean, not God, though there seemed little difference at this point.

"I fully expect to be booed on the field," Jones predicted correctly.

But for now, Jerry was a king of the village, taking congratulations from a receiving line of their club, a few sounding sincere. Everyone knew that Jones had craved Canton. Everyone does, but Jerry especially. He figured, with his three rings, work on the league committees, and all he had done to "build the NFL," this honor was past due. Kraft, of course, felt the same about Robert K. Kraft. And he was a ring up on Jones, two by the end of the night.

As I watched the old tycoons seated a few feet from each other, I wondered whether Jones would

trade his Gold Jacket for another Super Bowl ring—
or whether Kraft would trade one of his rings for
a Gold Jacket. I would get around to asking both
of them, but not then as they were busy getting
their rings and asses kissed before kickoff.

NOW THAT THE GAMES WERE DONE FOR A
while, it was time to return to the dueling Caligulas. Who was first among billionaires? Seasons
come and go but another Big Game is perennial—
the struggle to be considered the biggest, swing-
ingest member of the Membership. Was it Jones,
the devilish Arkansas wildcatter who owns the
league's most valuable team, or Kraft, emperor
of the league's presiding dynasty? The frisky sep-
tuagenarians had a shadow rivalry going. They
competed for rings (Kraft 5, Jones 3), Gold Jackets (Jones 1, Kraft 0), franchise value (Dallas
$4.8 billion, the most valuable team in the NFL,
per **Forbes**; New England finished second at
$3.7 billion), and other intangibles. Kraft was the
first owner to buy a dedicated team plane, a Boeing 767 christened **AirKraft**. He has led trips to
Israel with several Hall of Famers; Jones traveled
with a half dozen Gold Jackets to the Vatican.
Both men prized the limelight and company of
celebrity friends. Both go way back with Donald
Trump, and yes, competed for his public affection, too.

It was not lost on Jones that Trump had so conspicuously cozied up to Kraft during his 2016 presidential campaign. And did so even more after Trump won the presidency and Kraft's team won another Super Bowl. Within a few days of the game, Kraft joined the newly inaugurated President Trump and Prime Minister Shinzo Abe of Japan for an exclusive dinner at Mar-a-Lago. (This inspired the political journalist Sasha Issenberg to tweet that Abe should "reciprocate by forcing Trump to have dinner with the owner of the Nippon Ham Fighters.")

Some of Jones's fellow owners had described Jones as the NFL's Donald Trump. He was a big-talking billionaire showman easily dismissed as a carnival barker. He has a tendency to believe he runs the league, or should, or that his own exceptionalism should prevail over the plutocratic socialism he and his thirty-one fellow owners have entered into. "Jerry sometimes forgets that it's a kibbutz," Kraft has complained to his partners. When I asked Jones how he felt being compared with Trump, he was thrilled. Trump's rise, he said, "is one of the great stories in America. And let me tell you this," he went on: "The president ain't no joke. He's got as good a chance to be right as any of them."

Kraft is more demure in his self-grandeur but no less transparent. He does his best to be calculating and please as many audiences as he can.

Like any politician, Kraft tends to say quite different things for public and private consumption. In our interviews, he was constantly going off the record. This could become annoying, as he would then sometimes contradict something he had just said for the record.

Kraft's friendship with Trump provides a case in point. Kraft loves being a presidential buddy, but is also aware that many of his high-rent friends don't approve. So Kraft is quick to mention to his friends—privately—that he disagreed with Trump on many issues, and with many of the incendiary things the president has done and said. But he would rather have the presidential ear and try to be a positive influence. He tried selling Arthur Blank on this line, which the Falcons owner was not buying.

"I said, 'You fucker, you've given him a lot of money,'" Blank told Kraft. "'You have influence and spend time with him,'" Blank persisted. "'Robert, there are things he's saying and doing that are not great for this country. And the smartest people in the world today, you know they're viewing him as a four-year mistake.'"

This is the same Krafty jujitsu he deploys when the topic of Roger Goodell comes up. As an "influential owner" with a national profile, Kraft has been tireless in his support. Within the Membership, Kraft is eager to be considered the commissioner's ranking mentor—the so-called assistant commissioner. But when talking to "our fan base," Kraft is eager to pass himself off as their kindred soldier, just another fan still aggrieved over Deflategate.

I asked Kraft, in an interview at his Gillette Stadium office early in the 2017 season, whether he still counted himself a supporter of the commissioner's. It was clear he was. Kraft that summer had been a prime mover behind a new contract for Goodell. But there was also his Goodell-hating "fan base" to consider: at the season opener against the Kansas City Chiefs a few days earlier, Pats fans had greeted Goodell by waving seventy thousand towels bearing the commissioner's likeness adorned with a clown's nose.

Kraft paused to ponder my question about whether he supported the commissioner. He looked across his desk at Stacey James, his PR bodyguard. "Yes, yes," Kraft said finally, pushing the word out. "I think it's a very difficult job. I've learned to compartmentalize." He said he only wants what's in the best long-term interests of the NFL.

"And you think Goodell is the best person to be leading the NFL?" I asked again, maybe betraying skepticism.

"Can we go off the record?" Kraft said.

By all accounts, Myra Kraft's death in 2011 devastated Robert Kraft. He mentioned "my sweetheart" several times during our discussions.

He spoke to me about how "the guys in the locker room saved me after I lost my sweetheart." One senses with Kraft a bit of a weary soul, no matter how many red carpets he walks, how many billions he has, or how many "guys in the locker room" have become honorary family members. "I cried myself to sleep every night for a year after my wife died, until I met my girlfriend," Kraft told me. Hearing Kraft say this, it's impossible not to feel compassion and even warmth for the man. But then Kraft repeated the words nearly verbatim in my subsequent two visits to his office, and the sentiment—while no doubt sincere—started coming off like a line.

At the time of this particular conversation, Kraft's girlfriend was a blond shiksa/actress/dancer named Ricki Noel Lander. She was nearly forty years Kraft's junior. They met at a dinner party about a year after Myra's death, at the home of Giants co-owner Steve Tisch in Beverly Hills.

When Ricki-Bobby first became an item, the age difference between the couple was widely remarked upon. Kraft then turned up in a strange and heavily mocked audition tape featuring the bikini-clad Ricki, the latter of whom was trying out for a role in the film **The Internship**, starring Vince Vaughn and Owen Wilson. The clip of Kraft's not-quite-Oscar-worthy performance ends with Kraft's punching some guy in the face while uttering the immortal words "Fuck you, pussy." (Just watch the thing—it's all over the internet.) Kraft would issue an apology and promise to "stick to my day job" in the future. The audition tape was filmed at a studio in the basement of NFL headquarters at 345 Park Avenue; it was Goodell himself who authorized Kraft and Ricki to use the studio, though it is unclear whether he knew the exact nature of the eventual audition tape. (Sadly, Ricki did not get the part.)

Ricki-Bobby dated on and off for a few years. In between, Kraft has been seen at various functions with much younger blond friends. At the commissioner's party a few nights before the Super Bowl in Houston, Kraft was accompanied by a stunningly gorgeous blonde in a very tight dress, who couldn't have been older than thirty. When you mention Kraft's name around the league, his collection of "friends half his age" is often the first thing people mention. They do so with both mockery and envy. In the case of NFL owners, moral high ground in this category is not crowded. No shortage of them has lacked for much younger playmates. There is apparently some overlap, too. At the end of a heated session during an owners' meeting in New York in late 2017, Jones rose to deliver a Kumbaya speech. He mentioned the owners' unique brotherhood, according to a source in the meeting, which included league officials and about half the Membership. This occurred during a period of discord over players' protesting the national anthem. "We've shared great success and adversity," Jones said. "Even girlfriends," he added, breaking into his devious smile. It was not clear to my source exactly which owner(s) Jones was directing this last part to.

Late in the 2017 season, rumors began circulating that Ricki, who lived in Los Angeles, had given birth to a new daughter, assumed to be Robert's. Kraft, then seventy-six, threw a party at his Brookline mansion the night before the 2017 AFC Championship Game in which "Robert's baby" was the subject of much whispering among the guests. The **New York Post** broke the news of Ricki's baby a few weeks later, leading the usually buttoned-up Patriots to issue a statement saying, "Robert Kraft is not the biological father." Beyond that, the team said, they would have no further comment, and subsequent inquiries were met with the paternity equivalent of "We're on to Cincinnati." It is not known whether Jerry Jones sent flowers.

From a pure ego perspective, it nagged at Kraft that Brady and Belichick are considered the twin masterminds of his dynasty. Kraft feels he deserves equal billing. And perhaps he does, as the owner who hired Belichick in 2000, who drafted Brady and then kept the machine together for approaching two decades. But of the trilogy, Kraft is by far the hungriest for recognition. He is always reciting his team's accomplishments under his watch (nine Super Bowl appearances, thirteen trips to the conference championship game). The old football reproach against excessive endzone celebrations—"Act like you've been here before"—has been lost on Kraft.

Once, when I was in Kraft's office, I asked him if he felt he received enough credit for his team's success. "Since there is so much focus on Brady and Belichick," I clarified, aware that I might have been picking a scab. "Sweethaht," Kraft said in his Boston-accented honk (he addresses people as "sweethaht" sometimes, often when agitated). "When you own the team, at some point someone figures out that ownership can mess it up. And maybe if you look around the league, you'll see maybe that has happened. I'll tell you, they'll be no team in the NFL that will win consistently without having good ownership, so I don't worry."

I admit that I felt a measure of fondness for Kraft, and not just because he owned the team I rooted for. He was such a familiar and smaller-than-life figure. He felt accessible. I knew a lot of people like him when I was growing up in Newton, Massachusetts, not far from where he and his sons would stop en route to the stadium on Sundays to pick up roast beef sandwiches from Provizer's Deli on Commonwealth Avenue. He used the term "tush" a lot. At the beginning of our discussions, Kraft would make a point of saying that he agreed to talk again because he "felt a connection" to me. And maybe he did, but again. When he said this a third time, it began to feel manipulative.

Still, it was a little endearing, too, that Kraft would take such an impish and even vulnerable approach to ingratiating himself. He also, on two of my visits, presented me with a half dozen organic eggs from chickens raised by a caretaker at his Brookline mansion. "I eat these eggs every day," Kraft told me. "That's the reason I still have hair." It was probably too late for me, hairwise, but this was still a nice gesture by Mr. Kraft, like Charlemagne handing out opals and diamonds. The eggs were tremendous.

In the middle of one of our interviews, Kraft took a call on his cell phone from one of his granddaughters, an undergraduate at the University of Michigan. She was calling Kraft back after he had called her earlier for her birthday. "Hi sweetie pie, how ah ya?" Kraft said, with a big smile. He put her on speakerphone. "I'm actually sitting here with a reporter for the **New York Times** who went to Michigan, a graduate," Kraft said. We exchanged pleasantries, me and the granddaughter ("What dorm do you live in?"). Kraft took her off speaker. He said he didn't know what to get her for her birthday so was "just going to send you something" (guessing a check). "Oh, I love YOU," Kraft said warmly. "Thanks, I love you.

Thanks for calling sweetie pie, I love ya." It was sweet.

"Some of the gals I date make fun of me," Kraft told me, after hanging up. I wasn't sure what he was referring to, but I thought he might have been making a joke about how he's old enough to be some of his girlfriends' grandfather. "Is she older than any of them?" I joked, referring to Kraft's granddaughter and the "gals" he mentioned. This was a little edgy on my part. I regretted the attempt at humor instantly. When Kraft didn't react, I worried that I'd fallen on my tush. Luckily, his ADD kicked in, and Kraft started racking his brain over what we had been talking about before his granddaughter called.

Kraft says he feels no rivalry at all with Jerry Jones. If there is a rivalry, it's all on Jerry's side, or in Jerry's head. "I really bear envy towards no one," Kraft told me. "Since I put dirt on my wife's casket, I really realized what's important. The things we worry about are paper clips."

Still, enshrinement in Canton would represent the ultimate paper clip for Mr. Kraft. He wants that megarecognition badly, preferably before he dies. Kraft has a compelling case. He has served on many of the league's most important committees. He was instrumental in negotiating the league's massive broadcast contracts and its last collective bargaining agreement. There is also the Patriots' gaudy run of on-field success.

He would never admit this publicly, but it does bother Kraft that he is not in the Hall of Fame— and also that Jones got there first.

Would Kraft trade one of his Super Bowl rings for Jones's Gold Jacket? "No way," Kraft told me. Hall of Fame voting tends to be political. "A ring is earned," he said. "It means you've outmanaged your competition and you've managed excellence at the highest level. To me, that's more of a turn-on."

26.

THIS MAN'S LIVER
BELONGS IN CANTON

March 2017

Jerry Jones had been turned on pretty much since
the night before the Super Bowl. News that he'd
be inducted into the Hall of Fame further en-
gorged Jerry's already healthy ego like a perpetual
Viagra drip. It represented a milestone, sanctify-
ing Jones's status as first among members. People
in the league noticed an immediate change.

I ran into Jones in March, at the league's annual meeting at the Arizona Biltmore Hotel in
Phoenix. He was with his son Stephen, having a
beer at the bar in the middle of the afternoon.
I approached their table, congratulated Jerry on
his honor, and asked Jones if he would now be
the only "active owner" in the Hall of Fame. By
"active," I meant living, but Jerry took a more

nuanced definition. This depended, he said, on whether I counted Dan Rooney as being "active." Rooney, the Hall of Fame chairman of the Steelers, had been in failing health. He died a month later, at eighty-four, officially rendering himself "inactive," and leaving Jones as the only Gold Jacket owner still strutting the earth.

Across the bar and just off the lobby, Raiders owner Mark Davis was in the midst of a small commotion of angry Raiders fans. Davis had just won the right—per a 31–1 vote from his fellow owners—to move his team from Oakland to Las Vegas. That would make the Raiders the third NFL team to relocate in a fourteen-month period. Rabid Raider rooters from the Bay Area were the latest fan cohort to be aggrieved, and several of them traveled to Phoenix to tell the Captain Kangaroo–haired carpetbagger how they felt about his coming abandonment. In the spirit of confronting his victims head-on, Davis approached one of them, Godfather Griz Jones, the leader of a Raiders fan group called Forever Oakland. Davis extended his hand, but was rebuffed. Cold!

Davis pleaded for dialogue. He told Griz he wanted to talk about "the team's future," and how meaningful it would be if only they could all work together to support their beloved Raiders in their new home in the desert.

"There is no future," Griz said.

Ouch. Davis looked wounded, but rebounded quickly—near-billion-dollar stadium subsidies (from Nevada in this case) take the edge off such snubs. In the friendlier confines of the Membership, Davis was being treated more like a conquering hero. Few maneuvers are more respected among NFL owners than finagling a sweet stadium deal from a sucker municipality. Even more impressive in this case was that it was the nutty Mark Davis who pulled it off, someone who "surprises people if he can roll out of bed and put on his pants," as one owner put it to **ESPN The Magazine**.

Davis then headed off to receive an audience of well-wishing insiders at a Biltmore restaurant. **Sports Illustrated**'s Peter King, who was dining nearby, asked Davis if he had thought that day about his late father, Al Davis.

Having Al Davis as a dad must have been quite the fraught setup. My favorite story of Davis family pathology involved the great Raiders receiver Cliff Branch, who for a time had hired Mark Davis to be his agent—with hopes that Mark could get more money out of his dad. "I got kicked out of the house," Davis said. But then Branch scored two touchdowns in the Super Bowl, Mark recalled, and all of a sudden he was back in the family's good graces.

"I think about him every day," Mark Davis said of his late father, and then entertained the logical follow-up question: What would Al Davis think of the Raiders' moving to Las Vegas?

Mark paused and assumed a quizzical look. "I really don't know what he would think," Mark said.

Back at the bar, I stopped again at the Joneses' table. Jerry, who had moved on from beer to something amber colored in a tumbler, waved me over and said he had enjoyed my previous "visit" (everything constitutes a "visit" to southern men of a certain age, even a thirty-second drop-by at his table, such as my earlier "visit"). I seized this chance to remind Jerry that the two of us had had a fine visit in Dallas about a year earlier and I looked forward to visiting with him again in the future. He replied that he had enjoyed visiting before, and would very much look forward to that. I thanked him and headed off. Another good visit!

Our next visit would take place in Dallas about a month later. Jerry Jones was sitting aboard the Cowboys' bus, in the parking lot of a golf course not far from the Dallas–Fort Worth Airport. He was taking a break from the Cowboys Golf Classic, the tournament the team hosts every spring. As a general rule, the Dallas Cowboys' bus is not a place for the faint of heart, or liver.

At two p.m., Jones was sipping from a cup of tea. He had been battling a cough. But after about a half hour, the namesake King of Jerry's World was done messing around. He was not just any Hall of Fame owner, but an **active** Hall of Fame owner, especially when his habitat is amply stocked with his favored libation, Johnnie Walker Blue. "I do like to have a drink," Jones confirmed, something I'd heard from a few people over the years. "Do you want a shot of Scotch?" Jones asked me. Sure, I said, not realizing that by "shot," Jones was talking about blue twenty-four-ounce plastic stadium cups bearing the Cowboys' logo, soon to be filled—and refilled—to the top.

"This ought to take care of that cough," Dr. Jones proclaimed, raising his big cup and welcoming me to Dallas. It is not easy keeping up with the Joneses. I learned this the hard way.

One of the drivers in Jerry's employ, an African American gentleman named Emory, opened a back cabinet stocked with $250 bottles of "Blue." No doubt Jones could afford the smooth booze, but he also mentioned a qualifier. "It's the stuff it makes you do after you've had it that you might not be able to afford," he said. I relay this by way of transparency into Jones's inhibitions, which after a few more supersized pours from Emory were weakening fast.

After meandering around for a bit, I presented Jones with a flipped-around version of the question I had previously asked Kraft: Would Jones trade his Gold Jacket for one of Bob Kraft's rings?

Jones was nowhere near as definitive as Kraft was on the Gold Jacket versus ring question.

"Oh boy," Jones kept saying. "Boy. Boy! Boy! Boy! Boy." His face filled in a kind of sloppy and happy grimace, befitting this high-class dilemma. He suggested an alternative riddle. How about if I asked whether Jones would pay a quarter billion dollars for another Super Bowl ring?

"Why don't you ask me that?" Jones proposed. "If you could assure me of that, you'd walk out of here with a check."

Nope, can't do it, I said, and repeated my question: Would he trade his Hall of Fame jacket for another ring?

"No," Jones said finally. "No."

Sitting a few feet away, Rich Dalrymple, the Cowboys' longtime head of public relations, shook his head. "You messed that one up," he told his boss. Jerry tried to explain himself.

"I've been involved in Super Bowls," Jones said. He had three rings already, although none since 1996. He just loves his "babies," as he calls them. He has been known to slip one ring on each hand to announce his presence in places where he might not rightly be identified. Jones will walk into joints far from Dallas. He will slap his weighted hands down on the bar—**crack**—to break the ice with strangers.

"How 'bout them Cowboys?!"

No question, Jerry loves his babies, as if they were actual babies. But he still puts the experience of winning a Super Bowl a tad behind getting into the Hall of Fame. "Uh, well, let me think of how to say this," Jones said, trying to amend his answer to something more acceptable to Cowboys Nation. "I'm stumbling around here."

"He gets one mulligan, right?" Dalrymple tried to appeal to me. "Since we're on the golf course?"

Dalrymple wanted Jones to change his answer to the more politically correct "another Super Bowl." Fans would hope and expect to hear that from their first-class owner. It would reassure them that it's all about winning and rings. Otherwise it's just a rich guy's ego trip. But what a trip!

I was noncommittal on the mulligan. Actually, I was closer to inoperative at that point, as Emory had just inflicted a third massive cup of "love potion," as Jerry took to calling the Blue. My tape recorder, however, remained fully functional.

"Of course Rich would want me to say it's all about the Super Bowls," Jones said.

Dalrymple acknowledged that he was not at all surprised that Jones would value his Hall of Fame induction over another Super Bowl ring. The jacket is a more rarefied honor: a little more than three hundred NFL legends have received them, as opposed to the thousands who have gotten Super Bowl rings. "You're talking about immortality," Dalrymple said. "But I wouldn't want you to say that publicly," he added, looking back at Jones, who just did.

Jones grinned and shrugged. "I answered truthfully," he said. "I was trying to be truthful." Jones then raised his empty cup and jiggled the ice cubes to get the attention of Emory, who administered more truth.

It's important to have fun, Jones said, becoming philosophical. He's always managed to enjoy his various undertakings. As a young man, Jones said he did a stint as a shoe salesman, which he also loved. He then said something about "spending the afternoon masturbating over selling shoes."

Wait, WHAT?

"I've sold shoes," Jones said again, "and I've masturbated in my shoes."

Okay then. "We've all been there, sir," I said, trying to be reassuring. (Author's note: I have never masturbated into my shoes—or anyone's shoes.)

"We're deteriorating," Jones acknowledged. "But here is my point. I can tell you when I was selling them shoes, and I've sold a bunch of shoes, and I've sold insurance . . . I promise you the shoe itself won't get it done. The policy itself won't get it done, unless you're having fun."

Here I jumped in and made a parenthetical observation.

"I guarantee you that Robert Kraft is not sitting somewhere on a bus talking about masturbating in his shoes," I said. This is as safe of a guarantee as I have ever made to anyone. Jerry collapsed onto his side in a belly laugh. "And that's why he's not in the Hall of Fame," I added.

Dalrymple chimes in something about Kraft having a beautiful young girlfriend.

"Yep, Bob's got us all beat," Jerry announced.

"Let's put him in the Hall of Fame," Dalrymple suggested.

"Let's **do** put him in the Hall of Fame," Jones agreed. "He gets a Gold Jacket for that."

It was after five p.m., and we had officially blown past the three-hour mark of the interview. "The Johnnie Walker Blue sort of distorted our time," Jones said. That's not all it distorted. I was placing myself in the Cowboys' bus equivalent of injured reserve—not eligible to return.

Before leaving the vehicle, Jones invited me to lie down on one of its several couches. This was an excellent idea. No way was I in any condition to drive out of the parking lot, much less to my hotel. "I'm gonna tell Emory you're gonna take a nap," Jones said, as he struggled to open the door of the bus. "The only question is how do I get out of this motherfucker?"

Emory managed to liberate Jones, who headed off across the parking lot. Dalrymple would compare this encounter with a fifteen-round heavyweight bout in which "the guy from the **New York Times**" got buried in the thirteenth. He was being generous, since I am a middleweight, at best, and Jerry looked ready for another fifteen rounds. The Hall of Famer made a beeline for the clubhouse bar, where he ordered up some beers. "Hey, let's get some SEE-gars!" Jones was heard saying. This man's liver belongs in Canton.

Back in the recovery bus, I looked up from the couch to find the driver smirking down upon me. "I should have warned you about that, sir," Emory said. "We always warn people, you avoid the bus, or you're gonna pay. Everybody in the NFL knows that. It's **KNOWN**."

I closed my eyes, opened them again, and suddenly it was pitch dark and ten p.m. Knockout. **How 'bout them Cowboys?**

27.

"FAITH, FAMILY, AND FOOTBALL . . . PROBABLY NOT IN THAT ORDER"

April 18, 2017

Dan Rooney was a modest and humble gentleman, a throwback to a more modest and humble league. The longtime Steelers chairman was slight and stooped but a giant in the family business. His death, at eighty-four, was a Big Game, and his funeral was a mandatory rite for the lords of the league. If you love football, you have to respect Pittsburgh. The Steel City has a legit claim to being America's unrivaled mecca of the sport. A few other places might rate, maybe Green Bay, but I'd take Pittsburgh, factoring in: 1) the sustained excellence of the Steelers, whose six Super Bowl wins still lead the league; 2) western Pennsylvania's status as the country's most illustrious breeding ground of NFL legends, especially quarterbacks (Namath, Kelly, Marino, Montana, Unitas); and 3) football's roots as a factory game, which suit Pittsburgh's blue-collar identity like a windbreaker.

Football in Pittsburgh is for better or worse and till death do us part. And it is interchangeable with the Rooney family, whose patriarch, Art Rooney (Dan's father, known as "the Chief"), founded the Steelers in 1933. Natives discuss their **Stillers** in way-of-life terms, as their forebears used to speak of steel or coal mining. Life's a mixed bag, and so is love and so is football; sometimes you win, sometimes not; sometimes the factory closes and you get hurt on the field and nothing's supposed to come easy. Mr. Rooney's body was interned at Christ Our Redeemer Catholic Cemetery, not far from where Steeler Hall of Fame center Mike Webster's broken postfootball life, brain, and CTE discovery would be immortalized in the movie **Concussion**. For better, for worse.

I waited to pay respects at a public viewing held at Heinz Field the day before the patriarch's funeral. It was a warm spring day, late afternoon in solemn Pittsburgh. Irish bagpipes played "Danny Boy" echoing through the empty stadium. About half the people in line were dressed in suits and the other half were dressed for a Steelers game in November.

Most of the people I spoke to said they did not know Mr. Rooney well but appreciated what he did for Pittsburgh. African American mourners spoke with gratitude for Mr. Rooney's willingness to sign and draft black players and also for making them, as fans, feel welcome in a tribal, segregated, and majority-white city where they sometimes did not. (The NFL's "Rooney Rule," ensuring that minority candidates be interviewed for coach and executive jobs, was named for the Steelers' owner.)

"I love what he did for the black players," said lifelong Pittsburgher Camilla Ideley, an African American woman in a Steelers sweatshirt. She'd been rooting for the team her entire life but this was her first time at Heinz Stadium. She'd always had to work on Sunday during games and could never buy a ticket. But she left work early on this Monday to attend the viewing and pay her respects.

Funeral services were held the next morning at Saint Paul Cathedral, near the University of Pittsburgh. The proceedings had an end-of-an-era, won't-see-his-likes-again feel. It also had dignitaries—a former president (Obama), secretary of state (John Kerry), attorney general (Eric Holder), CEOs, dozens of Hall of Famers, two commissioners (Goodell and Tagliabue), representatives from the Nugget Industrial Complex, and Steeler royalty, past and present.

Art Rooney II, Dan's successor as Steelers chairman, paid tribute to his father on behalf of many admirers who wanted to. The Rooneys wished to avoid a fancy parade of eulogists, as anything too big-shotty would be unfit for Mr. Rooney. Art's speech lasted all of four minutes.

"Faith, family, and football" were his father's "core values," Art said, probably not in that order. He told brief stories: He was with his father once, attending daily Catholic mass during a visit to New York, when Dan's cell phone rang. To Art's surprise, his father picked up. How could he? In a cathedral? "I thought it might be the commissioner," Dan explained. God would understand, just as Art's mother, Patricia Rooney, understood when in 1968 Dan dropped her off at the hospital to give birth to their youngest daughter, Joan. "And then headed to the stadium to fire a coach," Art said.

I stood on the front steps of Saint Paul's and took in the assembled puzzle pieces: I met a city bus driver wearing a ragged Steelers jacket; a homeless woman and her daughter. Obama looked past the other dignitaries and made a point to shake the massive hand of Mean Joe Greene. (Rooney, a longtime Republican, had fallen hard for Obama and endorsed him early; Obama later appointed Rooney ambassador to Ireland.) Several owners—maybe two dozen here—milled around on the cathedral steps, waiting on Town

Cars. Would they get this number of owners at their own funerals? Would they get a president? (A cardinal? A Sal Pal?)

"Legacy" becomes a big deal to men of a certain age and wealth. Would they be remembered in the right way? Games end and scoreboards reset, but the final score goes in the books.

GOODELL WAS UNUSUALLY CLOSE TO DAN Rooney. It was Rooney who knocked on his hotel door in 2006 to tell him he would be the next NFL commissioner, after a series of deadlocked votes. Goodell, who tried to check in with each of the thirty-two owners at least once a month, told me he spoke to Dan Rooney almost every day. "It's hard to imagine this league without Dan Rooney," Goodell said.

Rooney died on the eve of what would become a tumultuous season for the NFL. For the second straight year, the league suffered a drop in television ratings.

Fracturing would occur at all levels—among owners, players, and fans; and along political, cultural, and racial lines. There were national anthem protests, fan furors, and the unprecedented circumstance of a United States president actively working to undermine the country's most popular and profitable sport. As in Donald Trump's rookie season in the White House, "division" was the inescapable watchword running through the turmoil of this campaign.

Players were divided among themselves, against the league and their owners; fans were furious with players, players mad at fans; fans with owners, owners with players, and owners with one another. "There's no question, this season has been probably unlike anything that I've been around," Art Rooney II told me at the end of 2017.

Among his many NFL roles, Dan Rooney used to chair the NFL's compensation committee, charged with determining the commissioner's salary. Falcons owner Arthur Blank, who succeeded Rooney as chairman, told me the story of the first owners' meeting he attended, in 2002, when Tagliabue was still commissioner. Rooney shuffled up to the microphone and announced he was going to issue a report on behalf of the committee. "He said, 'We've extended the commissioner's contract for five years, and if you have any questions, just call me,'" Blank recalled. That was it. Blank, the cofounder of Home Depot, was taken aback.

"I was like 'What the fuck?'" Blank said. "What kind of report was that?" The story underscores the uncluttered style of Dan Rooney and the relative simplicity of a process that, fifteen years later, would swirl into a mess.

Rooney was always stressing basic principles. Simplicity and modesty were foremost. David

Shribman, the executive editor of the **Pittsburgh Post-Gazette**, told me that whenever he went to lunch with Dan Rooney, "it always involved a tray," and usually took place at the Steelers' cafeteria. Shribman took me to dinner the night before Mr. Rooney's funeral (Thai food, no tray) and regaled me with stories of Rooney, usually landing on the theme of his everyman bona fides. "When pro football owners became highfliers, he remained grounded," Shribman wrote of Rooney following his death. "Dan Rooney was an ordinary guy in a field where there were no ordinary guys on the field."

Shribman told me about a lunch he had arranged with Rooney and Mary Leonard, a journalist who had moved to Pittsburgh from Washington to join the **Post-Gazette**. After the lunch, Shribman recalled, Leonard marveled about Rooney, how his kindness and lack of pretension stood in such contrast to the NFL owner she had left behind in her previous hometown. "He bears no resemblance at all to Dan Snyder," Leonard said of Rooney.

Rooney was never comfortable with the big business and audacious commercialism that had overtaken the modern NFL. He was rooted in a close-knit league of family businesses. There is a passage in Michael MacCambridge's bible of NFL history, **America's Game**, in which one owner speaks dismissively of Goodell's tendency to spew jargony business school terms such as "monetize" and "commoditize." The book also includes an account of Rooney sending Goodell an NFL jersey loaded up with advertising patches reminiscent of a NASCAR jacket. "This is what we're trying to avoid," Rooney wrote to Goodell.

Rooney also emphasized the importance of the Membership sticking together and putting the league before their self-interest. He urged his partners to solve problems "in house" and not let them spill into the press; and to avoid unnecessary drama. Dan Rooney would have hated the season to come.

28.

"WE NEED A BLACK
CHARLTON HESTON"

August–December 2017

They could have been any two billionaire schmucks taking an evening stroll through Manhattan. Robert Kraft and Arthur Blank had met up at the Plaza Hotel, where Kraft keeps an apartment. It was a warm night in August, and they decided to forgo the usual limo and head to dinner on foot.

Passersby who recognized them on the street expressed mild surprise that Kraft and Blank, the rival owners from the last Super Bowl, would be seen together. Kraft and Blank shared a few laughs over this. They are in fact close friends of similar age (mid-seventies), background (observant Jews from the Northeast, Blank from Queens and Kraft from Brookline, Mass.), means (multiple billions), and tastes (bespoke suits, younger women). Blank, however, needed to unburden himself of a minor beef with Kraft. It involved the aforementioned Super Bowl 51 rings that Kraft insisted be embedded with those 283 diamonds to commemorate the 28–3 deficit the Patriots overcame against the Atlanta Falcons. Blank, who bought the Falcons in 2002, mostly took the loss and the attendant trolling in stride. But the ring stunt bothered him. He found it unnecessary and tacky. "I said to Robert, 'You didn't have to do the 28–3 in the ring,'" Blank told me. "It kind of pissed me off."

In recounting the exchange, Blank mimicked Kraft's whiny, faux-sheepish response. "Well, you know how it is," Kraft replied to him. In fact, Blank does not know because his Falcons have never won a Super Bowl (and in case anyone forgot, the Pats had now won five). Kraft did not apologize. On the contrary, he told Blank that he should not be mad at him, but at the Falcons coaches. The exchange, which lasted all of about thirty seconds, ended there.

But Blank and Kraft had more important matters to discuss. They had come to New York in their capacities as members of the six-person compensation committee to iron out details of a contract extension for Commissioner Goodell. The dinner confab—held in the private room of the Midtown restaurant Aretsky's Patroon—felt like a formality.

Yes, Goodell had issues, and not small ones: the self-made imbroglios, the loathing that so many fans and players reserved for him, and the low-grade grumbling about the commissioner of the "can't we do better?" variety from several owners. Ultimately, though, the NFL is a conservative outfit whose stakeholders have a strong bias for the familiar. Goodell, for all his flaws, has been at the league thirty-six years and was part of the NFL furniture. More important, he performed splendidly in his primary role of making obscene amounts of money for his obscenely wealthy bosses.

Everything appeared to be on track for Goodell to receive a five-year contract extension with minimal friction—and maximum money, which could reach $200 million by 2024 if the league hit its financial targets (his current deal was set to expire after the 2019 season). Along with Blank, the committee chairman, and Kraft, the panel included four other influential owners chosen by Blank—Art Rooney, John Mara of the Giants, Bob McNair of the Texans, and Clark Hunt of the Chiefs. Jerry Jones had been sore that Blank had not chosen him to be on the committee. Jones had been agitating for a greater role in NFL governance and complaining for years that the league office had become bloated and that its executives were overpaid. This included the commissioner, whom he had otherwise given high marks, grading Goodell an "A-plus-plus" and "10 out of 10" as recently as 2016.

His fellow tycoons knew Jones had strong feelings about how the NFL was being run, and how important it was for him to be heard. In fact, Blank had told partners that he had grown tired of Jones's always being in his ear about the commissioner's deal. He decided to keep Jones involved in a semiofficial capacity by making him a nonvoting "adjunct" member of the committee.

As it was, Jones managed to gate-crash himself into the middle of the most divisive issues roiling the league in 2017. Dan Rooney's old committee would be the battleground on which the season's biggest points of contention would be waged—the commissioner's salary, Goodell's knack for turning player discipline matters into litigious fiascos, and the anthem protests that would unleash the president of the United States on his rival reality show, the NFL.

Goodell was in Colorado on the Friday night in September when Trump, at a rally in Alabama, called on NFL owners to fire players who knelt during the national anthem. "Get that son of a bitch off the field right now," Trump said. Joe Lockhart, the NFL's chief spokesman, called Goodell at 5:30 a.m. the following morning to discuss how to proceed.

Colin Kaepernick's initial protests in 2016 had inspired a dozen or so players to do the same or similar. But for all the media attention they received, the demonstrations had never reached a critical mass of players or prompted any significant fan resistance. Trump's provocation in Alabama changed that. "The week before the president made his statement, four people kneeled," Arthur Blank told me. "The president then said his thing, and then four hundred people kneeled." And even that response, Blank went on, showed signs of dying down within a few days, only to flare up again when Vice President Mike Pence waged (or staged) his own counterprotest, leaving an October 8 Indianapolis Colts game he was attending at taxpayer expense after a group of visiting 49ers knelt during the anthem.

Trump and Pence appealed to a vocal subset of NFL fans. They booed kneeling players and called for boycotts; teams argued politics among themselves, and some former players criticized current ones. ("It's the first time I've ever been ashamed to be a Patriot," the longtime New England lineman Matt Light said after a dozen current Patriots took a knee.) "No one was expecting this to happen, and it was hard to see coming," the Steelers' Art Rooney told me. "I think there was no question it hurt the league."

Certainly the situation went well beyond "distraction," which itself became a term of offense among protesting players. Russell Okung, an offensive tackle for the Los Angeles Chargers, said that the sequence of events—begun by Kaepernick, propelled by Trump—had turned the notion of "distraction" into something that could become a new period of activism in sports. "Never has our generation been presented with these historic choices," Okung told me. There could be ramifications within what has been an iron-fisted hierarchy inside the NFL. That's the nature of movements: they don't necessarily respect boundaries.

DONALD TRUMP IS NOT ONE FOR BOUNDARIES himself. As with so many things Trump, his cannonball into a relatively contained pool of player protest set off waves in all directions. In the absence of any great backlash to the initial Kaepernick-led demonstrations, the NFL could at least tacitly endorse the players' right to use their platform. But then suddenly not only the president of the United States but also a significant share of Americans were saying "Stand up and stick to sports." It moved the argument onto much more historically explosive—and, in a league where the owner-player divide is also largely a white-black divide, racially charged— grounds. During a tense owners' meeting at the height of the anthem protests in October, Texans owner Bob McNair said: "We can't have the inmates running the prison," according to an ESPN report. Most people construed the remark as an insult with racial overtones against protesting players, nearly all of whom were African American. (McNair later apologized and claimed that the "inmates" he was referring to were not the players but executives at the league office.)

In another less publicized meeting that took place a few days after Trump's "sons of bitches" rally, Goodell convened a group of about thirty players, owners, and league officials at 345 Park Ave to essentially talk past one another for three hours, albeit in feel-good tones. The owners and players sat in alternating seats around the table to demonstrate unity. Given the scrutiny they were under, Goodell emphasized the importance of maintaining secrecy.

"Let's make sure that we keep this confidential," the commissioner said to begin the session— an audiotape of which someone was nice enough to share with Belson and me.

The commissioner and owners spoke in elevated terms about their endeavors. They quoted Thomas Paine (Blank), invoked Dr. Martin Luther King's march on Selma (Miami's Stephen Ross), and expressed great hope for what they all could accomplish together ("This can go for a long, long time," San Francisco's Jed York gushed).

After a while, the players seemed to grow tired of the happy talk. They wanted to discuss why Kaepernick was still without a job and effectively being blackballed. "The elephant in the room," in the words of Kaepernick's former teammate and fellow kneeler Eric Reid.

"If Colin was on a roster right now," added Philadelphia Eagles defensive lineman Chris Long, "I feel like all this negativeness and divisiveness could be turned into a positive."

Long said that he did not wish to "lecture any team" on personnel matters, but "we all agree in this room as players that he should be on a roster." Other than a few nods from owners, the response was noncommittal. Eagles owner Jeffrey Lurie said that fighting for social justice is not "about one person."

Robert Kraft pointed to another "elephant in the room": "this kneeling," he called it. "The problem is, we have a president who will use that as fodder to do his mission that I don't feel is in the best interests of America," Kraft said. "It's divisive and it's horrible." (A related elephant in the room that went unremarked upon: Kraft's ostentatiously close friendship with Trump.)

Lurie, who derided Trump's presidency in the meeting as "fucking disastrous," cautioned everyone "not to be baited by Trump or whatever else. A black kid is going to get killed in some urban environment unnecessarily. We have to find a way to not get baited."

Bills owner Terry Pegula anguished over the uncertainty of when their Tormentor in Chief would next strike. "All Donald needs to do is to start to do this again," Pegula said. "We need some kind of immediate plan. All of us now, we need to put a Band-Aid on what's going on now."

Pegula complained that the league was "under assault." He then unloaded a dizzying flurry of nautical metaphors to describe their predicament. "This is like a glacier moving into the ocean," Pegula said. "We're getting hit with a tsunami." He expressed his genuine wish that the league no longer be "a glacier crawling in the ocean."

McNair played to his caricature as the good ol' boy, brave enough to tell people what's what. The players, McNair said, needed to knock off the damn kneeling. "You fellas need to ask your compadres, fellas, stop that other business."

The "fellas" across the table made no assurances about halting their "other business."

This inspired Miami owner Stephen Ross to suggest a "march on Washington," featuring both owners and players. Ross, a New York real estate developer worth $7.6 billion (per **Forbes**), thought this would be a great idea. He had a dream!

But Eric Reid had enough. "Everyone in here is talking about how much they support us," the 49ers defensive back said. He wanted to talk more about Kaepernick. The room fell quiet. "Nobody stepped up and said we support Colin's right to do this," said Reid, who wore a Kaepernick shirt over his dress shirt and tie. "We all let him become

Public Enemy Number One in this country, and he still doesn't have a job."

Thankfully, Bills owner Pegula had diagnosed the problem. The league, he said, was battling a perception and "media problem." He had a solution. Wouldn't it be great for the league to find a compelling spokesperson—preferably a player—to promote all of the good things they were doing together? He suggested that the league could learn from the gun lobby in this regard.

"For years we've watched the National Rifle Association use Charlton Heston as a figurehead," Pegula said. "We need a spokesman."

Yes!

Also, the NFL's Charlton Heston would need to be black.

"For us to have a face, as an African American that could be in the media," Pegula said, "we could fall in behind that."

With that, Ross felt it was important that everyone know that Dr. King's march on Selma was "the most important thing in my lifetime."

The meeting concluded with the commissioner and owners going on about how positive the session had been and how proud they were. More summits would be convened, Goodell assured everyone.

"We have a chance to do something monumental," declared Giants owner John Mara.

"I think this is great," said Kraft.

"This is obviously great," affirmed Jacksonville's Shad Khan.

Belson and I wrote a story for the **Times** about the meeting. One response from a reader struck me as on-point: "Does Mr. Pegula not realize that Charlton Heston has been dead for 10 years?"

A week later, I met Arthur Blank in the family office he keeps in Buckhead, the suburban Atlanta neighborhood, with a personal golf range in the basement. Blank is known for his sleekly tailored suits and the pride he takes in them. "I say to the players, 'You put your uniform on every Sunday, the owner should, too,'" Blank said as he slurped up the culminating drops of a massive Nutella milk shake he had brought in from a nearby Steak 'n Shake.

Blank gave off a vibe of exasperation, largely over the anthem protests and counterprotests that were then in full rage. "A lot of what the players are protesting in my view is very legitimate," Blank told me. When Trump weighed in as he did, he said, "it became a manhood issue" for many of the teams—"or in some cases a brotherhood issue."

Blank's relative outspokenness also reflects the demographic makeup of his customers. The Falcons' African American season-ticket base, at 40 percent, could well be higher than that of any professional sports team in America. Likewise, Kaepernick's 2016 protest, and York's support for it, were bound to receive a more sympathetic hearing in liberal San Francisco than they would have in, say, Dallas, home of the Cowboys and dominion of Jerry Jones.

$200 Million Buys a Lot of Therapy

Before the 2017 season started, there was growing sentiment inside the league that Jerry Jones had been flying closer to the sun than usual. Variations on a "Jerry thinks he runs the league" complaint have flared from time to time since Jones bought the Cowboys in 1989; but even by Jones's outsized standards, 2017 was extreme.

The Cowboys were coming off a 13–3 season in 2016, led by star running back Ezekiel Elliott, and the team had been picked by several experts to go to the Super Bowl the following year. Jones also remained stuffed with self-approbation over his Hall of Fame selection. He celebrated his August induction with a blowout party at Glenmoor Country Club in Canton, under a white tent fit for a circus. He assured me this would be an epic party. He was not wrong.

Cowboys past and present showed up en masse, an entourage of Gold Jackets as well as Jones's extended network of family, staff, partners, and random celebrity friends (Warren Buffett, Jon Bon Jovi, Chris Christie).

Guests passed through three checkpoints before getting taken the rest of the way to the party
tent via golf cart. I stood in the golf cart line behind Raiders owner Mark Davis, who wore an
all-white suit over a white sweatshirt and was
guzzling from a large bottle of Poland Spring
water. Davis appeared to have gained considerable
weight since he announced his team's move to
Las Vegas—those $1.99 buffets on the Strip can
kill you. This scene was itself a splendid buffet of
Jerry-mandered humanity: Earl Campbell made
his way into the party tent in front of me, with
the aid of his walker. Cowboys cheerleaders—
dressed in gold—lined both sides of the front
entrance to welcome us. Hall of Famer Warren
Sapp wore a bizarre pajama top–like sweatshirt
with bright-colored NFL logos, and practically
tackled Jones upon greeting him in the middle of
the party floor. Nutty former coach Barry Swit-
zer parked himself outside the men's room and
posed for selfies. Cocktail napkins were imprinted
with inscrutable "Jerryisms," memorable lines that
Jones had uttered in public over the years (e.g.,
"You don't have to spend a lot of time going over
and kind of circumcising the mosquito"). Guests
received sleek black boxes filled with miniature
donuts.

Jones was a late arrival, as he was held up at
the Gold Jacket dinner back at the Canton Civic

Center—where Paul Anka performed again, naturally. I had stopped by the dinner earlier, long enough to see longtime NFL insider Ed Werder receive the Dick McCann Award for excellence in NFL reporting from the Pro Football Writers of America. Werder worked for ESPN for twenty years before being laid off a few months earlier along with about a hundred other employees at the network, many of them well-regarded journalists. No one was better wired for Cowboys nuggets than Ed Werder—he fed millions of fantasy players every week. "I relied on him every Sunday to tell me how DeMarco Murray was looking in pregame warmups," my wistful colleague Mark Mazzetti said of Werder upon news of his departure. (Mazzetti added that his interest in DeMarco Murray was purely fantasy-related, and that he hates the Cowboys.)

ESPN had been moving toward more personality-based opinion shows, as opposed to the news gathering—or nugget gathering—from the Werders of the world and his ESPN colleague John Clayton, also let go. That wasn't really their game, the yelling and personality racket, although Werder did manage to get his photo taken with Lady Gaga at midfield before Super Bowl 51, which is no small consolation (nugget credit to **SI**'s Peter King for that).

There would be more layoffs coming at ESPN, as well as **Sports Illustrated** and other "insider" destinations. Suddenly these were dark days in the House of Nuggets.

"I was recently laid off by my employer," Werder said in his award acceptance speech. "Now I'm getting an award for lifetime achievement. Someone might be telling me something." Werder did not bother thanking ESPN in his remarks, or even mentioning the network, which was kind of awesome.

Jones entered his party to the Script's "Hall of Fame" and the requisite fuss. "The greatest owner in the history of sports is being honored tonight" is how Justin Timberlake described the guest of honor during the private ninety-minute set he performed. "This is such a great, great night," Jones kept saying as he greeted guests, nursing a tumbler of "something cold."

The party felt like it would rampage forever. Cowboy tight end Jason Witten finally grabbed the mic around 2:30 a.m. and told his teammates to head to the buses. They handed out fat cheeseburgers in golden foil on our way out. Sunday's Hall of Fame Game went off without getting canceled. It was, as always, utterly meaningless, but even "utterly meaningless" draws 8.2 million viewers in the NFL.

Goodell was among the dignitaries under the

tent. We had a brief exchange at the bar. He asked me what this book would be titled, and I said I didn't know. "How about 'The Shield'?" Goodell suggested. I think he might have been serious.

The commissioner greeted Jones with a hug. Goodell did not happen to mention a piece of business he knew would put a damper on Jones's big weekend. A few days later, the NFL would announce it was suspending Ezekiel Elliott for the first six games of the 2017 season following accusations of assault from a former girlfriend. (Elliott was never charged.)

Jones was not happy with this verdict, to say the least. When the commissioner called with the news, Jones promised, in so many words, to make Goodell's life a living hell. Jones compared himself with Robert Kraft, who had made a big stink against Goodell after he whacked Brady over Deflategate. "If you think Bob Kraft came after you hard, Bob Kraft is a pussy compared to what I'm going to do," Jones told the commissioner, according to an account of the conversation that appeared in **ESPN The Magazine**. One owner familiar with Kraft's thinking told me the Patriots' owner was "really, really upset" by Jerry's pussy characterization. Manhood, challenged! There would be more conversations between Jones and Goodell in the coming days, none pleasant.

Members of the compensation committee said Jones never raised objections to the particulars of Goodell's contract until the Elliott decision came down. But after Elliott, Jones changed his position and went aggressively rogue. Blank's committee became the main battleground through which Jones would wage his uprising.

He told at least two owners that he represented a silent majority, giving voice to the noncommittee owners' frustration over the commissioner's leadership. Jones tried to rally support to not only scuttle Goodell's new contract but also, as some owners interpreted it, topple him altogether. He hired the powerhouse litigator David Boies, and, in a conference call with members of the committee, vowed to sue them all if they went forward with Goodell's new deal.

Jones also became more vocal in his disapproval of how the NFL was handling the anthem protests. He tore into the Clinton alum Joe Lockhart, who he believed had been too aggressive in response to Trump's attacks on the league—and disrespectful to the president himself. "Everyone should know, including the president, that this is what real locker-room talk is," Lockhart said in a September conference call with reporters. It was a clear shot at Trump's attempt to explain away a leaked **Access Hollywood** video in which he infamously described grabbing women by their genitals.

As alternative programming to the anthem controversy, the NFL was offering up all different sorts of bad news. On a single October afternoon, these were the top headlines I found on ESPN.com:

Texans DE Watt Fractures Leg, Out Indefinitely

Dolphins Assistant in Video Snorting Powder

Chiefs' Reid: TE Kelce Had Trouble Remembering

Raiders LT Penn Confronts Fans in Parking Lot

OBJ Breaks Ankle as Beat-up Giants Fall to 0–5

Also on that day, Jones announced that any Cowboys player who did not stand during the national anthem would not take the field. This contrasted with some of the unsavory Cowboys Jones had allowed to play—Greg Hardy being a recent example. Jones's ultimatum was deemed unhelpful by many of the owners struggling to quell the issue, and by Goodell, too. "I think Roger's feeling on it was that any ultimatum would only prompt a larger protest if you attempt to enforce it," the Giants' John Mara told me. Some owners, like Jones and Washington's Snyder, might have believed Goodell should have "put the hammer down," Mara said. "But I think most of us believed that would cause more problems than it would have solved."

Not surprisingly, Jones's threat to would-be kneelers also caught the attention of Trump, who promptly tweeted approval: "A big salute to Jerry Jones, owner of the Dallas Cowboys, who will BENCH players who disrespect our Flag. 'Stand for Anthem or sit for game!'" This was a week and a half after Trump advertised that he had spoken to Jones ("Jerry is a winner who knows how to get things done"). If there's one thing Trump understands, it's how to manipulate needy billionaires.

Jones had drawn considerable resentment at an October league meeting in New York where he described himself as the "senior ranking owner" in the room. In fact, many of the owners had been in the league much longer than Jones, who purchased the Cowboys in 1989 for $140 million. Other than a few smirks and quizzical looks, Jones's "senior ranking owner" remark went unchallenged at the time. But it would linger, even as the season sputtered forward, the anthem controversy receded, and Goodell's contract extension moved closer to a done deal. Blank moved to complete the new deal for Goodell before the owners were scheduled to meet again at the Four Seasons in Irving, Texas, in December. Blank would present the final details of the contract there to the rest of the membership.

Blank was wary of celebrating too early (as one

would expect from the owner of a team that blew a 28–3 lead in the Super Bowl). He expected that Jones would make a final gambit to blow up the deal. "When Jerry stands up, it's like Showtime," Blank told me. "It's just entertainment. I'm being serious." He contrasted that with the more understated owners—next to Jones, basically all of them.

Sure enough, Jones delivered a "Showtime" speech in Dallas, complaining that the thirty-two owners did not have enough say on how the league was being run. The "big government" force at the league office had run amok, he said. But Jones's message appeared lost on most of the room. "Jerry, you just spoke for about forty minutes, and I have no idea what you're talking about," Kraft said after Jones finished.

Some of the "legacy owners" with long family ties to the league had taken offense at Jones's "senior owner" diatribe. Chief among them was Chicago Bears chairman George Halas McCaskey, grandson of the team's fabled coach and founder, George Halas. Collegial and mild-mannered, McCaskey would nonetheless become an unlikely source of resistance against Jones, telling at least two partners before the meeting that he was insulted by the Cowboys owner's attempts to undermine the compensation committee. "I'm sick of this shit," McCaskey told another owner before the meeting. "Look out." He ran into Goodell at the hotel gym that morning and said the same thing.

McCaskey stood up during the owners-only session and listed the several owners in the room who were more "senior" than Jones: the Maras of the Giants, the Rooneys of Pittsburgh, the Hunts of Kansas City, and the Bidwells of Arizona, among others. "Jerry, you don't represent me," McCaskey said to close his remarks. "The committee represents me."

Jones had almost no allies in the room, except for his friend and sidekick Daniel Snyder, the Redskins' owner. Snyder typically says little in league meetings—"because," as one NFC owner theorizes, "his face is buried in Jerry's colon." (Normally I would not include such a gross and unsourced slander in a mature and dignified book such as this, but the image is irresistible.) Snyder did make a generalized complaint in Dallas about how badly he believed the league had been run in certain areas. He took particular aim at Lockhart, who he said was using the league to carry out "a political platform." Snyder was one of several owners who had donated to Trump's campaign and inauguration.

The only other owner to cast any aspersions on the process was Jim Irsay, the flighty owner of the Colts, who walked in an hour late and expressed confusion over Goodell's presence. "I thought this was owners only?" Irsay said. It had been owners-only, he was told. But after about a half hour—before Irsay had arrived—the partners agreed to invite Goodell back to hear their feedback. This was before Irsay showed up. He still appeared confused.

Beyond whatever that was, the meeting was a romp over Jones, ending with the Cowboys' owner being repudiated, if not humbled. David Moore, the Cowboys beat writer for the **Dallas Morning News**, declared December 12 to be a "good day for Jerry Jones." How so? "The Cowboys owner wasn't forcibly removed from the grounds of the Four Seasons Resort," Moore wrote.

Everyone agreed that it was time to end this chapter and move on to the final weeks of the season. In a news conference after the meeting, Goodell was asked if he took Jones's rebellion personally. "Do I look like I take it personally?" Goodell replied. No one knew how to answer that. "Jerry, do I look like I take it personally?" Goodell said, pointing to Jones, who was standing behind him and didn't seem to know how to answer that either. Regardless, $200 million can buy a lot of therapy.

Goodell vacated the dais in favor of Jones, who promised to be "uncharacteristically brief" before launching into a (characteristically) rambling set of remarks. Jones concluded by saying that he appreciated how much Goodell loves the

National Football League. "He should love it even more right now," he added, to laughter.

Goodell flashed something between a grin and a smirk. He had a plane to catch back to New York—his own plane. He did not stick around for the rest of Jerry Jones.

29.

JUST COMPARTMENTALIZE, BABY

January 8, 2018

I went to see Goodell at NFL headquarters on a Monday in January, the morning after a sluggish docket of first-round playoff games. He had spent the weekend crisscrossing the country to catch two contests—Los Angeles on Saturday night to see the Falcons and Rams, Jacksonville on Sunday for the Bills and Jaguars.

The commissioner was sitting in his sixth-floor office, sipping water and battling a cold. Goodell, who was about to turn fifty-nine, wore a beige V-neck sweater and looked somewhat worn down but freshly worked-out; he had just come from a Pilates class. Regrettably, there had been no time for a Sunday workout: Goodell had to wake up at 3:30 a.m. in L.A. to fly to Jacksonville in time for

Bills-Jags. He also told me he had gone through two canisters of Purell over the previous two days. He is a beast.

It had been a rough season—"challenging," to use the language of the undaunted leader. There are never "problems" for this commissioner, only challenges. Goodell was now finishing his twelfth season as head of the league, thirty-sixth overall. He has been through strikes, lockouts, rival leagues, "existential" lawsuits, litigious owners, Al Davis, 9/11, Ray Rice, and, now, Donald Trump. It would be a bad look to complain, especially at his price. "We've always had our challenges," he said. But even by Goodell's embattled standards, this had been quite a year.

Goodell walked me to a small conference table in the far end of his office. I took a seat next to the shiny silver rendering of an NFL Shield. I mentioned to Goodell that I had met his wife, Jane, at a cocktail party during the league meetings, and that she had suggested—presumably joking—that her husband had a tattoo of the Shield. Roger Goodell laughed at my retelling of the exchange but also felt the need to set the following straight for the record:

"If there's one thing I can assure you," Goodell said sternly, "I have zero tattoos." Noted.

While Goodell's position has made him an expert at managing billionaire megalomaniacs, this season had exposed him to an entirely different breed of them—namely, the one who now occupied the White House. Trump had injected more politics into the NFL than the league had suffered through in years. Traditionally, culture-war critiques of the NFL had been confined to the left. Liberals were more prone to suspicion of football for its violence, militaristic sensibility, and over-the-top displays of patriotism. But Trump had now struck a throbbing nerve on the right, making the NFL an improbable symbol of permissive leadership and political correctness. And double bonus points for how prominently the NFL has figured into the president's ledger of personal grievance and unreturned affection.

Pete Rozelle's dim view of Trump—whom he saw as a clown and con man—trickled down to his protégé Goodell. Goodell told me he has met Trump at least twice over the years, once at a Yankees game about fifteen years ago and then a few years later at a dinner gathering. Goodell found Trump to be pleasant and solicitous in those limited encounters—maybe because Trump was still, at the time, angling for a place in the Membership. After losing out on buying the Bills in 2014, Trump began insisting that the NFL, particularly Goodell, was intent on freezing him out, on account of his history with the USFL.

Goodell comes from a notable Republican lineage, albeit of the mostly extinct northeastern-moderate subspecies. But he is carefully diplomatic in his public politics, and especially as they relate to the current president. "It's interesting times we live in" was as much as Goodell allowed himself to say. When I asked Goodell whether he or anyone on his staff had any communication with the White House, back-channel or otherwise, he smirked (I took this as a no). "Our focus is on what we do," he said. "Our focus is on the game itself." Nevertheless, owners and league officials close to Goodell said he was more supportive of the protesting players than they would have expected. He mostly received decent marks for his handling of the anthem protests, though often backhanded. ("Only Donald Trump is dumb enough to make Roger Goodell look smart," the Eagles fan and former Pennsylvania governor Ed Rendell said on Twitter.)

For as taxing—**challenging**—as this season had been, Goodell's demeanor betrayed a mix of relief and fatigue, and also a strong whiff of his usual self-satisfaction. The latter would be burnished by Goodell's muscular new contract, his ability to put down a rebellion by the NFL's most powerful owner and withstand an attack on the league from the most powerful man in the world.

Still, I was slightly surprised at Goodell's swagger given the vulnerability that had been laid bare in the league that season. When I suggested as much, Goodell assumed a seen-it-all-before jadedness. "Remember, I came into the league in 1982," Goodell told me. "We were facing litigation about the Raiders' move" (from Oakland to Los Angeles), he said. "We were on strike for nine weeks. There was a competing league. We had a lot of issues going on."

By comparison, he said, 2017 had merely been a year of "transition." Discussing the dealings between players and owners during the anthem turmoil, Goodell enthused about the "unprecedented dialogue" they had engaged in. "One of the players said, 'We're sitting here not in a locker room, not on a field,'" Goodell told me. "'We were sitting in a boardroom and dealing with each other as partners.' That understanding and listening was remarkable, and really a powerful thing for us as a league." The NFL pledged that it would donate $89 million over seven years to social justice organizations after several discussions with "the Players Coalition," a group of player-activists led by the Eagles' Malcolm Jenkins.

It's easy to be cynical about this, and dismiss the league's financial commitment to community and social-justice initiatives as just a way to placate the agitators. A group of players, led by then–San Francisco's Eric Reid, wound up quitting the coalition, believing the commitment was just that. Kaepernick is still unemployed and remains a flash point in the dispute. Reid, now a free agent, remains unsigned as of this writing, despite having been a starting safety for the 49ers for the last five years.

"How do we make sure this doesn't happen to anyone else?" said the Chargers' Russell Okung, one of the players who wound up leaving the Players Coalition, referring to Kaepernick. "Reparations need to be made in some manner," he said.

Goodell and the NFL survived 2017, but the commissioner and his league seem to be at the mercy of uncertain and uncontrollable events. The conflicts of 1982 that Goodell evoked might have been more dramatic and certainly "distracting"—that year's regular season was shrunk to nine games after a players' strike. But they were also more easily resolved. The dilemmas of today are more profound: There is no obvious common ground between Jerry Jones's vision of the football field as a respite and Kaepernick's vision of it as a platform. The players weren't kneeling to gain leverage or extract donations, or anything else Goodell could give them. They were trying to make themselves heard. "I talked to a lot of players who were saying, 'Man, I don't need to be quieter, I need to be louder,'" the Bengals' Eric Winston, the NFLPA union president, told me. "That to me was the key takeaway from this season."

And what happens if an owner like Jones decides to take matters into his own hands and "fire" players if their protests continue? "Our focus is on what we do," Goodell said, punting.

NFL owners don't pay Goodell so much to be interesting or revealing in interviews. In this regard, he is very good at being commissioner.

He added that everything was now fine between him and Jerry Jones. A nation exhales. The Cowboys' owner had congratulated Goodell on his new contract. They had just been discussing a bunch of other unrelated league business. It underscores a core fact of life among the billionaires' cartel and the soldiers of the Shield who serve them: Just compartmentalize, baby.

I pushed further: What happens, I asked Goodell, if players keep kneeling in future seasons? What if Trump tries to rekindle the issue, as you figure he'd love to do, just in time for the 2018 midterm elections or his reelection campaign in 2020—or, for that matter, fires off a tweet calling on viewers to turn off the Super Bowl if any players kneel, prompting the players to do exactly that?

"You're dealing with hypotheticals," Goodell said. "You can come up with five scenarios of what could happen."

Football is always generating new scenarios. That's part of what makes it so great and so fascinating. But not all scenarios stay between the sidelines—or stay hypothetical.

30.

THE LAST VISIT

It had been a long and jangled night.

—HUNTER S. THOMPSON,
"FEAR AND LOATHING AT THE SUPER BOWL,"
ROLLING STONE, FEBRUARY 28, 1974

"It's been such a long season," Giants co-owner John Mara was saying. He had only three wins for his troubles. He'd fired his coach, Ben McAdoo, after two years, had just found his replacement (Vikings offensive coordinator Pat Shurmur), and now just wanted to get out of town to somewhere warm. There would be no Super Bowl in Minnesota for John Mara.

Main Event LII had more mogul no-shows than usual. Usually there's a decent showing, if only as a gesture of respect for the commissioner.

Goodell tends to notice who comes to things like his State of the League press conference (Wednesday) and his annual Super Bowl party (Friday).

But Goodell's presser had more empty seats than it had media haircuts. For those who did come, the production reeked of tribal obligation. Goodell's canned podium spiel had a phoned-in quality. Even the planted-kid question was humdrum (something about Roger being someone whom a lot of kids look up to—questionable premise).

The one nugget discharged at the event was the NFL's news that it would be holding another regular-season game in Mexico City in 2018, between the Rams and Chiefs. Three questions were granted to Mexican journalists, including one reporter who was still **muy enojado** over something Coach Belichick had said in November after the Patriots played the Raiders there. El Hoodie was no fan of South-of-the-Border football. "Personally, I wouldn't be in any big rush to do it again," Belichick said on WEEI after the game. "We're fortunate," he added, "there was no volcano eruptions or earthquakes, or anything else." Trump could have named him secretary of state for that.

Kraft, meanwhile, sampled guacamole back at the hotel with a reporter for ESPN Deportes, who insisted that "Roberto" take a shot of tequila with him. I have no idea if the video of this has gone viral, but it should, if only to expose fans to the dulcet tones of Kraft saying "**Gracias**, Juan" in a perfect Brookline-Jew accent.

Stylish Stan Kroenke wore a scarf over his blazer to Roger's Friday night shindig. Rep. Kevin McCarthy, the House Republican leader, was working the room (he is apparently a regular at Super Bowl and Emmy parties: both potential donor goldmines). Demi Lovato performed, or someone like her.

Steve Tisch was present along with the stunning Katia, his future (third) wife. Katia is more than beautiful—she speaks five languages, Tisch will always remind people—though she is certainly beautiful, too. Fellow owners are quick to pay tribute ("Nice job there, Tush"). Other than Super Bowl rings or hot young stadiums or perhaps yachts (Jacksonville's Shad Khan leads the league with his five-decked, $200 million **Kismet**), there is no greater object of envy for an NFL owner than having a drop-dead gorgeous "friend." Jerry Jones is a huge Katia fan. Whenever he sees her, he makes a point of telling Katia that "Steve is such a nice boy," but that he, Jerry, is a **Man**. Katia told me this and thought it was funny. She planted a kiss on the Tush's mouth in a show of devotion. (Alas, while doing some last-minute fact-checking in May, I was saddened to learn from Tisch that the marriage was off and his fairy tale with Katia was no more—so, so much for all that.)

We were all waiting to pay respects to Gold Jacket Jerry. Jones was receiving supplicants at the Cowboys' table, close-talking at that moment with Al Michaels. If Jones was chastened by the slam-dunking he'd received at the hands of his partners a few weeks earlier, or by the Cowboys' disappointing season (9–7, no playoffs), he wasn't showing it. Jones seemed to be living large as ever, as large as the tumbler he hoisted upon seeing Katia and Steve waiting off in the wings—and again, Steve is **such** a nice boy.

When it was my turn, I approached Jerry's throne gingerly. This was the first time I'd spoken to Jones since our blurred-out horror show aboard the Cowboys' bus the previous May. I wondered if he would remember me. Of course he would remember me! "That was such a great visit," Jones said, nostalgically. "I remember that visit very fondly." Nice to know. Jones said that he was rooting for the Eagles in the Super Bowl. "Because I'm so jealous," he explained, presumably of the Patriots, or maybe just of Bob Kraft.

Anyway, it was good to see me, Mr. Jones said. Good visit. We agreed to visit again, one day, Jerry and I, or maybe this would be our natural endpoint.

THE NIGHT BEFORE THE BIG GAME, TOM BRADY Sr. invited me to a "small family gathering" at a bowling alley in Edina, Minnesota, about twenty minutes from downtown Juneau, or wherever we were.

Galynn Brady, Tom's mom, grew up two hours north of here in Browerville. This fluke of maternal origin lent her son a claim to local roots throughout the week. As we heard several times, Tommy and his sisters used to spend their childhood summers in Browerville, enabling the GOAT, years later, to regale media hordes with tales of milking cows.

The Brady family reunion overtook a second-floor stretch of the bowling alley. There was no sign of Tom or Gisele but about 150 Bradys or Brady satellites were here—Bradys by birth, proxy, or marriage, and also Kevin Youkilis, the former Red Sox infielder now married to Tommy's sister Julie. "**Yoouuk**," I said, upon seeing him, as the Fenway crowds used to howl when he came to bat—Youk still gets this a lot, I'm guessing.

Brady Partiers wore their #12 and Pats gear. They pronounced **Tahhmm**y with Minnesota accents. One of them—a cousin, I think—got everyone's attention and yelled out news that "**Tahhhmmy** won the MVP, it was just announced." Everyone cheered for the quasi-native son, and then went back to their bowling.

Tom and Galynn looked eager for game day to arrive and the deep freeze to end so they could get on with being proper Californians. If Tom Senior had his way, he told me, he'd like the NFL portion of his son's party to end altogether. "Absolutely," he said when I asked whether he wanted his son to retire. But then, TB Senior doesn't get a vote on this. "Of course not," he said. "Did your dad get a vote when you were forty?" (No, but in fairness I was out of the league at that point.)

Gisele does get a vote, and it's clear she's with her father-in-law on this. She has ceded the final call to her husband, but for how much longer? The question touches everything in the Not for Long: it comes for eternal quarterbacks, wives, parents, Hall of Fame coaches, and really, the whole cavalcade. Clock management is a lie.

In Brady's case, there's little doubt his wife would prefer having a husband around who better approximates what a normal one might be like; someone who doesn't spend his autumns in "scheduled car crashes" with three-hundred-pound unicorns in helmets. "If you want to compete with me, you have to give up your life," I've heard Brady say a few times, underscoring his commitment to **sustained peak performance**. "Because that's what I'm doing."

Good for him, but you can see how that might be a drag to be married to after a while. "Sustained peak performance isn't about changing one or two habits in your life, it **is** your life," Brady wrote in **The TB12 Method**, a coffee table book published in 2017 that lays out his rules of the road. They include, among other things, lots of "pliability" work, hydration, and no coffee, thus freeing coffee tables to showcase this glossy cinderblock. Tom was nice enough to send me a copy of his book in November—and he even inscribed it (yes I checked, and immediately). The author said he wished the best for me always!

A FEW WEEKS AFTER PHILADELPHIA'S SUPER Bowl win over New England, Eagles offensive lineman Lane Johnson called the Patriots "a fear-based organization." He claimed that players do not enjoy playing for the team, no matter how much they win. "When they go to do interviews, they act like fucking robots," Johnson said of Patriot players on Barstool's **Pardon My Take** podcast. "You only get to do this job one time, so let's have fun while we're doing it."

Johnson has never played for the Patriots, but his perception of a smothering mirth-free environment certainly rings true. It was also hard to dismiss that Johnson had given voice to a common belief around the league about Foxborough—including from within the fortification itself.

As notable as Johnson's words were, more so was that almost no Patriots players, past or present, were compelled to defend the Patriot Way (one exception being ESPN's Tedy Bruschi, a three-ring Super Bowl champ with the Pats). Rob

Gronkowski, who as of early spring 2018 had not said whether he wanted to keep playing football, has told numerous people how sick he was of going to work in such a dreary monolith. After veteran receiver Danny Amendola signed with Miami in March, Gronk paid tribute via Instagram and implored his teammate to "Be FREE, Be HAPPY."

"The Patriots don't play with joy," Tom Brady's father agreed after I read him the quote from Lane Johnson. "But I don't know of any sustaining organizations that play with joy." He went on to compare his son with the "lead dog" in Belichick's pack. By allowing himself to be beaten, the Alpha had demonstrated by example that lesser canines should also fall into line.

Mr. Brady was not the first to apply the battered-canine metaphor to a taskmaster coach. The late Hall of Fame defensive tackle for the Packers, Henry Jordan, famously quipped that Vince Lombardi "treats us all the same—like dogs." It was a funny line, and leavened with affection for Lombardi in the retelling. But the dynamic inevitably gets old, and usually well before eighteen years (Lombardi lasted only eight in Green Bay). "After a while, you're going to bite your owner," Mr. Brady said.

No question, his son had become fed up himself with the Belichick culture. Brady was now biting back, in his own way. He has spoken— to friends, teammates, and relatives—about how playing in Foxborough had indeed become a dismal grind. He felt he had earned more deference and gratitude from a coach who probably owes his Hall of Fame career more to him than to anyone else. "He tells me, 'I love it so much,'" Bündchen said about her husband and playing football in **Tom vs Time**, a behind-the-scenes documentary released in early 2018. "'I just want to go to work and feel appreciated and have fun.'" The conspicuous implication here was that Brady presently was not having fun. "These last two years have been very challenging for him in so many ways," Bündchen said.

Brady knows that his legend status in the NFL is every bit as potent as his coach's. He had grown impatient with Belichick's self-aggrandizing propaganda: the "how we did it" testimonials, via NFL Films, that Belichick would participate in following Super Bowl wins. In these productions, the likes of Brady and his teammates are portrayed as interchangeable cyborgs privileged to toil inside Bill's genius lab. **"Do Your Job." "No Days Off."**

Brady was becoming more aggressive in telling his story, and on his own terms. The six-part **Tom vs Time** was released into the digital wilderness on something called Facebook Watch. Brady granted his filmmaker friend Gotham Chopra an up-close view of his "method" as he conducted his subversion campaign against the

expectations of NFL longevity. **Tom vs Time** also represented Brady's subversion campaign against the colorless code of the Belichick Method. It is not clear whether Brady even told his coach about the project, which dropped right on the eve of the playoffs.

What was clear, and becoming more so, was that the Patriots machine was showing strain. In December, a report in **ESPN The Magazine** described grumblings along several fault lines: tension between Brady and Belichick; between Belichick and Guerrero, whom the coach banished from team facilities; between Belichick and Kraft, after Kraft ordered Belichick to trade Brady's backup and possible heir apparent Jimmy Garoppolo (Kraft was in turn angry with Belichick for getting only a second-round draft pick from the 49ers in return for the coveted Garoppolo). "Division from within can be the biggest enemy in the NFL," Kraft told me in an interview about a year earlier. He had described the Patriot Way to me as the ability to keep these divisions at bay, or at least out of public view. "With all due respect to the media, they don't know what's really going on," Kraft said. "No one would believe what's really going on." I heard this as something between tantalizing and a thrown-off taunt. Regardless, the divisions had become hard to miss.

It was a wonder that the Patriots' dynastic foundation had held together as long as it had.

Even more remarkable was that somehow the Patriots managed to scrape themselves into another Super Bowl, and nearly win the wacky game in Minneapolis. They had the ball on their own 33, down five, with over two minutes left. The Brady comeback routine was cued up perfectly. Philadelphia fans wore resigned looks. But then the center failed to hold. And the right guard failed to block—in this case block the Eagles' Brandon Graham.

Graham strip-sacked Brady. Philly recovered the fumble, and euphoria ensued from the beaten-dog fans of the green jerseys. And what right did spoiled-rotten Pats fans like me have to feel crestfallen? None, for sure, but I did anyway. If NFL owners can be greedy, why can't we? Nothing's fair in love, or rational in rooting.

"Yeah, that sucks," Brady distilled after the game. "But no one's gonna feel sorry for us. That's football."

I MADE A FINAL RUN AT BRADY AFTER THE SEAson. We'd emailed back and forth from time to time over the months. In March, as I was finishing this book, I asked Tom if he was up for talking to me once more. He invited me to send questions to him by email. "Interviews" by email are less than ideal, certainly from a reporter's standpoint, but you can see where it would suit a message-conscious celebrity obsessed with control.

I held off on the email questions, figuring I was in touch with enough people in Brady's life to know that he remained unhappy with the state of play in Foxborough. His relationship with Belichick was strained beyond what it had been in years, maybe ever. The arrangement between the Patriots and Guerrero remained unresolved. Kraft and Brady had at least one conversation that Brady came away from less than satisfied that anything would change. "You go, 'What are we doing this for?'" Brady said three days after the Super Bowl in the final **Tom vs Time** installment. "'What are we doing this for, who are we doing this for? Why are we doing this?'" The question hung unanswered for months as Brady remained aggressively noncommittal about his plans through the off-season.

Along with Gronk, Brady blew off the Patriots' voluntary team workouts in April and May, something that would have been unheard of before. He kept ducking questions about his future. In addition to unsettling Bob Kraft, the possibility of Brady's walking away was unsettling for me, too, selfishly speaking. If Brady wouldn't be back in September, it would be good for me to know this now, before this book went to press in early May. Finally, I emailed Brady a bunch of questions, the most important one being whether he planned to still be the Patriots' quarterback in September. He didn't answer for a week.

I bugged him again. "Hey, Tom," I wrote. "Sorry to be a pain in the ass. I know you're busy. You have a chance to look at those questions? I can re-send if you want—or I can just send them to your dad and he'll answer them filterless."

This made Tom laugh, at least in that email way (**"Hahahahaha funny"**). He told me he was still "thinking through" the questions and wasn't sure there were many he'd want to weigh in on.

I crossed out all but three of the questions and sent them back, to streamline things. Another few days passed. **Me vs Time**, directed by Tom.

On a Friday morning, just before six a.m., I got an email from Brady that said simply, "Let me know if this helps." Attached was an audio file, about ten minutes long. It was Brady, sleepy-voiced, reading through my questions and riffing on them. I'd never had an interview like this before, if you'd call this an interview. But here was Brady, in my phone, and in full control of the game. I guess, in my case, you just take what the defense gives you.

"Whassup, Mark," Brady said. "I apologize. It's just been sooo busy. Let me answer these as best I can. Some of them are obviously pretty deep."

The first question—which was probably unfair, but I asked anyway—was a redux of the earlier "void" question, the riddle of what could possibly replace football for Brady, perhaps the most football-consumed person on the planet? Brady's answer couched football in creative terms, not competitive ones. "I still love being involved in creating things," Brady said. "And there's definitely ways to fill this creative outlet that's been filled by football for so long." Brady concluded that he did not think about the end very often.

When I first met him, in the summer of 2014, one of the things Brady talked about was the always-unfolding mystery of the next move. He was speaking in the context of a team growing and evolving. He told me that that spring, he had been watching game film of Peyton Manning's previous season with the Broncos, which ended in a Super Bowl loss to the Seahawks. Brady said he had focused on how Manning was able to change and improve the Denver offense from September to February. Brady was studying a peer-genius's in-season evolution. He had become fascinated by the puzzle of adaptation; as if change itself was an art form, and the quarterback was a painter. The best ones can ascertain patterns and find nuances, fine-tune a machine on the fly and drive it downfield.

A hallmark of the Patriots' success over the years has been the team's ability to overhaul game plans from week to week, depending on their opponent. They also are known for overhauling their rosters from year to year, depending on what tools were available and which ones brought the best value to the widget factory. "You're always changing, you're always evolving," Brady said in the audio file. That would seem obvious, not quite revelatory. But hearing Brady talk, I'm struck by how he described his life in terms of shifting game plans and unfolding conditions. "Your kids are growing, another year goes by, you have a career," Brady said. "But you're going through your life as well. You're trying to find what works in your life, and those things change from year to year."

Again, this can come off as obvious, if not simplistic, but I was struck by Brady's positing the process of growth as the key to getting "back to center" from season to season. "Alex and I always spend time in the off-season trying to learn from the previous year," he said. "This year, I want to work on having more quickness in the pocket, more speed from under center." Those, he says, are "things just in my sport." Otherwise, Brady said, he is devoting these months to his kids, his wife, and his parents, which he acknowledged "I haven't necessarily done as good of a job of in previous years."

So would Brady still be the Patriots' quarterback this fall? "It's April, and I don't intend to retire," he said. "And I certainly don't intend to get traded." He added that "they can do whatever they want." It was pretty clear that things were not great between "they" and Brady right then; my sense is—informed by talking to some people close to him—that it wouldn't kill Brady if the Patriots were to release him into free agency, allowing him to control his next move. But that wasn't going to happen, so here we were, and the game continued.

Brady seemed to catch himself after saying "they can do whatever they want," as if he was concerned he might have sounded more abrupt than he intended. "I don't mean that in a negative way," he added. "It's just, I'm training and getting ready to play like I always do, so that's not in any controversial way, that's reality." He made a point of adding, "Obviously, I love Coach Belichick." If I had a follow-up, I would have asked if he slipped the "obviously" in there for sarcasm.

Brady emphasized that I could quote only from the audio file for the purposes of this book— nothing should appear anywhere before that time. In other words, he seemed content to keep the bastards guessing about his plans for a while, not least his employers.

"Anyway, that's it man, hope you're doing well," Brady said. "Hopefully this helps you out in some way. Let me know if you need anything else."

I imagined Tom lying in bed, still in his bio-dynamic sleepwear, talking into his phone. Was Gisele asleep next to him? Or was she out in back, in the yoga and meditation sanctuary? Was Tom in the car, headed off somewhere?

I am writing this at the end of April, or—by the official NFL calendar—Day 3 of the 2018 draft. I used to waste beautiful spring Saturdays indoors watching the draft on TV; today I'm wasting a beautiful spring Saturday indoors trying to finish off this beast. I'm not sure this counts as an evolution. If I wasn't doing this, I'd almost certainly be watching the draft—and maybe catch something like an orangutan named Rocky announcing the Colts' fourth-round selection (that actually happened—as USC O-lineman Zach Banner can attest). Now I'm back to the scheduled car crashes of covering politics in Trump, D.C. The league held its annual meetings in Orlando a few weeks ago. I thought about going but decided to stay away—because football seasons have to stop sometime, including my own.

The Patriots' PR department was good enough to post on its website a "Best of Robert Kraft at Owners' Meetings" montage, like one of those K-Tel Greatest Hits albums from the 1970s. The big news of the week was that Kraft's on-again girlfriend, Ricki, was at the resort with her (their?) baby daughter. The baby's name: "Monarch." Like the butterfly. Or maybe they meant to honor the commissioner. I miss these people already.

In other news, Kaepernick remained unsigned

and is suing the league for collusion while simultaneously trying to get hired by some team (he showed up in a black Kunta Kinte T-shirt to attend a four-hour deposition of Texans owner Bob McNair). The league suffered its worst Super Bowl ratings in nine seasons in February and reported its highest number of concussions in six. It was another nonstop Christmas for the NFL doomsayers. Meanwhile, the league just kept printing money to buy new presents. How worried can you be when Fox is spending more than $3 billion for the rights to broadcast five years of **Thursday Night Football** (or "Poopfests," as Richard Sherman called them). Likewise, the Carolina Panthers fetched a sale price of $2.2 billion for disgraced owner Jerry Richardson. That compares with the $206 million Richardson paid in 1993 for the right to found the Panthers. They don't make doomed sports leagues like they used to.

Everything was back and forth, a whiplash of outlooks to rival the pinball of a Super Bowl. Nothing feels settled or resolved. I'm back to just watching, despite myself, and happy to leave the existential cliff-hanger to the pros: Is this the decline of Peak Football we are watching in still-massive numbers? We await the replay.

Acknowledgments

It starts with a whistle and ends with . . . the acknowledgments.

So much gratitude to Arthur and A. G. Sulzberger, Dean Baquet, Mark Thompson, and everyone at the **New York Times** for your support professionally and personally. You run the most essential newspaper in the world, now more than ever. Just as important, you know what matters.

Big Game thanks to Jake Silverstein, a great boss, editor, and rabbi; and to everyone at the **Times Magazine**, where parts of this project got started: Bill Wasik, Jessica Lustig, Mike Benoist, Charlie Homans, Erika Sommer, Kathy Ryan, Liz Gerecitano, Nandi Rodrigo, Rob Liguori, and alumni that include my friends Jon Kelly, Hugo Lindgren, Joel Lovell, and many others.

Thanks to the **Times** D.C. bureau for letting me live there. I never take for granted the osmosis factor of going to work in such a killer newsroom. Gratitude to bureau chief Elisabeth Bumiller and longtime pal Bill Hamilton; the essential Ron Skarzenski, Jeff Burgess, Clif Meadows, Tahirah Burley, and everyone who makes it work. I'd be lost (and stranded) without **NYT** travel whizettes Robin Deblinger and Beth Ryan.

Gratitude to my friends and colleagues who keep it fun and make me better: Peter Baker, Julie Davis, Michael Shear, Binyamin Appelbaum, Maureen Dowd, David Brooks, Maggie Haberman, Jonathan Martin, Glenn Thrush, Mike Schmidt, Mark Landler, Helene Cooper, Jennifer Steinhauer, Jim Rutenberg, Emmarie Huettemann, singer-songwriter Carl Hulse, and nugget consumer Mark Mazzetti; Ashley Parker and Matt Flegenheimer (dammit!) and Rebecca Corbett. Janet Elder, you're an angel, and missed every day. Likewise, the incomparable David Carr and Robin Toner.

To everyone in the **Times** Sports department, for letting me hang in the toy store. Ken Belson was a great "compadre," as Mr. McNair would say. Game balls, too, for Jason Stallman, Terri Ann Glynn, Joe Drape, Michael Powell, and Ben Shpigel.

Also receiving votes: Paul, Train, and all the

Farhim; David Maraniss, Jeffrey Goldberg, Mike Barnicle, Tom Brokaw, Chuck Todd, Joe House, John Dickerson, Nem Hackett, Josh King, Ned Zeman, Matt Brune, Peter Canellos, Jake Sherman, Jessica Yellin, Nicky Dawidoff, Charlie Pierce, Mark Salter; Good ol' Maggie Jones (for helping me navigate Catholicism in Pittsburgh) and Gotham Chopra, whose Boston fanboy and artistic fellowship I much enjoyed; Tom and Galynn Brady are GOATs in their own right.

So many sportswriters and Men Wearing Makeup took me into their guild and made me feel at home: **SI**'s Peter King is a big-time mensch. Old pal Sally Jenkins is a beast; it was terrific to meet and commiserate with Tom Curran, Ben Volin, Bob Socci, Mike Reiss, Judy Battista, Amy Trask, Seth Wickersham, Peter Schrager, Don Van Natta Jr., Dan Kaplan, Mark Ganis, and many others.

My **Times** colleague Lindsay Crouse is the research equivalent of the fast-closing corner who thwarts disaster in the end zone. "Fact-checker" sells her short. Thanks also to Courtney Harrell for the reporting assist in Pittsburgh; and photo wrangler Thea Traff. All errors of fact and oversight are of course my own.

Grateful to the run-stuffers at 345 Park Avenue for their professionalism and good humor throughout this process, such as it was. Same goes for a great and ever-helpful collection of friends at the "clubs." If I start naming people, I'll leave some out; or worse, leave some **in**. You know who you are, I hope.

Elyse Cheney graduated from "Agent" to "Super Agent" a long time ago, not to mention "Friend" to "Super Friend." You are the best in the biz. Dinners owed through 2057, at least. Thanks, too, to the Super Team at Cheney Agency: Alex Jacobs, Claire Gillespie, and Peter Finnerty.

David Rosenthal is the spiritual father of this whole journey/ordeal. David understood and indulged me in all the right ways, which I'll never not be thankful for. Special thanks to Aileen Boyle and Marian Brown, whose friendship endures even if Blue Rider does not.

Scott Moyers at Penguin Press proved not only to be a lights-out relief pitcher (hey, they can't all be football clichés) but also a blast of an editor/publisher. I'm so lucky to have landed with Scott. Big thanks also to Ann Godoff, Mia Council, ace publicist Liz Calamari, Matt Boyd, and everyone at Penguin.

I will always cherish our Kibbutz with the Rosinplotzim: David, Hanna, Noa, Jacob, Giddy, Ma, Pa, Mumi, and Eli. It takes a village, and you are the village. Hugs to all—and good riddance to the minivan.

Never-ending love to my family in their assorted units: I'm especially grateful to my mom, Joan Leibovich, and sister, Lori Leibovich, for, well, everything—you are always with me, and me with you. Much love to bonus parents Ted Sutton, Betty Grossman, Jack and Barbara Kolbrener, the latter of whom I miss all the time. Hermano Larry Kanter (**still** of Resistor) and bonus kids Carlos and Clara Kanter; big love and appreciation for Michael Kolbrener and Bill Kolbrener and their great families.

This book is dedicated to my father, Miguel Leibovich, who died in February 2017, a few days after yet another Super Bowl that he didn't care about. He encouraged me from the start, and I'll carry him with me to fiesta's end. Eternal love, also, to my late dear brother, Phil Leibovich, a blue-chip football fan and friend, who remains at my side (and, Phil, you'll never believe what happened to that lousy football team we used to root for when we were kids).

Best for last: Such indescribable love to my daughters, Nell, Eliza, and Frances Leibovich, who astound and amaze me with the great people they're becoming. You are forces of wonder, and I couldn't adore you more. Likewise, to my Hall of Fame wife, Meri Kolbrener, who's made me better and wiser in every way, and who has made this whole caravan possible, beautiful, and fun. So damn lucky!

Notes

INTRODUCTION: FOOTBALL, IN SPITE OF ITSELF

xix "America can survive": "Football's True Believers Circle the Wagons and Insist the Sport Is Just Fine," **New York Times**, January 30, 2018, p. B8.

xix "In twenty-five years": Chuck Klosterman, **But What if We're Wrong?: Thinking About the Present as if It Were the Past** (New York: Blue Rider Press, 2016).

xxi By Friday, the warring: "30 Surprising Facts About the Mall of America," **BuzzFeed,** July 8, 2014.

xxi "I will always live": Steve Rushin, "Show and Nice," **Sports Illustrated**, January 29, 2018.

xxvi "Much of its popularity": Michael MacCambridge, **America's Game: The Epic Story of**

How Pro Football Captured a Nation (New York: Random House, 2004).

PROLOGUE: RESPITE

19 **"I can't think of another"**: Leigh Steinberg, **The Agent: My 40-Year Career Making Deals and Changing the Game** (New York: Thomas Dunne Books, 2014), pp. 209, 210.

CHAPTER 1: THE SUPER BOWL WITHOUT JOCK STRAPS

25 **"Hey, even the worst bartender"**: Eric Winston interview with CSNNE, January 30, 2015.

27 **the next month's draft**: Source of credentialed media numbers: NFL media relations department.

30 **"He's made the NFL relevant"**: Pat McManamon, "Joe Thomas Rips Deflategate Probe, Roger Goodell's 'Ridiculous Witch Hunts,'" ABC News, August 23, 2015.

CHAPTER 2: THE MONKEY'S ASS

43 **truck-stop operator**: Tony Dejak, "Haslam-Owned Truck Stop Chain to Pay $92 Million Fine over Rebate Scam," AP, February 11, 2014.

43 **$84.5 million in compensatory damages**: Ben Horowitz, "Judge Announces Damages of $84.5 Million Against Wilfs in Long-Running Lawsuit," NJ.com, September 24, 2013.

43 **"organized crime–type activities"**: Ben Horowitz, "Real Estate Mogul and Family on Losing End of Epic Lawsuit Filed by Business Partners," NJ.com, April 5, 2013.

43 **an antigay initiative**: Katherine Driessen, "Texans Owner Bob McNair Donates $10,000 to Anti-hero Effort," **Houston Chronicle,** October 15, 2015.

43 **to a Walmart heiress**: "Ann Walton Kroenke Profile," **Forbes**, March 6, 2018.

48 **Johnson was hopeful that**: Peter King, **Monday Morning Quarterback**, SI.com, January 23, 2017.

CHAPTER 3: NUGGETS

57 **on Secretary's Day**: Greg Bishop, "Blocking for the Patriots Coach so He Can Do His Job," **New York Times**, February 3, 2012, p. D1.

64 **Goodell is apparently required**: **Monday Morning Quarterback**, SI.com, August 8, 2016.

72 **"sex scandal with his wife!"**: Nicholas Dawidoff, **Collision Low Crossers: A Year Inside the Turbulent World of NFL Football** (New York: Little, Brown, 2013).

CHAPTER 5: "BEWARE THE PISSED OFF PRETTY BOY"

110 **Al Davis used to wear padded suits**: David Harris, **The League: Inside the NFL** (New York: Bantam Books, 1987), p. 58.

CHAPTER 6: GARISH FIST ORNAMENTS

125   **"guilty of retiring early"**: Brett Favre to Greta Van Susteren, **On the Record**, Fox News, July 14, 2008.

125   **"God only knows"**: Brett Favre, interview with WSPZ-AM, Washington, D.C., October 24, 2013.

125   **"We get brainwashed to believe"**: Tom Brady interview, WEEI, October 12, 2015.

127   **"scheduled car crash"**: Tom Brady, **The TB12 Method: How to Attain a Lifetime of Peak Performance** (New York: Simon & Schuster, 2017), p. 19.

CHAPTER 9: NO ONE BUYS TICKETS TO WATCH A MORALITY PLAY

165   **"my candy store"**: Frank Deford, "Welcome Commissioner Pete Rozelle and Wife Carrie," **Sports Illustrated**, January 21, 1980.

165   **"We can't hopscotch franchises"**: John F. Steadman, **From Colts to Ravens: A Behind-the-Scenes Look at Baltimore Professional Football** (Centreville, MD: Tidewater Publishers, 1997).

165   **"It was the worst feeling"**: MacCambridge, **America's Game**, p. 398.

CHAPTER 11: WHUPPINGS

185   **It spent a fortune:** Alan Schwarz, Walt Bogdanich, and Jacqueline Williams, "NFL's Flawed Concussion Research and Ties to

the Tobacco Industry," **New York Times,** March 24, 2016, p. 1.

184 **"You have no choice":** Pete Rozelle interview (unbylined), "Backtalk: From a Retired Pete Rozelle, Some Points After," **New York Times,** September 18, 1994.

CHAPTER 12: "WE PAY HIM DAMN WELL TO BE NEUTRAL"

206 **Even the head of the nation's:** Ken Belson, "Goodell's Pay of $44.2 Million in 2012 Puts Him in the Big Leagues," **New York Times**, February 14, 2014, p. D1.

209 **He was known as cerebral:** Bryan Curtis, "Mr. Goodell Goes to Washington," **Grantland**, February 4, 2013.

209 **"I no longer wanted":** Suzanne Pollak interview with Roger Goodell, "Remembering Mom," AOL Build, May 8, 2015.

213 **"The job is like attending 10 weddings":** Sam Farmer, "No Consensus Yet on a Replacement," **Los Angeles Times**, March 21, 2006, p. 2.

214 **"I inherited a strong constitution":** Deford, "Welcome Commissioner Pete Rozelle and Wife Carrie."

214 **"Dammit, don't be telling us":** MacCambridge, **America's Game**, p. 317.

215 **"He's the face of the owners":** The **MMQB**, SI.com, July 19, 2016.

CHAPTER 14: ROGER AND ME

242 **complaining in open settings:** Gabriel Sherman, "The Season from Hell," **GQ**, January 19, 2015.

259 **He infamously patronized Peyton Manning:** Jay Feely interview, **The Michael Kay Show,** ESPN Radio, February 14, 2014.

259 **He also wondered:** Ibid.

CHAPTER 15: THE BIG SPLAT

273 **"The game lets you know":** Jermichael Finley, "They Basically Reset My Brain," **The Players' Tribune**, May 23, 2017.

274 **"bullet in his chest":** Ibid.

CHAPTER 16: IMMORTALITY GETS OLD

299 **Baker referred to the Hall:** Daniel Kaplan, "Canton Puts Up Some Hall of Fame Numbers," **SportsBusiness Journal,** July 28, 2014.

CHAPTER 17: "START BLOW-DRYING TEDDY KOPPEL'S HAIR 'CAUSE THIS ONE'S DONE"

305 **"you played some, man":** Ben Smith, "Travels with Joe," **Politico**, September 18, 2008.

CHAPTER 18: AMERICAN CARNAGE

321 **More than 83 percent:** http://blogs.reuters.com/great-debate/2014/05/30/nfllast-sports-bastion-of-white-male-conservatives/.

321 **Nearly 70 percent of the players:** http://nebula.wsimg.com/1a7f83c14af6a5161767402

44d8afc46?AccessKeyId=DAC3A56D8FB782
449D2A&disposition=0&alloworigin=1.

323 **"This makes football akin"**: Klosterman, **But What if We're Wrong: Thinking About the Present as if It Were the Past** (New York: Blue Rider Press, 2016), p. 187.

327 **"They just saw him as this scumbag"**: Tim Marcin, "Trump's NFL Fight Dates Back to His Failed USFL Experiment in the '80s," **Newsweek,** September 25, 2017.

CHAPTER 19: PATRIOTISM

338 **"face to face with my gangsters"**: William C. Rhoden, "Connections That Go Far Beyond Wins," **New York Times**, January 29, 2008.

CHAPTER 20: CHEESEHEAD ELEGY

350 **"We don't talk about Fight Club"**: Michael Eisen, "The McAdoo Report," Giants.com, January 6, 2007.

CHAPTER 22: "I'M DRUNK, I'M STUPID, I'M A PATS FAN," THE MAN TOLD POLICE

379 **"I hope to Christ I never again"**: Hunter S. Thompson, "Fear and Loathing at the Super Bowl," **Rolling Stone**, February 28, 1974.

CHAPTER 23: THE TV REPORTER IN THE BILL BELICHICK UNDERWEAR

386 **They went as far as scrubbing**: Benjamin Hoffman and Ken Belson, "No Trump or

Goodell at Super Bowl, at Least According to NFL Transcripts," **New York Times**, January 31, 2017.

388 **"lower your own IQ"**: Buck Harvey, "If Watt Is Earl: How Some Stories Last," **San Antonio Express-News**, October 1, 2016.

388 **"The hardest-hitting running back"**: Frank Luska, "Campbell Leaves His Legend," **Los Angeles Times,** August 20, 1986, p. 32.

CHAPTER 24: CLOCKS AND SITCOMS

408 **"taking a great Chagall"**: **Mornings with Maria**, Fox Business Channel, February 13, 2017.

CHAPTER 26: THIS MAN'S LIVER BELONGS IN CANTON

426 **"surprises people if he can roll out of bed"**: Seth Wickersham and Don Van Natta Jr., "Sin City or Bust," **ESPN The Magazine**, April 24, 2017.

CHAPTER 27: "FAITH, FAMILY, AND FOOTBALL . . . PROBABLY NOT IN THAT ORDER"

440 **"When pro football owners"**: David Shribman, "Dan Rooney: Pittsburgh and N.F.L. Royalty, and an Ordinary Guy," **New York Times**, April 14, 2017, sports section, p. 8.

Photograph Credits

Insert page 13, bottom: Heather Harvey/ESPN
    Images
Insert page 14: Kevin Reece/Icon Sportswire
Insert page 15: Everett Collection/Alamy
Insert page 16: Roy K. Miller/Icon Sportswire

Index